The Environment and the Human Condition

An interdisciplinary series edited by faculty
at the University of Illinois

D1015922

Books in the Series

Agricultural Biotechnology and the Environment

Sheldon Krimsky and Roger P. Wrubel

Agricultural Biotechnology
AND THE **Environment**

SCIENCE, POLICY, AND SOCIAL ISSUES

University of Illinois Press   Urbana and Chicago

This book is printed on acid-free paper.

An earlier version of chapter 11 was published as "The Cultural and
Symbolic Dimensions of Agricultural Biotechnology," by Sheldon
Krimsky in *Issues in Agricultural Bioethics*, ed. T. B. Mepham, G. A.
Tucker, and J. Wiseman (Nottingham: Nottingham University Press,
1995).

Library of Congress Cataloging-in-Publication Data

Krimsky, Sheldon
    Agricultural biotechnology and the environment : science, policy,
and social issues / Sheldon Krimsky and Roger P. Wrubel.
        p.   cm. — (The environment and the human condition)
    Includes bibliographical references (p.   ) and index.
    ISBN 0-252-02164-9 (cloth). — ISBN 0-252-06524-7 (pbk.)
    1. Agricultural biotechnology. 2. Agricultural biotechnology—
United States. I. Wrubel, Roger P. (Roger Paul), 1949–   .
II. Title. III. Series.
S494.5.B563K75   1996
338.1'62—dc20   95-32490
                                                          CIP

Dedicated to Robert S. Cohen
—S.K.

For Roberta and Ari
—R.P.W.

Contents

Tables

Figures

Acknowledgments

We wish to express our appreciation to the Center for Environmental Management at Tufts University for funding much of the research that contributed to this book. Two funded grants were titled "The Potential for Pollution Reduction in Agriculture" and "Improving the Assessment of Transgenic Microorganisms Released into the Environment: An Integrative Approach." The projects were supported under assistance agreements CR813481 and CR820301 between the U.S. Environmental Protection Agency and the Tufts Center for Environmental Management. Some of the material for the book was derived from the final report titled *Agricultural Biotechnology: An Environmental Outlook* issued in 1993.

Although segments of this book were derived from studies funded by the U.S. Environmental Protection Agency under assistance agreements with the Center for Environmental Management, the information and opinions in this volume do not necessarily reflect the views of the agency or the center, and no official endorsement should be inferred.

There are several people who deserve special mention. Peter Stott served as a reseach and editorial assistant in various stages of the work.

We thank the following individuals who commented on earlier versions of individual chapters: D. Andow, K. Bergmann, J. Callahan, P. Carlson, H. Coble, J. Dekker, S. Duke, D. Fischhoff, W. Gelernter, R. Giaquinta, R. Goodman, F. Gould, J. Gressel, T. Hankinson, J. Hebblethwaite, D. Hess, L. Kim, M. Law, H. LeBaron, W. Lockeritz, P. Marrone, S. Padgette, J. Panetta, D. Pimentel, J. Rissler, J. Ryals, R. Sandmeier, A. Sorensen, S. Uknes, and G. A. de Zoeten.

Leah Steinberg contributed the media analysis in chapter 8, and our colleagues Stuart Levy and Richard Wetzler served as collaborators on a challenging interdisciplinary project on genetically modified microorganisms.

Agricultural Biotechnology and the Environment

Introduction

Two decades after new biological methods for recombining hereditary material in living organisms were introduced into science and industry, it now seems clear that biotechnology has a secure place among major technological breakthroughs of the twentieth century. Although the industry is still young, there is sufficient evidence for its future growth in pharmaceuticals, diagnostics, and food production.

When historians consider the last quarter of this century, they will note that the discovery and commercial applications of biotechnology did not come without some social resistance and public skepticism. Initially, scientists called attention to potential hazards when gene splicing was first reported in the literature (Krimsky 1982). As the concerns over laboratory hazards waned, public attention was directed toward the technology, the manufacturing and agricultural processes, and the consumer products that resulted from biotechnology. The din of controversy spread over a broad spectrum of issues, including patenting of life, human genetic engineering, genetic screening and identification, the release of genetically modified organisms into the environment, and the production of genetically engineered food, plants, and animals.

As these controversies rise and fall, inevitably the question will be, What was all the fuss about biotechnology? Is applied genetics so different from other technologies? Have industrial nations created higher standards for the adoption of genetic technologies beyond those required for past technological innovations? Or perhaps we are naive in thinking that contemporary societies have selected biotechnology for special treatment. Nuclear and chemical technologies have certainly been met with a formidable degree of public opposition. Even computer technologies have their detractors. There is a notable difference, however. With biotechnology, the public's scrutiny has come at the early stages of innovation, before the technologies are on-line and before products are marketed. One cannot say the same about the introduction of nuclear and chemical technologies.

Nevertheless, countless thousands of innovations in products and technological processes are introduced into manufacturing plants and the consumer market annually, with citizens having little or no awareness of the changes. Perhaps we are more likely to take note of new technologies when we use them directly and when they offer a new function or a replacement for an old one. Material substitutions are noticeable to the consumer when the product differences are pronounced, such as a change from metal to plastic fabrication. For each innovation that is discernible to the consumer, scores of others are hidden from public view. How many people would be able to detect a change in the composition of a plastic container, or in the chemical sprays used on new clothing to maintain freshness, or in the type of pesticides used on vegetable crops? The entry of homogenized milk into consumer markets was immediately obvious, but the introduction of a microbially derived growth hormone (called bovine somatotropin) on cows will not be discernible by taste or observation.

A colleague at the Tufts University Medical School tells the story of how the controls of her experiment designed to detect the presence of chemicals that mimic the function of human estrogens were contaminated. She scrutinized her laboratory and every piece of equipment. She telephoned manufacturers to determine whether changes had been made in the formulation of plastic products. One manufacturer of tubing confirmed her suspicion. The polymers in the plastic tube had been modified, she was told, but the new formula was a trade secret. The medical school researcher had the plastic analyzed and discovered in the new composition another industrial chemical with estrogenic properties.

Notwithstanding the fact that changes in manufacturing processes and products take place continuously, technological innovations are rarely debated in the public arena or the media. Industrial societies have come to place great trust in technological change. The impulse for and nourishment of change in manufacture is part of the *Weltgeist* of the modern industrial state. As a consequence, the public has very little control over industrial innovations, which are presumed to be in the public interest by virtue of their success in the marketplace unless proven otherwise. Every state has some minimal ground rules for the adoption of a new product or technology, for example, that they not introduce unacceptable risks to human health and safety or to the environment. As long as the threshold conditions are satisfied, the norms of the market economy, for example, microeconomic efficiency and profit maximization, take over.

Over the past century some of the most notable achievements in technology have been in agriculture. Once a highly decentralized and labor-intensive system of production, modern farming is evidence that industrial mass production was applicable to the growth of crops and the production of livestock. Just as the size of factories increased to enable manufacturers and investors to capitalize on economies of scale, the concept of efficiency applied to farming sought the optimum use of land, air, water, soil, and germ plasm, eventually resulting in integral roles for electrification, mechanization, chemicals, and management science in food production. Innovations in agriculture also shape the system of social relations and the institutions associated with food production. For example, it has been noted that the cotton gin made it possible for the South's plantation owners to preserve slavery as an economically viable system.

American farmers have achieved among the highest levels of land and labor productivity in the world. A mere 1.5 percent of the U.S. population provides enough food for domestic and export markets. By 1990, 320,000 large farms produced 77 percent of the total national agricultural product (Cochrane 1993, 460). Biotechnology offers farmers and seed manufacturers the tools for securing additional improvements in agricultural yield. It began its ascendancy in investment circles as a blossoming but unproven high-technology sector about the same time the U.S. manufacturing industry began to decline internationally. As financial markets were bullish over biotechnology, hundreds of new firms were created with research ideas germinated in academic laboratories. According to the Office of Technology Assessment, "The boom in biotechnology company formation occurred from 1980 to 1984, with nearly 70 new firms begun in 1981 alone" (OTA 1988, 9). U.S. funding agencies began a massive research initiative to investigate the role of biotechnology in medicine and agriculture. In 1990 the federal government expended more than $3.4 billion in overall R&D in biotechnology-related projects. The bulk of those funds, $2.9 billion, came from the National Institutes of Health compared to $168 million and $116 million from the National Science Foundation and the Department of Agriculture, respectively (OTA 1991, 21). Between 1991 and 1993 the public investment in about one thousand American biotechnology companies amounted to $6 billion. Approximately fifty of these firms were involved in agricultural biotechnology, with investments exceeding $200 million annually (Caswell et al. 1994, 7). The innovative potential of gene engineering was often described as being without limits. At the same time, many R&D projects were not pursued beyond their early public relations announcements.

Some companies decried the lack of clear regulations; others struggled with negative public opinion of biotechnology. There were suggestions that regulatory obstacles had slowed the pace of innovation. The Congressional Office of Technology Assessment affirmed that "when regulation is untried in the marketplace, untested in the courts, or ambiguous in status and scope, the resulting set of uncertainties can become a dominant influence in selecting or rejecting an R&D objective and associated business strategy" (OTA 1988, 100).

For more than a decade, agricultural research has begun to respond to the promise of applied molecular genetics. New research centers blossomed at land grant colleges and other universities. Biotechnology industrial parks were sought as jump-starters for local economies. A number of states such as California promoted biotechnology investments in advertising campaigns directed at new companies. One city even used Housing and Urban Development Block Grant funds to provide loans to biotechnology firms that might locate there (H. Miller 1993, 5). Investing in America's future meant investing in biotechnology.

In 1991 the Office of Technology Assessment listed four areas where biotechnology would contribute to agriculture (99):

- gains in yield through new plants resistant to environmental stresses;
- lower costs in labor and agricultural inputs;
- higher-quality food and value added products; and
- environmentally benign methods of managing weeds and insect pests.

This book examines the directions of research and development for the first generation of agricultural products and generic product categories arising from the applications of new tools in genetic engineering. We are interested in why certain paths of innovation were preferred over others and which factors shaped the direction of new biotechnology products. What, for example, has been the impact of regulation or lack thereof in the investment strategy for agricultural biotechnology products? What has been the outgrowth of social and environmental concerns resulting from the choices of new technologies?

In the early 1980s when venture capital and Fortune 500 investments in biotechnology were being sought, many expectations were discussed for the fledgling industry. More than a decade later it is possible to compare these early expectations with the realities of current product development and research trajectories. For example, while biotechnology was being cast as environmentally friendly, the industry has not been embraced by environmental organizations. Quite the contrary, major environmental groups have spoken critically of new biotechnology products. In this volume we have sought to answer whether current trends in agricultural biotechnology are likely to promote safer insecticides, promote sustainable agriculture, create more biodiversity, or reduce dependency on fossil fuel and chemically intensive farming.

We also focus on the public reception to the first generation of biotechnology products. To what extent does the progress of innovation match the public's expectation? What are the sources of public apprehension? How deep are society's ideological divisions over biotechnology?

This book is organized around generic product types such as disease resistant crops and transgenic animals. Each chapter provides a systematic overview of scientific developments. Some chapters include interview data from leading-edge biotechnology companies on the state of the art in product development. The technical analysis of research and product development leads to consideration of other contextual issues, such as the anticipated economic benefits, environmental effects, public perceptions, and the social and ethical implications associated with the research agenda.

Chapter 1 explores the issue of change in agricultural biotechnology through a general discussion of technological innovation and diffusion in agriculture. The innovation pathways in biotechnology are fashioned by a superposition of government policies, technological maturation, technology transfer mechanisms, regulations and incentives, and social values. The significance of these factors is sorted out through specific cases.

Chapters 2–5 examine the science and social issues associated with transgenic crops; each chapter focuses on a generic class of products and research programs. Chapters 6–8 address transgenic microorganisms in three agricultural applications: insecticidal, nitrogen-fixing, and frost-inhibiting bacteria. Chapters 9 and 10 discuss transgenic animals, the former examining current science, ethics, and social considerations and the latter human health and animal safety issues. Chapters 2–10 focus on topical applications of biotechnology. The chapters begin with a scientific overview followed by a discussion of new developments, economic impacts, social and political responses, environmental implications, and ethical considerations. Although these divisions are useful for purposes of analysis, they should not be mistaken for the actual form or chronology of social and scientific controversy where many factors are at work concurrently at the time the technology is being introduced and evaluated by the scientific community, by government, by the media, or by the broader public.

Chapter 11 and the Conclusion are devoted to an interpretation of the current state of development in agricultural biotechnology. Chapter 11 reexamines the early expectations of biotechnology in terms of a set of myths and anti-myths. The Conclusion looks more closely at the impact that biotechnology is having on the system of food production and examines alternative social interpretations of the place of biotechnology in the future of agriculture.

We seek answers to five groups of questions. First, what have been the direction and goals of agricultural innovation through biotechnology? What explanations are there for the particular pathways to innovation? What impact has regulation had on biotechnology R&D or product commercialization? Second, how do the current developments in biotechnology measure up to early expectations? Are the widely touted tools of applied molecular genetics living up to their potential? What can be viewed as successes, failures, or limitations? Third, what impacts is agricultural biotechnology having on, or what contributions is it making to, the problems of the environment? Will biotechnology be a kinder and gentler technology in its effects on natural systems? Will it advance the cause of sustainability? Will it help us remediate environmental problems of the past? Will it make a contribution to pollution prevention? Of particular interest on this point is the research program on herbicide resistant crops and its impact on chemical herbicide use, both volume of use and toxicity. Fourth, will biotechnology cause or contribute to structural change in the agricultural sector? Is it likely to introduce new modes of production, new relations of production, and new forms of ownership or alter significantly the scale or concentration of industrial sectors? Fifth, what significance can be made of the public debates over new products in biotechnology? Are there discernible patterns in the social criticism and political discourse around issues of genetically modified organisms? How may we understand the perspectives of alternative constituencies such as technologists and anti-technologists, molecular biologists and ecologists, and mainstream agriculturalists and alternative agriculturists or small-scale versus large-scale farmers. We will return to an analysis of these issues in the Conclusion.

1 Technological Innovation in Agriculture

Humans began cultivating crops between ten and fifteen thousand years ago, however, most of the technological innovations we attribute to agriculture have taken place within the past two hundred years. These include mechanization, plant breeding, hybridization, chemically based pesticides and herbicides, and chemical fertilizers. The discovery of recombinant DNA in the early 1970s rapidly opened new frontiers for the next generation of innovations in food production. The application of biological processes in agriculture has a venerable tradition involving the selection, modification, or use of living organisms to achieve improvements in crop cultivation, animal husbandry, or food manufacture. Pisano (1991, 238) describes several stages in the evolution of biotechnology. At first, biological production processes were improved by the selection of natural strains that carried desirable traits. Eventually, individual organisms were manipulated through hybridization, a process in which whole cells are fused from different parental sources, making it possible to create crosses between distinct but not vastly unrelated crops. The use of chemicals and radiation to create mutant strains opened another chapter in the development of biotechnology. And now, through genetic engineering, plant, animal and microbial cells can be designed with specific phenotypic characteristics.

Many predictions have been made about the future prospects of biotechnology, but few bear the weight of optimism expressed in a statement from the Monsanto Corporation (cited in Busch et al. 1991, 3–4): "Biotechnology would revolutionize farming in the future with products based on nature's own methods, making farming more efficient, more reliable, more environmentally friendly, and more profitable for the farmer. Moreover, plants would be given the built-in ability to fend off insects and disease and resist stress, animals would be born vaccinated, pigs would produce leaner meat and grow faster, cows would produce milk more economically and food crops would be more nutritious and easier to process."

Optimism can also be found among independent scholars who extol biotechnology's future environmental assets to agriculture: "Biotechnology offers the prospects for achieving a sustainable agricultural program in the United States and the world. If plants can be induced to exude their own pesticides, if animals can be designed to produce more healthful meat, and if organisms can be developed that more effectively fix atmospheric nitrogen and digest animal waste, biotechnology will have realized the promise of even its most fervent exponents" (Molnar and Kinnucan 1989, 254).

Finally, many see biotechnology not simply as an innovative means to consumer products, but as the key to the future in agriculture, health care, energy sources, and new materials. Referring to the public anxiety over the introduction of bovine somatotropin, an animal growth and lactation promoter, Hecht (1991) states, "The implications of BST are broad. They may affect millions of people who are waiting for cures for cancer, for AIDS, and for a variety of other fatal diseases. Biotechnology holds the best hope for conquering these monumental human afflictions. If the progress of biotechnology were slowed or stopped, many people would never have the chance to benefit from the efforts of our scientists."

It is generally recognized that plant, animal, and microbial molecular genetics has much to offer the agricultural sector. The possibilities for innovation that occur when an important scientific revolution is brought to the doorstep of a major sector of the global economy are vast and greatly exceed the actual paths chosen. Russell (1991, 11) states that "ideas industries like biotechnology typically generate much more innovation than they can cope with." This raises some important questions about the possible applications of biotechnology that will be supported by public and private investments. Why are certain product development opportunities chosen and others left behind? Is scientific promise transformed into social use through a public choice rationale or through some technological imperative that operates in industrial societies? Is there a theory or set of explanatory paradigms that helps us understand the technological innovations taking place in agricultural biotechnology? Finally, how does the path of innovation—and the factors that influence it—determine who benefits from technological changes?

A. Innovation as an Area of Study

The study of technological innovation in general, and for agriculture in particular, has been a subject of interest among historians, sociologists, economists, and business scholars. Each discipline approaches the problem of innovation somewhat differently. Much is written in the economics literature about the organization of industrial sectors and its relationship to the emergence of innovative enterprises. Economist J. A. Schumpeter's (1934) division of technological change into three components provides a useful framework for examining disciplinary approaches to the study of innovation. Invention refers to primary discovery; innovation is the application of primary discoveries to commercial products or processes; and diffusion of innovation refers to the adoption of the innovations within or among industrial sectors. Hamilton (1990, 142) offers a variant of this scheme in his three phases of technical advance: scientific research, technical development, and commercial application. Each phase associated with the evolution of technological change suggests a different set of historical, sociological, and entrepreneurial questions. Not all innovations follow the path from science to device to commercial success. Historically, many innovators began as tinkerers. And when changes came slowly, they were the result of generations of trial and error. The sequence of scientific research, technical development, and commercial success is only one developmental path, but it happens to be the one that most resembles the early period of innovations in agricultural biotechnology.

1. Scientific Research

Historians study the conditions, favorable or unfavorable, to scientific and technological change. Why did the industrial revolution develop in England? What is the relationship between Protestantism and the Industrial Revolution? After impressive achievements in ancient science, why had China ceased to be the place where modern science took hold? With respect to biotechnology, historians focus on the conditions that nourished the development of molecular genetics and eventually recombinant DNA techniques (Bud 1993).

Certain discoveries are generative. We may call these primary innovations. From these multiple pathways are possible secondary innovations in product development. The modern industry we call biotechnology, usually defined as the industrial use of recombinant

DNA, cell fusion and novel bioprocessing techniques (OTA 1988, 28) arose directly from basic research in molecular genetics. The research was focused on studying higher order organisms (eukaryotes). Most of the nuclear DNA in higher organisms consists of very long DNA molecules that are difficult to study. In the 1970s biologists learned that one way to study the function of specific genes was to move the genes from a host organism to a simpler biological system. A novel protein found in the new organism could be correlated with the foreign gene segment. Early methods involved the transfer of bacterial genes into mammalian cells by hooking them on to a mammalian virus. The purpose of these experiments was to determine whether bacterial genes could be expressed in the cells of higher organisms. Subsequently, the genetic transfer process became simplified by the use of extrachromosomal DNA particles called plasmids. Mammalian DNA was transferred by this method to bacterial cells.

Sociologists study the institutional roles of innovation, linking the achievements of individuals to other contextual events. The training, values, and ideals of scientists are relevant data. Where do nontraditional ideas come from and what makes the innovator innovate? Molecular geneticists having turned en masse to the commercialization of knowledge raises questions about the changing norms of scientific institutions (Kenney 1986).

2. Technical Development

How do major scientific and technological discoveries become applied to product development in the private entrepreneurial sector? Innovations in agriculture emanate from varied sources: mechanical technologies, management, microbiology, genetics, and embryology. Not all are derivative from basic science (see table 1 for a list of key innovations in the dairy industry). Each primary innovation, for example, one that comes directly from basic research and is generative of many secondary applications, such as gene splicing or cell fusion, can be advanced along many development pathways. Not all of these pathways are chosen. How do we explain the direction of technological change? One might posit a set of stages for innovation that include discovery, patenting, technological feasibility, economic evaluation, regulations, markets, and competition. An innovation may fail to meet the threshold criteria at any of these stages of development. For example, although the idea of implanting functional nitrogen-fixing genes from microorganisms into plants was widely acclaimed, it had technological limitations (chapter 7).

Table 1. Some Notable Innovations in
the Dairy Industry

Scientific feeding	1920
Dairy head improvement testing	1925
Mechanical milking	1930
Artificial insemination	1940
Electronic farm counting	1960
Milking parlors	1960
Bulk tanks	1960
Free stall housing	1960
Embryo transfer	1980
Bovine somatotropin	1994

Source: Adapted from Yonkers 1992

Economists study the role of technology and technological choices
in contributing to social wealth. Why do some technologies take
hold and others fail? What are the economic promoters of technological innovation? Why do some sectors innovate more rapidly than
others? What is the relationship between technological innovation
and the structure of an industry, for example, whether the industry
is competitive or monopolistic? Hacking (1986, 22) stresses the
importance of elasticity of demand in a firm's choice of product
investment: "What a firm is willing to invest in is related to elasticity of demand. The higher the elasticity of demand, the lower the
risks which are deemed acceptable and the lower the research ex-
penditure."

Business scholars approach innovation from the standpoint of the
firm: How can or does government establish economic incentives
for innovation? How does technological innovation affect competitiveness? What are the respective roles of innovation and tradition
in the commercial success of the firm? What are the stages or patterns of development of the industry, and what strategies are pursued by established and emerging firms? What organizational forms
evolve to govern innovation (Pisano 1991)?

Much of what we call innovation in biotechnology emanates from
"publicly-financed entrepreneurial firms" (Ostrach 1991, 27) whose
intellectual capital derives predominantly from academic scholars
in contrast to large, established companies with substantial R&D
budgets supported by profits from successful products. According to
Nelson et al. (1988, 220), "In recent years the natural ways to advance recombinant DNA technology have, in general, not required

massive resources and giant laboratories, but have been pursuable by small companies, or even by individuals with access to modern laboratory equipment." It has been reported that institutional investors have shown unprecedented interest in biotechnology companies. This is reflected in the significant growth in new stocks issued and the rising value of the shares (*Economist* 1991).

In this volume we seek, in part, to understand the patterns of development resulting from the applications of applied molecular genetics to agricultural products. What choices are firms making in the development of new products and what are the factors that shape those choices? Are there product opportunities not being pursued? If so, Why? Many of these questions require a detailed study of business decisions, but there is also a larger context that defines the linkage between knowledge and commerce.

3. *The Commercial Success of Innovation*

To succeed, agricultural innovations must be received by farmers and consumers in society. Innovative ideas are like seeds. Their growth depends on a proper substrate. The adoption and diffusion of agricultural innovations has been the subject of many studies by rural sociologists (Cochrane 1993; Summers 1983) who seek to explain the differences among user groups. Their studies examine the knowledge and receptivity of the farm communities, the structure of agribusiness, and the type of sector transformation. Because few biotechnological products in agriculture derived from gene splicing have actually reached the marketplace, adoption and diffusion research has not extended, as yet, to this area. Many of the generic products discussed in the following chapters are in their nascent stages of development. One product that has entered the market, however, is bovine somatotropin (BST) alternatively called bovine growth hormone (BGH). A number of recent studies of BST shed light on both farmer and consumer receptivity to innovations in veterinary products (chapter 9). BST has created a schism within the agricultural community, pitting traditional and alternative concepts of agriculture squarely against one another. The controversy over the development of lactation enhancers like BST also highlights issues pertaining to autonomous technology, a term used to characterize the transition from technological success to adoption as inevitable.

In the United States, most research that gave rise to the primary innovations in biotechnology was funded by the National Institutes of Health. The commercial value of recombinant DNA is often cited as an unexpected byproduct of basic research. There are many other sources of primary innovation aside from the publicly funded basic research published in the open literature. Classified military research has produced spinoff technologies from radar, computers, material sciences, and chemical warfare materials. Another path to primary innovation is through industrial research. The birth of the industrial revolution witnessed numerous innovations in hydropower and textile manufacturing that were brought about by private entrepreneurs. Conditions of resource scarcity provide economic incentives for firms to develop substitution products. During World War II, scarcities in rubber and nylon provided the incentives for companies to develop synthetic fibers and plastics. Thus, factor scarcity, intense market competition, and efficiency are the key motivators of industrial innovation.

Aside from the state's role in funding basic research, national policies in the United States and other industrialized nations were vital in creating economic incentives for technology transfer (Krimsky 1991; Orsenigo 1989; Pisano 1991). As noted by Hacking (1986, 281), "Some of the high risk associated with biotechnology is now being reduced by government policies, subsidies, grants, capital allowances, the U.S. capital gains tax and so on."

B. The Growth of the Biotechnology Industry

At the time that gene engineering was spawning a new configuration of industrial activities, the economic organization of technological innovation was already changing. Large industry sectors and their R&D affiliates were not the source of the most exciting innovations in such fast growing fields as microelectronics, microprocessors, and computer software. Similarly, much of the early growth in biotechnology came from new firms created by venture capital investments (Krimsky 1991, 37). Hamilton, Vila, and Dibner (1990, 76) report that 350 new venture firms in biotechnology were formed in the United States between 1971 and 1987.

In 1978, Monsanto, Du Pont, and Eli Lilly were the few established companies that had in-house research programs in biotechnology (OTA 1984). Multinationals first entered the field cautiously and then made substantial investments in the early and mid-1980s. By 1982 Monsanto was spending 28 percent of its total R&D budget on biotechnology, Schering Plough 47 percent, and Eli Lilly 22 percent (Harsanyi and Schneider 1984, 16). In a 1988 study of the industry the Office of Technology Assessment surveyed 296 dedicated biotechnology companies and found 24 firms (8 percent) devoted to plant agriculture (OTA 1988, 10). The application of biotechnology to therapeutics was the fastest growing sector, with mean R&D budgets of dedicated biotechnology companies of nearly $9 million. In the survey, plant agriculture came in second, with a mean budget of about $5 million.

Highlighting prior expectations, the report cited biotechnology as having the potential "to modify plants to resist insects and disease, grow in harsh environments, provide their own nitrogen fertilizer, or be more nutritious (OTA 1988, 13). Burrill and Lee (1993) report a $22 million R&D budget for public biotechnology firms in 1991. Therapeutics dominated the R&D expenditures at 61.1 percent, with agriculture second at 17.7 percent and diagnostics third at 14.1 percent (figure 3, page 30). Commercially successful rDNA-derived pharmaceuticals like human insulin, interferons, and tissue plasminogen activator elevated investor confidence in biotechnology drug development. Agricultural products had a longer latency period in reaching commercial markets, in large part because of controversy over regulations. Hacking (1986, 286) argues that pharmaceuticals generally have a higher inelasticity of demand compared to agricultural products (people cannot as easily substitute drugs as they can food products), which is why drug companies are inclined to invest heavily in research where expenditures can be recouped in the price of the product. Nevertheless, by 1992 fifteen agricultural biotechnology firms reported R&D expenditures amounting to $168 million, a 40 percent increase over the previous year (Spalding 1993).

C. Factors of Innovation

Technological innovation in agriculture may be divided into several stages: the origins of ideas, the cultivation of those ideas into prototype technologies, the commercial development of the technology, the diffusion of the technologies (their adoption by farmers), and the longevity and success of the innovations. What determines which technological ideas are developed and which are left behind? How are technological options determined in the firm and what screening mechanisms are used? This problem is complicated by the fact that decisions of this nature take place over a period of time. Also, many variables may affect the outcome. The choice of product development may be compared to a system of filters. Each innovative idea faces a series of filtering mechanisms (economic, social, regulatory, and managerial) that determines whether the idea is kept viable. In biotechnology the source of a seminal idea is as likely to come from academic research scientists as from industrial scientists. Concerning the source of new ideas in a fledgling company, Russell (1991, 11) writes:

> Ideas come from everywhere, from outside the company just as much as within. Everybody is continually in touch with the world outside through constant reading, talking, looking, and listening. Other people's ideas taken in via public channels or through private conversation often provoke the spark which sets a group of potential innovators thinking. Those ideas from outside might have come from a totally unrelated context; oftentimes they originate from government agencies indicating new areas of interest, from the business world at large, from competitors' publicity as they go about their own marketing and public relations activities and, of course, from the world's universities and research institutes.

Academic scientists by the scores have sown their ideas in private for-profit firms in return for equity, licensing fees, or management control. The idea is then met by a number of institutional queries and constraints. Transition from the concept to the product stage is highly variable and depends on markets, assessment of development feasibility and time, and the persuasiveness of the individuals who advocate the research direction. The firm's choice of innovative products is in part shaped by its positioning strategy for "exploiting the opportunities presented by technological change" (Hamilton, Vila, and Dibner 1990, 80). The strategies differ for firms that are technology or market derived, externally or internally oriented.

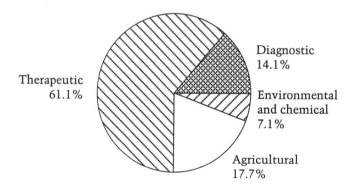

Figure 1. Biotechnology R&D Spending in 1991 by Market Segment. *Source:* Burrill and Lee 1992

The following factors represent some of the key variables in the timing and choice of innovation as well as the direction of R&D for agricultural biotechnology.

D. Problem Maturation

Many new biotechnology companies were formed on the promise of a creative application of a scientific idea. To what extent is the scientific problem that defines the innovation ripe for solution? The scientific problem may involve transferring certain traits from one organism to another, for example, as in making certain plants insect resistant. The maturation of the problem may be reflected in several questions. Are the genes for the trait well characterized? Has a model system for transferring the trait been developed? Is the science well understood?

If a laboratory strain of the desired organism has been developed, there are still many hurdles to face in evaluating the effectiveness of the organism in the field. Will the additional genetic baggage reduce the efficiency of the organism? How many years will it take from successful laboratory tests to field trials?

Some of the early enthusiasm for biotechnology products was dampened subsequently when it was learned that the science that had yielded them was more complex than originally thought. Plants that can be genetically engineered to fix their own nitrogen, and thus become auto-fertilizing, were widely publicized in the mass media and in popular science magazines during the early 1980s. Accomplishing this, however, has proven to be a much more formidable task than originally conceived, and companies have placed in abeyance the aspirations of achieving this result in the near future (chapter 7).

Another obstacle to biotechnology development is the gap between product success in the laboratory and success under field conditions. Brill (1991) noted that microbes proven effective in the laboratory often do not survive well when released into the environment. Because publicity about new products usually comes after the completion of successful laboratory experiments, it is not unusual for the path of development to stop or slow down when the product fails to perform under field conditions.

E. Consistency of Innovation with Existing Agricultural Paradigms

Agricultural improvements have been distinguished from agricultural innovations (Fliegel and van Es 1983). Improvements refer to the modifications of existing technology, whereas innovations represent departures from the latter. Faced with a variety of new ideas, companies tend to assess the viability of the product within the existing system of agricultural production. Products that may be desirous on energy or environmental criteria may be too far afield from the methods or norms of current agricultural practice. Innovations are more likely to be additive and incremental because there is less risk in improving an operating production system in which existing markets are secured.

Companies that manufacture pesticides and herbicides are also investing in biotechnology R&D that could have an impact on their markets. It seems reasonable to assume that the choices these companies make about which products to develop may be influenced by their existing markets. Some of the newer and smaller biotechnology firms advertised their research efforts as moving away from the existing paradigm of chemically intensive agriculture. They were seeking new market niches through which they could capitalize on the public's interest in an environmentally sound agriculture.

According to Goodman, Sorj, and Wilkinson (1987), the dominant paradigm that has guided the transformation of agriculture is expressed by the concepts of *appropriationism* and *substitutionism*, whereby the rural base of agriculture is being displaced by an urban/industrial base. The authors argue that biotechnology continues in this tradition of the "industrial appropriation of the rural production process." The paradigm provides an important selection pressure for agricultural innovation before questions of efficacy, economic efficiency, and markets are considered. "A 'technological paradigm' defines contextually the needs that are meant to be fulfilled, the scientific principles utilized for the task, and the material technology to be used" (Dosi et al. 1988, 224–23). Campbell (1993, 287) cites the importance of production-enhancing innovations as a primary explanation for agricultural adoption of technologies. The author refers to the term *technological treadmill*, introduced by Cochrane (1958), which signifies a continuing process of farm technological advance associated with capital intensification, increased output, and the redistribution of productive assets in agriculture, "The adoption-diffusion literature suggests that production-enhancing technological innovations, in combination with the inelastic demands characteristic of agricultural markets place all farmers on a technological treadmill."

But the term *production enhancing* is not sufficient to explain a choice of technological path because there may be alternative ways to increase production, some more resource intensive, some tending toward capital concentration, and some tending toward decentralization. We can have production-enhancing techniques within sustainable, organic, and rotational grazing systems of agriculture or within chemically intensive feedlot farming. A broader envelope of factors shapes the path of innovation.

F. Government Policies

The federal government's matrix of policies, regulations, tax laws, centers of excellence, and funding of research creates a complex tapestry of incentives and disincentives for innovation. For example, the Orphan Drug Law makes it economically worthwhile for some companies to develop certain drugs that will have limited use. Innovations that are not patent protected may not succeed in the corporate agenda. In biotechnology this presents special problems. As noted by Marrone and Sandmeier (1991, 228), "While the patent process is very clear and very well understood for chemical pest control agents, it is not clear for biological agents, and a large backlog in processing biotechnology patent applications has not helped industry gain confidence that it will have a guaranteed return on investment."

Companies that produce agricultural pesticides are faced with chemical and biological approaches to protecting crops. However, the regulatory requirements for these approaches may be vastly different. "The regulatory environment can be seen as a staging area for innovations before market mechanisms, social networks, and diffusion agencies can make products available and facilitate their use" (Kinnucan, Molnar, and Hatch 1989, 117). New chemical products often face a fairly stable but exhaustive set of toxicological studies. In contrast, biological products, particularly those modified by genetic techniques, face a less stable but often less rigorous regulatory regime. Garraway (1991, 460) reports that the costs of R&D and toxicological testing for chemical pesticides is twenty times what it is for microbial pesticides. This leads some companies to adjust their R&D goals to the real and/or perceived obstacles of regulation.

Nevertheless, the worldwide market for chemical pesticides is around $13 billion, whereas the annual market for microbial pesticides is about $20 million. There are more than a thousand known microbial pathogens of insects, however only a small number have been approved for agricultural use (Hacking 1986, 272).

After waiting five years before the genetically modified *Pseudomonas* strain called ice minus was finally field-tested in

California, Advanced Genetic Sciences decided it would pursue the development of the frost inhibitor through chemical rather than rDNA processes (chapter 8). Efforts on the part of the Bush and Clinton administrations have been directed at removing regulatory obstacles to new biotechnology products. The administrations' goals are to remove the controls over small field tests, establish a fast track for large-scale use of transgenic organisms in the environment, and deregulate genetically engineered food products so that they are treated like new crop varieties rather than food additives (see the Conclusion).

G. Market Demand for the Product

It is, of course, a simple and obvious truth that a product will not be successful if it has no market. But the relationship between technological innovation and markets has been a subject of much scholarly investigation. In order to distinguish between cases where the innovation responds to factors of production and where it arises, sometimes serendipitously, from creative discovery, J. R. Hicks wrote in his classic work *The Theory of Wages* (1932), technological advance can be induced or autonomous. Contemporary economists speak of "technology push" and "demand pull" innovations. In the former case, the firm's scientific research group develops an innovation whereupon products and markets are subsequently sought. This is illustrated by the development of lasers that were then applied to surgery and music production. In the latter case, the ideas for the innovation derive from the marketing and production sectors of the firm, whereas the outcome is developed by the research group. An example cited by Kamien and Schwartz (1982, 34–35) is the development of transistors, which were developed at Bell Laboratories in response to AT&T's need for smaller and more efficient switches. Thus, some innovations and R&D programs respond to the current market demands while other programs innovate first and then seek or create the demand. Under the "demand pull" case, the incentives for innovation come directly from users; in the case of agriculture, that would be farmers or consumers. For "demand push," people do not know that they need a product until it is available, and then they can be informed about it.

Russell (1991, 13) maintains that biotechnology businesses are unorthodox in the sense that they did not come into existence to fill a need: "While it is true in most cases, [demand-pull] does not provide an accurate model of technology business such as biotechnology. The tools of biotechnology, the ability, for example, to move genetic information from one cell to another, even one species to another, were created and immediately recognized as having great commercial value before anyone articulated a specific market need. So it would appear that this is a clear case of the chicken coming before the egg."

If the "technology (or demand) push" model of innovation best accounts for biotechnology, it remains to be determined whether (1) biotechnology is responding to the needs of farmers; (2) selected farming sectors are benefiting; and (3) farmers are playing a role in shaping the innovation strategies of agribiotechnology research. Our research indicates that biotechnology products provide additional options that are not on the whole being sought after by farmers but are consistent with the general needs and interests of selected agricultural subsectors. Hacking (1986, 2) remarks that in biotechnology, "Technology push rather than market pull has tended to be the order of the day. In common with electricity a century ago, biotechnology is today a technology in search of applications."

H. Social Environment of Innovation

Increasingly, the products of innovative technologies are facing public scrutiny. It is no longer unusual for advocacy groups to campaign against specific technologies such as the supersonic transport, solid waste incinerators, and irradiated or genetically engineered food. Busch and Lacy (1983, 211) note that

> the agricultural sector has been confronted with increasing consumer interests and concerns about the products of this system. Consumers have begun to challenge agricultural research agendas that ignore nutrition and health and have demanded increased governmental regulation to provide for public health and safety. . . . the public has begun to raise broad questions about the fundamental goals for the nation's food and agricultural system, including such issues as equity, efficiency, resilience, flexibility, conservation, and consistency with other objectives of U.S. society.

Social factors have become palpably more visible in the diffusion of innovations. Some small dairy farmers, for example, opposed the introduction of bovine growth hormone because they believed it did not serve their economic interests. They were supported by animal rights activists, who campaigned against BGH as inhumane to animals, and consumer groups, who were opposed to it for health and safety considerations (chapter 9).

A second innovation in biotechnology that brought a social response is genetically modified food. The Food and Drug Administration issued its new guidelines for regulating food products resulting from genetically engineered crops. The Environmental Defense Fund, the Council for Responsible Genetics, and the American Association of Chefs protested that the regulations did not protect the public and had no provisions for labeling. The salient issues of public concern involved health, nutrition, and cultural values. For example, consumer surveys indicate that there is a significant expression of concern among respondents over mixing genes from animals to plants (chapter 5).

As evidenced by the rising demand for public opinion surveys, R&D firms have shown an increased interest in public attitudes toward biotechnology. The direction of innovation as a function of social attitudes is not as well studied as the receptivity of the public to the products of innovation. In most cases, public reactions to products takes place in the postmarketing phase of development. Biotechnology, however, has experienced an advanced notice of public reaction that provides companies with another input in the choice of R&D direction. Some companies had already become early targets of criticism when they contemplated products, such as herbicide resistant crops (chapter 2), that drew negative reactions from environmental groups.

During our investigations of innovation in agricultural biotechnology we inquired about whether social values, equity, regulation, or environmental factors played a role in shaping the firm's research agenda. Rarely have such examples been manifest. Unexpectedly, we learned that industry has taken a more socially pragmatic view toward investment in technology. We can no longer take for granted that efficiency, markets, and profits are the exclusive criteria for the development of new products. In large part, this is due to the influence of the public interest sector, which increasingly has raised issues about new products before those products reach consumers.

The various factors at work in determining the path of technological innovation are illustrated in figure 2, which identifies five sector roles: innovators, mediators, users, government, and social values. A comprehensive study of each sector role will fill out the empirical details of agricultural innovations in biotechnology. In this

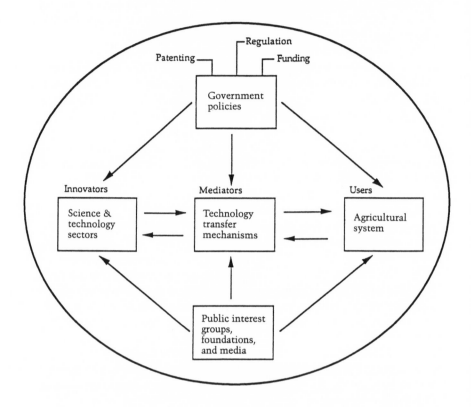

Figure 2. Institutional Roles in Technological Innovation for Agricultural Biotechnology. *Source:* Authors

framework, mediators are represented by venture capital institutions, other financial markets, and networks that make possible the capital flow to innovator firms, particularly new technology-based firms. For example, networks, or organizational structures for creating a social pool of information, have been identified as integral to creating markets for innovations (Teubal, Yinnon, and Zuscovitch 1991, 389). The role of government policies has been significant in shaping the pathways of innovation through funding of research, regulations or lack of regulations for biotechnology products, technology transfer legislations, and liberal patenting policies (Senker and Faulkner 1992).

I. Theories of Innovation

Why does technology develop in the fashion that it does? Does one sector role take precedence over others? How do the sector roles interact to create product pathways? These questions have prompted several theoretical explanations that address the forms of technical change derived from a primary innovation such as gene splicing. In the case of biotechnology, we are seeking to explain the priority of technological development. How is the rhetoric about environmentally sound uses of biotechnology products matched with the realities of commercial development? What explains why certain potentially environmentally friendly technologies have been left behind or at least have not advanced significantly?

Theories of innovation and technological change have been advanced to account for one or more of the three critical transitions: scientific and technological discovery, industrial investment, and use adoption. Each of the transition points defines a different set of questions. Philosophers and historians of science have addressed the conditions of primary scientific discovery. Differentiating factors such as continuous versus discontinuous and rational versus nonrational change help to distinguish among theoretical perspectives (Kuhn 1962; Lakatos and Musgrave, eds. 1970).

The diffusion model of innovation describes an ordered progression consisting of scientific discovery, technological application, product development, and product integration into commerce. Technology is advanced by order of discovery within the constraints of economic profitability. Innovation, in this model, is driven by science. Products and markets are sought once the technology is available. For example, advances in microchip technology resulting in the miniaturization of computers create products that seek out new markets before identification of a real demand or need. In biotechnology, examples illustrating the diffusion model are found in cases where innovation starts out with a pure scientific result. Scientific entrepreneurs then seek ways that the result can be used in some product. The model assumes unanimity over ends, which in agriculture usually means increased efficiency or value-added production. The diffusion model implies that the path of innovation is highly predictable once the outcome criteria are met. If the conditions of technological change are such that new discoveries drive new applications independent of prior needs or demand, the diffusion model may be the correct lens through which one can view innovation. The model is often criticized as far too simplistic, positivistic, and mechanistic. It does not address the broader array of contextual issues that affect industrial investment.

Another class of theories attempts to explain the investment direction of technology (e.g., whether firms develop one type of transgenic plant or another). The induced innovation model has its roots in the works of the economist J. R. Hicks (1932) and stresses the importance of economic parameters in the choice of research program. In agriculture, for example, technical innovations are said to be developed in response to factor scarcities (Binswanger and Ruttan 1978). Kinnucan, Molnar, and Hatch (1989, 108) cite the level of relative prices, a surrogate for factor scarcities in market economies, as the force behind innovation: "The changed relative prices will stimulate the search for new methods of production which will use more of the now cheaper factor and less of the expensive one."

The argument in support of this model is that agricultural science is closely linked to the market through the agricultural extension services and a variety of interlocking relationships between scientists and agribusiness. "Thus, for example, if labor becomes more expensive relative to capital, scientists and engineers will be encouraged to seek ways to economize on the more scarce input by developing new labor-saving machinery" (Kinnucan, Molnar, and Hatch 1989, 108).

However, the rapid development of applied plant molecular genetics brought innovations from a new breed of plant technologists who had little contact with traditional agriculturalists. Even at its best, the economic theories of innovation fail to account for other influences beyond relative factor scarcities and efficiency. For example, there are institutional frameworks that serve either as barriers or catalysts for the investment into technological innovation. Middle-range systems including venture capital firms, banks, the agricultural extension services, and legal and regulatory frameworks that mediate between scientific discovery and R&D development. The federal government plays a major indirect role in the entrepreneurial choice of research agendas through a variety of inducement programs on one hand and regulations on the other. Thus, the Technology Transfer Act of 1986 mandates public-private cooperation. The Supreme Court decision on patenting microorganisms, followed by the Office of Patent and Trademark's decision to accept patents for transgenic mammals, creates economic incentives for new products. Restrictive regulations also influence the choice of R&D agendas. "The regulatory environment can be seen as a staging area for innovations before market mechanisms, social networks, and diffusion agencies can make products available and facilitate their use. . . . The future of biotechnology is likely to be most greatly influenced by the political economy of regulation than the relative reluctance or receptivity of individual farmers to innovations (Molnar and Kinnucan 1989, 117).

A final group of theories are directed at the third leg in the innovation triad: the conditions under which farmers adopt technological change. The term *diffusion* is applied to theories that describe the spread of innovation (Rogers 1983). Among these, the treadmill theory (Cochrane 1993, 427) offers an explanation for farmers' behavior in adopting new technology. The theory distinguishes between early and late adopters. It relates the adoption of innovation to the reduction in the number of farmers, higher price for farmland, and the relationship between new technologies and cost-saving (Molnar and Kinnucan 1989, 105).

J. The New Path to Innovation through Transgenic Organisms

The search for ideal germ plasm is an ongoing one. But the qualities that make the germ plasm ideal have evolved as the social objectives of agriculture change. With more ultraviolet light entering the biosphere, germ plasm that is not damaged by the radiation is desired. As water becomes scarce in certain regions, plants that can thrive on less moisture are sought. And when arable land becomes scarce because of population pressures, crops that are productive when planted in dense plots become the ideal. In other words, the ideal germ plasm is an outcome of the environment we create.

We created an agricultural system that is heavily dependent on chemical adjuvants. In this system, the ideal germ plasm must be optimally efficient within the chemical support system. Now the opportunity arises whereby the germ plasm can be modified in a highly systematic way—gene by gene. For which environment do we seek an optimum germ plasm? There has certainly been a changing attitude toward chemical pesticides and fertilizers. Even established professional groups have expressed concern about the liability to the environment of continuing the chemical dependency. Many are now viewing the American farm as a dysfunctional system.

Policymakers, however, do not want to be responsible for reducing American farm output—which many view as the inevitable outcome of weaning farms of their chemical supports. Since the publication of Carson's *Silent Spring* (1962) the question has been which pesticides to use, not whether there should be pesticides. The transition that took place after *Silent Spring* was from highly persistent organochlorines to less persistent but more toxic (to mammals) organophosphates. In some cases the risks have shifted from consumers and wildlife to farm workers. In other cases, risks have shifted from carcinogens to endocrine disruptors.

The ideal germ plasm for the environmental age produces a plant that withstands wide swings in temperature, tolerates UV light, fertilizes itself, has an immune system to viruses, functions with limited water, and is not enjoyed by insects.

After forty years of agrichemical dominance, some mainstream agribusinesses are beginning to contemplate a new germ plasm that will offer higher yields with less chemical use. How realistic is this idea? What will happen to the industry that owes its lifeblood to the chemical fixes that keep farms profitable? Will the chemical industry, now so heavily invested in agriculture, reduce fertilizer and pesticide inputs? Will biological pesticide products and insect resistant strains provide a safer alternative? Innovation is not a pure scientific ideal. It has its own political economy.

2 Herbicide Resistant Crops

The creation of crops that are resistant to herbicides is among the most controversial applications of biotechnology to agriculture. A prominent theme of the agricultural biotechnology industry is that genetically engineered crops will reduce the use of pesticides and are thus environmentally beneficial and should aid in the development of sustainable agriculture. Crops engineered with protein products to kill insects or that resist disease have been cited by industry as examples.

But how can it be argued that herbicide resistant crops (HRCs) will reduce herbicide use and benefit the environment? Environmental and alternative agricultural groups that have been generally critical of industry and government efforts to develop biotechnology products for agriculture have seized on this apparent contradiction to publicize their case that the goal of companies developing biotech products is short-term profit and not the long-term health of agriculture and the environment. An analysis published by these groups describes herbicide resistant crops as "biotechnology's bitter harvest" (Goldburg et al. 1990). However, the companies developing these products have promoted HRCs as consistent with the responsible and wise use of biotechnology to solve pest problems in an environmentally compatible manner.

The possible scenarios involved in understanding the impact of herbicide resistant crops on agriculture and the environment are complex and not clear-cut. Differences of opinion regarding the benefit or harm from HRCs are largely based on attitudes about the safety of herbicides and the sustainability of the high-input type of agriculture practiced in the United States and other developed countries.

Since the 1950s, the use of herbicides in agriculture has increased dramatically (Osteen 1993). In 1966 about one hundred million pounds of active ingredient were applied to U.S. croplands (NRC 1989). From 1984 to 1993 usage averaged more than five hundred million pounds a year (Aspelin 1994). In the United States, herbicide use (pounds of active ingredient per acre) is greater than the combined use of insecticide and fungicides (figure 3). This trend holds for worldwide use as well. In the United States, more than 90 percent of the soybeans, corn, and cotton acreage typically receives at least one herbicide treatment each year, as does 50 percent of the wheat crop (USDA 1993). Even though the amount of herbicides applied has not increased significantly since 1986, herbicide expenditures have continued to increase steadily (figure 4).

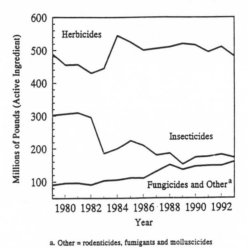

a. Other = rodenticides, fumigants and molluscicides

Figure 3. Agricultural Pesticide Use in the United States, 1979–93. *Source:* Redrawn from Aspelin 1994

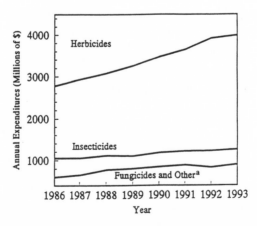

a. Other=rodenticides, fumigants, and molluscicides

Figure 4. Expenditures for Agricultural Pesticides in the United States, 1986–93. *Source:* Redrawn from Aspelin 1994

Herbicide resistant crops are very attractive to industry and are among the first products of biotechnology to become available to farmers (table 2). More than eight hundred of the 2,500 field tests of transgenic crops (produced with rDNA technology) conducted in the

Table 2. Herbicide Resistant Crops Approved for Field Tests in the United States from 1987 to July 1995

Crop	Herbicide	Research Organization
Alfalfa[a]	Glyphosate	Northrup King
Barley	Glufosinate/ Bialaphos	USDA
Canola (oilseed rape)	Glufosinate/ Bialaphos	University of Idaho
	Glyphosate	InterMountain Canola
Corn	Glufosinate/ Bialaphos	Hoechst-Roussel
		ICI
		UpJohn
		Cargill
		DeKalb
		Holdens
		Pioneer Hi-Bred
		Agsrow
		Great Lakes Hybrids
		Ciba-Geigy
		Genetic Enterprises
		AgroEvo
	Glyphosate	Monsanto
		DeKalb
	Sulfonylurea	Pioneer Hi-Bred
		Du Pont
		Monsanto
	Imidazolinone	American Cyanamid[b,c]
Cotton	Glyphosate	Monsanto
		Dairyland Seeds
		Northrup King
	Bromoxynil	Calgene[d]
		Monsanto
	Sulfonylurea	Du Pont
		Delta and Pine Land
	Imidazolinone	Phytogen
Peanuts	Glufosinate/ Bialaphos	University of Florida
Potatoes	Bromoxynil	University of Idaho
		USDA

Table 2, continued

Crop	Herbicide	Research Organization
(Potatoes, continued)	2,4-D	USDA
	Glyphosate	Monsanto
	Imidazolinone	American Cyanamid
Rice	Glufosinate/	Louisiana State University
	Bialaphos	
Soybeans	Glyphosate	Monsanto[c]
		Northrup King
		Agri-Pro
		UpJohn
		Pioneer Hi-Bred
	Glufosinate/	UpJohn
	Bialaphos	
	Sulfonylurea	Du Pont[b,c]
Sugar beets	Glufosinate/	Hoechst-Roussel
	Bialaphos	
	Glyphosate	American Crystal Sugar
Tobacco	Sulfonylurea	American Cyanamid
Tomatoes	Glyphosate	Monsanto
	Glufosinate/	Canners Seed
	Bialaphos	
Wheat	Glufosinate/	AgrEvo
	Bialaphos	

Source: Compiled by the authors from USDA data.
a. All crops were created using rDNA techniques except where noted.
b. Crops created by selection of plant parts (tissues or protoplasts) using in vitro culture techniques.
c. Commercially available in the United States.
d. Rhone-Poulenc, the herbicide's manufacturer, has been granted a time-limited tolerance by the EPA that allows the use of bromoxynil on up to 250,000 acres of Calgene's resistant cotton until April 1997.

United States have involved herbicide resistant traits (figure 5).[*] Herbicide resistant crops now available include genetically engineered soybeans and nongenetically engineered soybeans and corn. The latter two products were created using in vitro selection of plants parts (tissues or protoplasts) grown in culture media and exposed to the

[*]Data on field tests of genetically engineered crops in the United States were obtained from Biotechnology, Biologics and Environmental Protection, USDA, APHIS, 6205 Belcrest Road, Hyattsville, MD 20182 and from the USDA/APHIS World Wide Web server http://www.aphis.usda.gov/bbep/bp/.

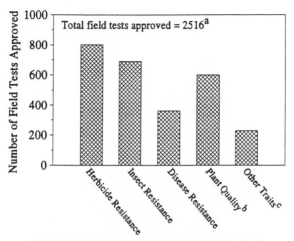

a. Some tests involve plants with multiple traits, so that the sum of the individual bars (2684) is greater the number of tests approved.

b. Plant quality includes, but is not limited to, modifications to chemical content, timing of ripening, and stress tolerance.

c. Other traits include marker genes, production of pharmaceutical and industrial proteins, and heavy metal sequestration.

Figure 5. Field Tests of Transgenic Plant Varieties in the United States from 1987 to July 1995. *Source:* Compiled by the authors from USDA data

herbicide of interest (Chaleff 1983). The plant parts surviving the herbicide treatment are regenerated into whole plants for seed harvesting. Many more crop varieties with genetically engineered resistance to one or more herbicides are likely to become available soon.

Can engineering or breeding crops to tolerate herbicides help farmers grow crops without harming the environment as industry and many weed scientists claim? Or, is this an example of the misuse of biotechnology solely for the benefit of large agrichemical companies, as critics charge?

A. The Creation of Herbicide Resistant Crops

1. Rationale

Plants exhibit varying levels of tolerance* to herbicides. Some plants are highly sensitive and are damaged or killed by very low doses of

---

*The terms *tolerance* and *resistance* are sometimes used interchangeably. Tolerance refers to the naturally occurring variation within a population to withstand some particular herbicides. These plants are referred to as susceptible. Other plants have high tolerance and are not affected by doses of herbicide that kill other plant species. For example, corn is highly tolerant to atrazine, whereas wheat and barley are tolerant to certain sulfonylurea herbicides at levels that control many weeds. If a crop is sufficiently tolerant to an herbicide, the herbicide can be applied to control weeds while the crop is growing in the field. This is called postemergence herbicide treatment. There are limited numbers of postemergence herbicides that can be used with an individual crop because most crops are sensitive to most herbicides. Many, especially the most effective broad-spectrum herbicides, are often applied before the crop is planted or emerges in the field. This is known as preplant or preemergence treatment. Sometimes specially designed applicators are used to avoid contact with the crop. Thus, the use of the most effective broad-spectrum herbicides is restricted by crop sensitivity.

Starting in the late 1960s, weeds exposed for many years to the triazine herbicide atrazine, applied extensively in corn and sorghum, developed resistance (Bandeen, Stephenson, and Cowett 1982). It became obvious that if weeds could acquire resistance there must also be genes that if transferred to crops would enable them to become resistant, too (LeBaron 1991). Early attempts to selectively breed crops for resistance to herbicides were largely unsuccessful. Classical breeding techniques were used to create new varieties of rapeseed (canola) and rutabaga resistant to the herbicide atrazine (Benbrook and Moses 1986; Beversdorf, Hume, and Donnelly-Vanderloo 1988). However, adding atrazine resistance resulted in significant yield reductions. Advances in molecular biology provided the tools for researchers to uncover the genetic basis for resistance to the triazines as well as the mode of action of other classes of herbicides. Using the new techniques of genetic engineering and plant tissue culture, researchers have now transferred to crop plants genes that confer resistance to particular herbicides (Gasser and Fraley 1989). In many cases, crop plants can be made resistant to herbicides by the addition of a single gene, making herbicide resistance amenable to the current level of genetic engineering competence.

---

dosage of a chemical without prior exposure to that chemical. Resistance is the ability of an organism to withstand exposure to a chemical (for pesticides, the field rate of application) because of natural selection of parental genotypes after exposure to the chemical. Neither definition precisely fits the genetically engineered situation. We prefer to use the term *herbicide resistant* crops rather than *herbicide tolerant* crops, the term preferred by most of industry.

A company will gain substantially if it can increase the market share for a herbicide to which it holds the patent. By creating crops resistant to its herbicides a company can expand markets for its patented chemicals. The U.S. agricultural market for herbicides is now more than $3.9 billion annually and dwarfs sales of insecticides and fungicides (figure 4). Revenue to companies from the sale of herbicides has continued to increase in contrast to insecticide revenues, which have been flat for many years. The market for HRCs has been estimated at more than $500 million by 2000 (Goss and Mazur 1989). As might be expected, herbicide resistance research by industry has been largely limited to herbicides under patent and large acreage crops. Work on creating crops resistant to off-patent herbicides and/ or making minor crops resistant has been conducted primarily by the United States Department of Agriculture (USDA) and university researchers.

Another feature of HRCs attractive to industry is their perfect fit into the existing agricultural system. In growing and harvesting the crop, a farmer need not do anything different when planting herbicide resistant seed than is done with nonresistant crops. The only difference might come in planting an herbicide resistant crop along with nonresistant varieties. Accurate record keeping is then required to prevent spraying the nonresistant crop with the wrong herbicide.

2. Techniques

a. Plant Transformation. Two new biotechnologies are recombinant DNA technology (rDNA), also known as genetic engineering, and plant tissue culture. The former involves the transfer of genes between reproductively isolated organisms, whereas the latter offers the ability to regenerate whole plants from plant protoplasts, single cells, or tissues. Both technologies have been used to create herbicide resistant varieties as well as plants with many other characteristics.

Several techniques developed over the past dozen years have proven effective in modifying the genome of plants and have led to a flourishing of activity in plant biotechnology. The first breakthrough came in the early 1980s, when a system using the plant pathogenic bacterium *Agrobacterium tumefaciens* was developed to transfer genes of interest into plants (Bevan 1984; figure 6). In nature *Agrobacterium* is able to transfer fragments of its DNA into plant cells, causing those cells to produce proteins used by the bacterium as a nutrient. The infected plant cells also proliferate, causing tumorlike growths on the plants, hence the name crown gall

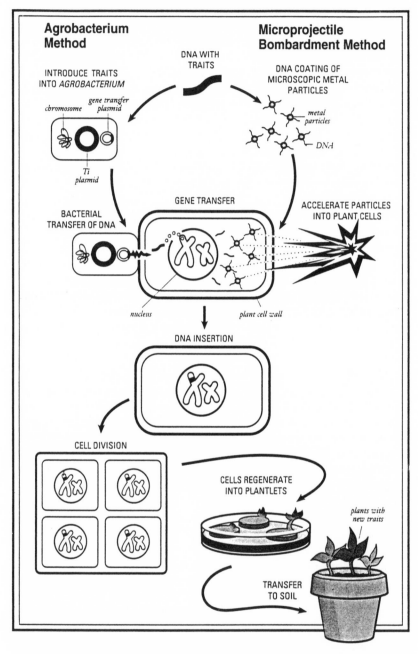

Figure 6. Two Methods for Transforming Plants. *Source:* Monsanto Co.

disease. To use *Agrobacterium* as a DNA transfer agent the disease-causing genes are removed and replaced by genes of interest such has those conferring herbicide resistance. Using plant cell culture techniques, the plant cells exposed to the recombinant bacteria are grown into whole plants.

A number of important agronomic species, including cereal crops, are not readily transformed by *Agrobacterium*. Other techniques have been developed to transform these species. Microprojectile bombardment is now the second most widely used method of gene transfer to plants. Crops recalcitrant to *Agrobacterium*-mediated transformation, including soybeans, oats, rice, wheat, and corn, have been transformed by this method. DNA is applied to the surface of metallic microparticles, and a "gene gun" shoots the particles into plant cells (Klein et al. 1988; Sanford 1988; figure 6). The holes in the cell wall and plasma membrane are quite small and close readily without damage to the plant cell.

Another generalized method of plant transformation involves plant protoplasts, which are cells that have had their cell walls removed by exposure to enzymes. Pure DNA can be transported across the plasma membrane surrounding the protoplasts using chemicals or electrical processes (e.g., Rhodes et al. 1988). The technique is limited by difficulties in regenerating some plants from isolated protoplasts.

b. Conferring Herbicide Resistance. Two main strategies have been used to create HRCs. The first strategy is to alter the active site of the herbicide in the plant, reducing the sensitivity of the plant to the herbicide while maintaining the plant's normal biochemical functioning. Glyphosate is a broad-spectrum systemic herbicide affecting both broadleaf and grass species. The target protein of glyphosate is a plant and bacterial enzyme, EPSP synthase, which is involved in the biosynthesis of amino acids (Padgette et al. 1989; Steinrucken and Amrhein 1980). Treatment of a plant with glyphosate results in aromatic amino acid starvation and cellular death. Early demonstration of the efficacy of this strategy was provided when tobacco plants were transformed with a mutant gene from the bacterium *Salmonella typhimurium,* coding for a form of the enzyme in which there was a single amino acid substitution. The transformed plants exhibited increased resistance to glyphosate compared to controls (Comai et al. 1985).

Sulfonylurea herbicides inhibit an enzyme, acetolactate synthase (ALS), in the biosynthesis pathway of the amino acids valine and isoleucine (Chaleff and Mauvois 1984). Using cell selection and tissue culture techniques researchers have successfully created tobacco plant lines containing a sulfonylurea-insensitive enzyme gene with a single amino acid substitution. Plants regenerated from the mutant cells are one hundred times more resistant to sulfonylurea than wild-type plants (Chaleff and Ray 1984). Also using cell selection and plant tissue culture techniques, researchers have created corn varieties with imidazolinone-insensitive ALS enzymes (Anderson and Georgeson 1989; Newhouse et al. 1991). The imidazolinones are another class of ALS-inhibitor herbicides widely used for weed control in soybeans.

A second strategy involves introducing genes into crops for metabolic detoxification of the herbicide. Plants and bacteria that are naturally tolerant to herbicides often have enzymes that convert the herbicide to a nontoxic metabolite. For example, cereal crops that have natural tolerance to sulfonylureas convert the herbicide to an inactive form (Saari, Cotterman, and Thill 1994). Stalker, McBride, and Malyj (1988) transferred a gene from the soil bacterium *Klebsiella ozaenae* to tobacco plants. The gene encodes an enzyme, nitralase, that transforms bromoxynil, a broadleaf herbicide, to an inactive form. Transformed tobacco plants showed high levels of resistance to bromoxynil. Similarly, a detoxification gene from the bacteria *Streptomyces viridochromogenes* transferred to tobacco conferred resistance to the broad-spectrum herbicide glufosinate (DeBlock et al. 1987).

B. The Current State of Development

Two conditions must be met for herbicide resistant crops to be competitive in the marketplace. First, the crops must be able to tolerate dosages of the herbicide that are sufficient to kill all or most of the sensitive weeds invading the crop. Second, the agronomic characteristics of the resistant plants, after treatment with the herbicide, must be comparable to nonresistant varieties. There are few published data comparing plant performance of genetically engineered herbicide resistant cultivars with nonengineered cultivars (Duke et al. 1991). However, yield deficits of 20 to 30 percent have been noted in classically bred atrazine resistant canola compared to nonresistant varieties (Beversdorf, Hume, and Donnelly-Vanderloo 1988; Goss and Mazur 1989). McHughen and Holm (1995) conducted a three-year study in Canada and found that two herbicide resistant varieties of flax yielded at least as well as the parental strain. However, another herbicide resistant variety underperformed its parental line. From this limited data it appears that genetically engineered HRCs are not necessarily agronomically inferior to classically bred varieties. At the same time, the development of some herbicide resistance products may be slowed or arrested because of yield and quality deficiencies (Duke et al. 1991).

We shall focus on the research and development of HRCs for four herbicides—glyphosate, bromoxynil, sulfonylureas, and imidazolinones—being conducted by Monsanto, Calgene, Du Pont, and American Cyanamid, respectively. Glyphosate is the active component in Roundup, a widely used nonselective (i.e., no crops are tolerant) postemergence herbicide. Monsanto, which holds the patent on and markets Roundup in the United States, is actively pursuing commercial development of genetically engineered resistance to glyphosate in a number of crops, including cotton, corn, soybeans, and potatoes. Field tests of glyphosate resistant tomatoes, sugar beets, and canola have also been conducted by Monsanto and other companies. The major developmental problem has been creating crop lines with commercial levels of resistance while maintaining yield and vigor qualities equivalent to nonengineered lines (Metz 1991; Padgette 1991). Monsanto was granted a label in May 1995 by the EPA for use of glyphosate resistant soybeans, which were developed with Asgrow Seed Company. Thus glyphosate resistant soybeans have become the first HRC to be commercialized fully.

Bromoxynil is the active ingredient in Buctril, a postemergence broadleaf herbicide manufactured by Rhone-Poulenc. Calgene, in association with Rhone-Poulenc, has been developing cotton resistant to bromoxynil. Commercial levels of protection have been reported along with yield and plant quality similar to nonengineered varieties (Goodman 1990; Salquist 1991). Since 1991 Calgene has conducted field tests at numerous sites across the cotton-producing states in cooperation with agricultural extension and university personnel. Calgene's petition to the USDA to deregulate bromoxynil resistant cotton was approved in early 1994. In 1995 the EPA issued a time-limited tolerance for bromoxynil, which allows Rhone-Poulenc and Calgene to treat up to 250,000 acres of bromoxynil resistant cotton until April 1997. The companies are required to collect data to determine whether the combination of herbicide and herbicide resistant cotton actually reduces herbicide use. Meanwhile, the EPA continues to evaluate the potential human health hazards of bromoxynil.

The sulfonylureas are a class of herbicides developed by Du Pont and several other companies. Wheat, oats, soybeans, and barley are naturally tolerant to certain sulfonylureas. Other crops, for example, sugar beets, are very sensitive to this class of herbicides. Many sulfonylureas are persistent, remaining active in the soil for more than one planting season. Farmers using sulfonylurea herbicides and rotating sulfonylurea tolerant and sensitive crops have sometimes suffered yield losses in the year following treatment. Using selection and plant culturing techniques, Du Pont has developed soybeans that are resistant to a newly developed short-residual sulfonylurea herbicide. The short residual characteristic of the new herbicide is designed to avoid the carry-over problem. The resistance trait has been designated "STS." Soybeans not carrying the STS trait are susceptible to the new herbicide. The STS trait has been incorporated into several soybean lines and is available commercially. Du Pont and other companies have been conducting field tests on genetically engineered sulfonylurea resistant varieties of corn and cotton.

Fourteen hybrid corn varieties resistant to the imidazolinone herbicide imazethapyr (Pursuit) became commercially available for the first time in 1993. Marketing has been concentrated in the northern corn belt. The varieties were produced through selection and culturing techniques, not genetic engineering. American Cyanamid, which holds the patent and markets the herbicide, developed some of the varieties with Pioneer Hi-Bred. Other resistant corn varieties were developed independently by Zeneca Seeds, Ciba Seeds, and Cenex/Land O'Lakes. American Cyanamid and others have conducted or are planning field tests of genetically engineered imidazolinone resistant corn, potatoes, and cotton.

This survey of the efforts by four of the major companies, along with the data presented in table 2, indicates that farmers will soon have a variety of HRCs from which to chose. We now analyze the impacts that HRCs will have on agriculture and the environment.

C. HRCs and the Quantity of Herbicide Applied

Intuitively, the development of HRCs would seem to make it easier to use herbicides on more crops and over longer periods of the growing season and thus increase the overall amount of herbicide applied. However, because the current use of herbicides is so prevalent—more than 90 percent of all corn, soybean, and cotton acreage receives at least one herbicide treatment each year (USDA 1993a)—it is unlikely HRCs will increase the overall use of herbicides (Giaquinta 1990; Goldburg et al. 1990; Iowa State University

1991). Rather, the likely impact of HRCs will be to shift the types of herbicides that are used, and farmers will increasingly rely on a few broad-spectrum herbicides.

HRCs can actually lead to reductions in the quantities of herbicide applied, at least in the short term, for several reasons. First, the application rates of some of the herbicides being promoted with HRCs, especially the ALS-inhibitors, are dramatically less than the rates of those they would replace. For example, the application rate for the imidazolinones in herbicide resistant corn is 110 grams per acre while the application rate of atrazine, the most widely used corn herbicide, is 1,200 grams per acre. Although reducing the amounts of active ingredient being released into the environment would seem beneficial in itself (Giaquinta 1990; Goodman 1990), critics counter that the lower application rate merely means that the chemical is much more phytotoxic—that it has greater plant "killing power" (Goldburg et al. 1990). Critics add that surfactants and other nonactive ingredients in herbicides may also have deleterious environmental effects and are often unregulated (Goldburg et al. 1990). Clearly, a lower application rate of a more dangerous chemical is not a desirable outcome. However, most of the herbicides for which crops are being made resistant, such as the ALS-inhibitors and glyphosate, are considered to have favorable environmental characteristics.

Second, for some crops several different herbicides are now used through the growing season to control the range of infesting weeds. With HRCs, multiple herbicide treatments might be replaced by use of a single broad-spectrum herbicide, resulting in a net reduction of the number of applications and the quantity of herbicide applied. Using this logic, scientists at Calgene claim that a single application of bromoxynil could replace up to three other herbicides now in use for broadleaf weed control of cotton in the southeastern United States, thus reducing the total amount of herbicide applied in cotton by 40 to 50 percent (Goodman 1990; Salquist 1991; Wrage 1994). Many herbicides are effective for control of either broadleaf or grass species but not both. Similarly, a single application of glyphosate, which can control both grasses and broadleaf plants, might replace applications of several narrower-spectrum herbicides used within a single crop.

In fact, weed control in practice is not so simple. Even an effective broad-spectrum herbicide usually does not control all weeds all the time. Farmers may still resort to multiple sprays to get the results they desire. Note that the level of control desired by farmers is often greater than the level of control needed to prevent yield loss.

Also, herbicides like glyphosate and bromoxynil are not persistent; their weed-killing ability dissipates rapidly. Weeds germinating after the initial spray may have to be controlled by additional treatments later in the season. It is hard to predict and harder to quantify the supposed benefits of HRCs for reducing herbicide applications.

Third, and most important from an environmental and an agricultural perspective, HRCs could promote integrated pest management of weeds by allowing a shift to a total postemergence approach to weed control. This could reduce the quantities of herbicides applied, the number of applications per growing season, and the number of acres treated. Herbicides are now commonly applied before weeds appear in a field as insurance against having to treat a weed problem once the crop is up. Postemergence treatment is more difficult because of the danger of harming the crop. Preemergence treatment is the antithesis of an integrated approach to weed management, which is based on treatment with herbicides only when it is known that weed populations are above the economic threshold for the crop. The economic threshold defines the crop damage level that economically justifies remedial action. Having effective and safe postemergence herbicide options, which would become available with HRCs, might convince farmers that they do not need to rely on preemergence herbicide treatment (Coble 1991). In this way, HRCs could be incorporated into integrated weed management programs and herbicides be used after nonchemical cultural and mechanical methods have failed to provide adequate control.

The success of HRCs does not necessarily mean that integrated methods will also be adopted. The outcome has much to do with who provides the information that influences farmers' weed management decisions. USDA surveys have shown that many farmers obtain advice on pest control decisions from pesticide manufacturers, not agriculture extension personnel at land grant universities (e.g., RTD Updates 1993a, 1993b). The herbicide business is very competitive, and the market system rewards those who sell the most chemicals. This push toward higher sales serves the short-term profit motives of industry but not necessarily the long-term interest of farmers, consumers, and the environment.

D. Environmental and Health Effects of Herbicides and HRCs

Opposing opinions regarding the merit of herbicide resistant crops center on different perceptions regarding the effects of herbicides on the environment and on our health and the necessity of using herbicides in crop production. There is a clear dichotomy of opinion regarding the safety of herbicides. As a general matter, environmentalists and alternative agriculturalists believe that all pesticides (herbicides, insecticides, and fungicides) carry undue risk. Some risks are known, but many others remain to be identified.

In contrast, most weed scientists distinguish herbicides from other pesticides and evaluate the safety of each herbicide individually. Weed scientists acknowledge that some herbicides have detrimental environmental or health effects and should be phased out (Duke et al. 1991). But most also believe that the majority of herbicides are safe, especially when used as directed.

In fact, insecticides and herbicides are very different types of chemicals. Many insecticides are nerve toxins, and these and others are broadly toxic to vertebrates, including humans, at field rates of application. In contrast, herbicides are designed to act on biochemical pathways that are unique to plants. Many inhibit enzymes that plants use in photosynthesis or in the synthesis of amino acids. These are enzymes and biochemical pathways that animals do not possess. Most herbicides have little or no acute toxicity to humans and wildlife at rates of likely exposure (Edwards 1993, 16–17).

The real unknown about herbicides and for that matter almost all xenobiotics (foreign chemicals introduced into the environment) is the health effects of low-level chronic exposures (Wilkinson 1990). Most research on the long-term effects of pesticides has focused on cancer risk, and far less attention and low funding priority have been given to neurological, immunological, developmental, and reproductive effects. Even for herbicides that are comparatively well studied, the evidence is often hard to interpret, even by the experts. For example, a panel of thirteen epidemiologists and toxicologists were assembled by the Center for Risk Assessment of the Harvard School of Public Health in 1989 to review the evidence that the herbicide 2,4-D was a human carcinogen (Ibrahim et al. 1991). After evaluating the literature consisting of animal studies and epidemiological studies of farm workers and pesticide applicators who are likely to have had the highest and most continuous exposure rates in the population, two experts thought it unlikely that 2,4-D was a human carcinogen, while eleven thought it possible. Of the eleven, one thought the possibility strong, while five thought it remote. How should the public deal with such a conclusion by the experts? The bottom line is that we do not presently have the tools to evaluate accurately the risk of long-term exposure to many chemicals, including herbicides.

While the health effects of herbicides remain controversial, they have some well-established environmental benefits. Before herbicides' widespread use in the years following World War II, farmers controlled weeds through frequent cultivation, which leads to high rates of erosion and compacts the soil. Herbicides not only reduce the cultivation needed to control weeds but also make no-till and minimum-till agriculture practical, eliminating the need for fall and spring plowing. To use these techniques, after a harvest a farmer either lets weeds cover a field or plants a cover crop. In the next growing season the farmer creates openings for a new crop by treating rows of the plant cover with herbicide and then sows seed directly into those rows. Thus, the farmer exposes virtually no soil, which dramatically reduces erosion, conserves soil moisture, and maintains good soil structure.

Proponents of the technology contend that HRCs will allow the replacement of older, widely used herbicides such as atrazine, alachlor, cyanazine, and metolachlor—which are suspected or known to have deleterious environmental or health effects—with newer herbicides having more desirable toxicological characteristics. These more favorable characteristics include rapid breakdown, low soil mobility to prevent movement into surface water and groundwater, and low toxicity to animals.

Companies recognized the importance of defending and promoting the environmental compatibility of their herbicides. But critics emphasize that not all of the herbicides for which herbicide resistant crops are being created have desirable characteristics and that there is nothing to prevent the expanded use of a suspect but legal herbicide. Bromoxynil is applied at low rates, degrades rapidly in the soil, does not accumulate in groundwater, and does not leave residues in food. However, environmental and alternative agriculture groups have staunchly opposed any expanded use of bromoxynil, citing evidence of birth defects in laboratory animals, possible human developmental effects, potential cancer-causing linkages, and toxicity to fish (Gene Exchange 1994a; Goldburg and Hopkins 1993; Rissler and Mellon 1993). In 1989 the EPA listed bromoxynil as a restricted-use herbicide because of evidence of birth defects from animal studies (EPA 1989). The restriction was dropped by the EPA in 1992.

Both the sulfonylureas and imidazolinones are promoted by their respective manufacturers, Du Pont and American Cyanamid, as being environmentally compatible because they are used at "ultra low rates" resulting in reduced active ingredients in the soil compared to other widely used herbicides, have very low toxicity to humans and wildlife, and contribute minimally to food residues. Glyphosate is described in a Monsanto publication as "environmentally friendly" (Schneiderman and Carpenter 1990) and as being essentially nontoxic to animals. Glyphosate is rapidly adsorbed onto soil particles and then degraded by microorganisms so that it does not leech into groundwater or accumulate in the soil (Duke 1988; Metz 1991). Because of its broad spectrum of activity, glyphosate could be used for weed control in no-till or minimum-tillage systems if resistant crops were available (Schneiderman and Carpenter 1990).

Critics charge that the biotechnology and agrichemical industries cannot be trusted to develop crop-resistance exclusively for safe chemicals (*Gene Exchange* 1994b; Rissler 1991). For example, atrazine resistant canola (classically bred) is available in Canada, and there is work to develop tobacco, potato, and cotton resistant to 2,4-D in Australia and the United States (Bayley et al. 1992; Lyon et al. 1989; table 2). Environmentalists consider both of these herbicides hazardous.

A report by the Council for Agricultural Science and Technology recommends that development of crop resistance to herbicides with poor environmental or hazardous toxicological characteristics should be prevented (Duke et al. 1991). Proponents assert that HRCs will encourage environmentally sound weed control and that the marketplace plus the strict toxicological testing requirements in the United States are sufficient to prevent the commercialization of crops resistant to undesirable chemicals. However, critics and proponents do not agree on which herbicides are risky and what mechanism should be used to limit development. Representatives of industry and some university scientists feel assured that the regulatory system as it now exists is sufficient to prevent the increased use of herbicides with unfavorable environmental profiles. Critics feel less sanguine and prefer stricter regulation rather than letting the market act as arbiter. There is no formalized mechanism that would prevent a company from developing crops resistant to environmentally undesirable herbicides as long as the herbicides had not been withdrawn from the market voluntarily or by EPA order.

The controversy surrounding certain herbicides and HRCs has affected the decision of researchers and companies to pursue commercial development of some herbicide resistant crops. In the Midwest, soybeans are often rotated with corn. Atrazine is a widely used herbicide in corn, but soybeans are sensitive to atrazine. When soybeans are planted in a field the year following atrazine treatment, there can be a carry-over effect that reduces soybean yield. Atrazine resistant soybeans would be an attractive product to prevent carry-over and possibly expand the use of atrazine in corn-soybean rotations. However, atrazine has been detected in surface and groundwater (Goolsby, Coupe, and Markovchick 1991; NRC 1989) and is listed as a possible human carcinogen (Goldburg et al. 1990). Several companies decided against commercial development of atrazine resistant crops because of environmental concerns.

Marketing personnel at Biotechnica, a biotechnology firm formerly of Cambridge, Massachusetts, reportedly planned to initiate a research program to develop atrazine resistant soybeans (Cannon 1990). Research personnel at the same company were against developing this product because of the adverse environmental attributes of the herbicide. The research program was never initiated (Cannon 1990). The Swiss-based company Ciba-Geigy had engaged in research on developing atrazine resistant crops, but that program was dropped in the late 1980s amid criticism from environmental groups and a decision by the company to restrict rather than expand the use of this herbicide because of environmental and health concerns (Chilton 1991; LeBaron 1991).

These examples may be illustrative of the new power of environmental criticism over certain paths of innovation. In such cases firms jettison commercial opportunities for new products if they feel public opposition and a fragile regulatory system could jeopardize the future success.

E. HRCs and the Evolution of Weed Resistance

The factor that most threatens the success and agronomic usefulness of HRCs is the potential for weeds to develop resistance to the associated herbicides. The extensive and continuous use of herbicides since the 1950s has resulted in the evolution of more than a hundred weed species resistant to one or more herbicides (Holt and LeBaron 1990; Holt, Powles, and Holtum 1993). While use of HRCs may not greatly alter the total number of acres treated with herbicide, it will shift the number of acres treated with particular herbicides. If HRCs are widely accepted, there will likely be increased reliance on a few of the newer herbicides, with the phasing out of older, less desirable ones. For example, it has been projected that the number of acres treated with glyphosate may increase from a few million to nearly 150 million if glyphosate resistant crops were available (Benbrook and Moses 1986). The widespread use of HRCs developed for resistance to single herbicides will accelerate the selection pressure on weeds to evolve resistant biotypes (Dekker 1991; LeBaron 1989; Wrubel and Gressel 1994).

Two families of herbicides for which HRCs are commercially available, the sulfonylureas and the imidazolinones, are particularly prone to the rapid evolution of resistant weeds (LeBaron and McFarland 1990). At least fourteen weed species have become resistant to the sulfonylurea herbicides since their introduction in 1982 (Saari, Cotterman, and Thill 1994), and imidazolinone resistant populations of common cocklebur, a serious weed of soybean and corn, have appeared at several locations in the southeastern United States (Wrubel and Gressel 1994). There is fear that HRCs will increase the acreage treated with these herbicides, exacerbating the resistance problem (LeBaron 1989; Wrubel and Gressel 1994).

In 1992, 47 percent of soybean acres in the United States were treated with an imidazolinone herbicide. Until 1993 use of these herbicides was restricted to soybeans, naturally tolerant to imidazolinones. However, now that imidazolinone resistant corn is available, the herbicide can be used in both of these large-acreage crops. Because more than 50 percent of farmers in the Midwest rotate corn and soybeans, a farmer who formerly rotated herbicides along with soybean-corn crop rotations now has the option to use an imidazolinone continuously. Some of the area planted in continuous corn or corn rotated with crops other than soybeans, which formerly never encountered imidazolinones, now will be exposed.

Industry has recognized that resistance to the imidazolinones and sulfonylureas is a problem and has come up with resistance management recommendations for farmers. However, farmers must voluntarily adopt the industry recommendations, which are likely to increase weed control costs. In addition, a review of the industry recommendations questions their effectiveness to prevent or delay the evolution of weed resistance (Wrubel and Gressel 1994).

Some herbicides are considered less prone to weed resistance problems. LeBaron and McFarland (1990) classified glyphosate and bromoxynil as relatively low-risk herbicides for development of weed resistance. No weeds resistant to glyphosate and only a single species, *Chenopodium album* (lambsquarters), resistant to bromoxynil have been reported (Holt and LeBaron 1990). However, the increased use of these nonpersistent herbicides, resulting from the promotion of HRCs, may still result in weeds developing resistance, even if more slowly (Dekker 1991; LeBaron 1991). The development of cross-resistance among weeds presents an additional and serious problem. Cross-resistance is the appearance of resistance in weeds that have not been exposed to the particular herbicide. Some weeds have developed cross-resistance to herbicides that have similar modes of action. For example, weeds resistant to sulfonylureas can be cross-resistant to imidazolinones, both of which inhibit the activity of the same plant enzyme. More disturbing, there have been a few instances of weeds developing resistance to herbicides that do not have similar modes of action. It appears that weeds, under selection pressure from a single herbicide, have evolved generalized metabolic pathways that are effective in detoxifying unrelated herbicides (Gressel 1988).

HRCs have the potential to increase the evolution of resistant weeds and with it the loss of effectiveness of some of the more environmentally favorable weed control chemistries. Thus, industry has a responsibility to commercialize HRCs only after having a compulsory and proven resistance management plan in place.

F. Herbicide Residues in Crops

If resistance is conferred on a crop by making the active site insensitive to a herbicide, residues of the herbicide as well as degradation products may build up in the plant. If herbicide resistance is conferred by transferring a gene to a plant that detoxifies the herbicide, the degradation products will build up in the plant. Before a herbicide is approved for registration, residue levels of the herbicide in the new crop and any metabolic products of the herbicide in the plant must be determined and the data presented to the EPA, which is responsible for establishing acceptable levels of pesticide residues in plants and plant products.

Critics of efforts to develop herbicide resistant plants have argued that the acceptable residue levels established by the EPA underestimate the true danger of herbicides to human health because few long-term studies on the chronic effects of herbicide exposure are available (Goldburg et al. 1990). Critics point out that the inert ingredients in herbicides, including surfactants and solvents added in formulations to improve application and spreading on plant surfaces, can be more acutely toxic than the active ingredients (Goldburg et al. 1990; Goldburg 1992). Industry and weed scientists reason that any crop that is resistant to a herbicide, whether it be natural tolerance or engineered resistance, has to store, process, or excrete the herbicide or its metabolic products. This is not a new problem, and they argue that the regulations regarding registration of herbicides for the new HRCs are stringent and should not be any different than they are for nongenetically engineered crops.

G. Economics of HRCs

If HRCs are successful in reducing the use of herbicides, farmers should not expect to reap the full savings, because companies will likely charge a premium for the seed (Wrage 1994). However, farmers will accept HRCs only if they believe there is a significant economic benefit in their use compared to ordinary seed. Because there are many weed control options for all major crops, farmers need not switch to HRC varieties without convincing evidence of their effectiveness. Seed and chemical companies must prove that their products have a significant economic advantage derived from lower overall weed control costs and/or more effective weed control leading to higher yields and improved crop quality. Because the herbicides for which HRCs are being designed are almost all under patent, they will be more expensive than many of the herbicides they are intended to replace. Herbicide resistant crops are unlikely to be economically beneficial for all crop-herbicide combinations.

Few economic product evaluations have been published for HRCs. Analysts at Calgene estimate annual cotton seed sales at $100 million and herbicide costs at $150 million. By switching to bromoxynil for broadleaf weed control in cotton, Calgene projects savings to farmers of up to $37 million each year from reductions in herbicide purchases of 40 to 50 percent. If these projections hold, the company could charge a premium for HRC cotton seed and still provide an economic incentive to farmers to purchase the product.

Hayenga et al. (1992) analyzed the economic impacts of herbicide resistant hybrids of corn and processing tomatoes. They found that a shift to herbicide resistant crops would cause a shift in the types of herbicides used and reduce the overall cost and amount of herbicides applied. The reductions occur because the technology allows a shift to broader-spectrum herbicides, reducing the number of sprays required and the amount of herbicide needed per application. Because of differences in production methods, cost savings for tomatoes could be significant, while savings in corn less so.

Homer LeBaron (1991), formerly a weed scientist at Ciba-Geigy, which has discontinued its HRC development program, is pessimistic about the economic viability of HRCs. He notes that it takes years to develop a resistant crop, produce sufficient seed, and test its performance in the field. Meanwhile, crop breeders are busy developing new lines that have superior traits. LeBaron argues that companies will have trouble charging a premium for products if they are unable to develop HRCs quickly enough to get them into the newest crop lines favored by farmers.

H. The Need for HRCs

Is there really a need for additional herbicide options in the crops for which HRCs are being designed? Herbicide resistance is being engineered almost exclusively into the major-acreage crops of the United States and the other developed countries (table 2). Large numbers of herbicides are already available to treat most weed problems for all these crops, and HRCs are largely unnecessary in these systems (Coble 1991; Dekker 1991). In Iowa, where rotation of corn and soybeans is the dominant cropping system, thirty to forty herbicides are already available to control weeds (Iowa State University 1991). Probably only 5 percent of the acreage in Iowa has uncontrolled weed problems. However, even in major crops that have many herbicide options available difficult weed problems can sometimes benefit from treatment with more effective herbicides. For example, although most broadleaf weeds are effectively controlled in cotton with a combination of cultivation and chemical treatment, morning-glory remains a significant problem and causes economic loss in the southern and southeastern United States (Coble 1991). Bromoxynil might be a solution for this problem.

Because most of the HRC research is industry-supported, the choice of crops selected for genetic engineering are those that will return significant profits rather than those for which farmers have unresolved weed problems. There is a greater need for developing HRCs in some of the minor crops, where fewer or no good herbicides are available for postemergence weed control (Duke et al. 1991; Gressel 1993; LeBaron 1991). These crops are largely ignored by herbicide manufacturers for economic reasons.

Weed problems in third world countries have also gone unmet. Jonathan Gressel, a weed scientist at the Weizmann Institute for Science in Israel, contends that herbicide resistant vegetables and beans should be created to treat the "most destructive and pernicious group of weeds in the third world"—parasitic weeds (1993, 155). Parasitic weeds cause yield losses of up to 50 percent in North and West Africa, the Mideast, India, and Southern and Eastern Europe. There are no herbicides that can control parasitic weeds without harming the crop. Systemic herbicides would be useful in controlling parasitic weeds only if the crops were made resistant. Herbicide resistance to a broad-spectrum systemic herbicide, such as glyphosate or a sulfonylurea, would double yields without any increase in fertilizer or irrigation (Gressel 1993). Greenhouse experiments demonstrate that the invasive weeds can be controlled in herbicide resistant tobacco and canola without harming the crops (Joel et al. 1995). However, companies have been unwilling to lend their genetic engineering expertise to creating herbicide resistance in the affected third world crops (Gressel 1995).

Perhaps the greatest need that HRCs could meet in the United States would be in making available effective and selective postemergence weed controls that promote integrated pest management (IPM) of weeds (section C). IPM is a control strategy that relies on determining the pest population level that will cause economic loss in a crop sufficient to dictate remedial measures (NRC 1989). Researchers are developing models to predict the economic effect of weeds on crops based on the number of weed seedlings germinating in a field early in the growing season (Coble 1991). If it is determined that the weed population is above the economic threshold, then agricultural extension agents can recommend appropriate nonchemical and chemical remedial measures to treat the problem. Farmers who adopt IPM practices and give up preemergence herbicide treatments must feel that effective postemergence herbicides are available to treat a weed problem if all other alternatives fail (Coble 1991). HRCs could provide this assurance.

I. Herbicides versus Nonchemical Weed Control

Although HRCs may not necessarily increase herbicide-treated acreage in the United States, HRCs do encourage continued dependence on these chemicals, which critics view as harmful to the environment and human health. Alternative agriculturalists argue that nonchemical methods of weed control can be implemented immediately to decrease dependence on herbicides and that research into better alternatives needs to be intensified. Among the alternative techniques are the reintroduction of crop rotations where they have been abandoned, cultivation designed to minimize erosion, timing of planting, high-density plantings, cover cropping, intercropping, and biological control (Cramer et al. 1991; Liebman and Janke 1990). Combinations of these techniques are being used effectively in some agricultural situations (NRC 1989). For example, long-term field experiments run by the Rodale Institute in Pennsylvania and the

Practical Farmers of Iowa show that herbicide-free management can produce equivalent yields to crops grown with conventional methods (Iowa State University 1992; Peters, Janke, and Bohlke 1992). However, many mainstream weed scientists argue that the alternative methods, primarily increased cultivation, have adverse environmental consequences, including erosion and soil compaction, and that herbicides cannot now be replaced. There is skepticism within the weed science community that alternatives can be developed that will significantly reduce the need for herbicides. But there is also a growing feeling among some weed scientists that an extreme reliance on herbicides for weed control is an unsound and unsustainable agronomic practice that may indeed have harmful environmental consequences. Accumulating evidence on the presence of herbicides in surface and groundwater and the accelerating discovery of weeds resistant to herbicides has fueled reexamination of the direction of weed science and the responsibility of weed scientists to promote a more judicious use of herbicides. More weed scientists are calling for increased emphasis on the study of weed ecology and population biology to design weed management strategies that complement herbicides and result in an overall reduction of herbicide use.

At least since the early 1980s, however, research efforts by weed scientists have been concentrated on herbicides. The number of research articles appearing in *Weed Science* and *Weed Technology*, publications of the Weed Science Society of America, that exclusively deal with herbicides has far outnumbered those on nonchemical control and integrated weed management (figure 7; Norris 1992; Thill et al. 1991).

J. Conclusions

The development of herbicide resistant crops best illustrates the interplay of all factors in the innovation framework of chapter 1 (figure 2). The agricultural system is in a constant state of readiness to address weed problems. Therefore, innovations in this area, if not stimulated directly by farmer demand, are certainly welcomed in the perpetual struggle against weeds. To farmers, HRCs represent an innovation that enables them to simplify herbicide applications to a few broad-spectrum chemicals. This is also a case where the new techniques in molecular genetics fostered breakthroughs in developing HRCs when classical selection methods had largely failed. Agrichemical companies viewed this as a way to increase the value

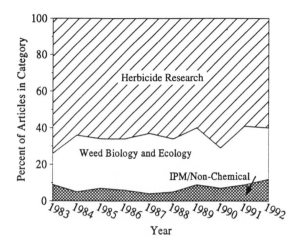

Figure 7. Research Classification of Articles in *Weed Science*, 1983–92

of certain herbicides by expanding their range of uses. Few in industry expected the harsh criticism of HRCs from the public interest community and international nongovernment organizations. Our research indicates that it is quite likely that some innovations in developing HRCs to more problematic herbicides, such as atrazine, were jettisoned because of social concerns. In this particular case, social selection may have taken place among economically viable opportunities. Social selection did not happen at the regulatory level but rather at the stage in which some companies were evaluating product choices. Despite public interest group opposition to bromoxynil resistant cotton because it would lead to increased uses of this suspect herbicide, the cotton has been given limited approval by the EPA and full approval by the USDA and FDA.

Clearly, HRCs are part of and an extension of high-input, chemically intensive agriculture in the United States. As such, the technology is rejected outright by those demanding a shift to low-input agriculture. For the critics, herbicide resistant crops increase the dependence of farmers on chemicals, delay the development of alternative weed control methodologies, and are heavily promoted because of industry self-interest to the detriment of environmentally sound agriculture. However, for those taking the more moderate position that herbicides have a place in weed control and if used appropriately can have positive impacts on agriculture, herbicide resistant crops represent a technology that could have a beneficial effect in modifying the current system.

Both the agrichemical industry and its critics need to examine HRCs thoughtfully. Herbicide resistant crops could help phase out environmentally damaging herbicides, reduce overall herbicide use, and make integrated weed management more attractive to farmers. But HRCs could just as easily result in reliance on a few chemicals, eventually leading to herbicide resistant weeds.

Because HRCs will certainly become a weed control option, farmers must be provided with information enabling them to use these crops in integrated weed management programs that both reduce herbicide use and avoid the rise of resistant weeds.

In our view, herbicide resistant crops are being released without adequate weed resistance management programs in place. Most farmers rely on their agrichemical dealers for pest control advice. However, industry pressures to increase herbicide sales conflict with the wise use of herbicides and the long-term health of agriculture. More federal and state financial support needs to be provided for researchers and extension personnel at land grant universities to design and implement integrated weed management programs that include HRCs where appropriate. With more support for outreach, agricultural extension agents could convince farmers to forgo early chemical treatments and employ effective sampling methods to predict the need for postemergence herbicide applications only where required.

3   Insect Resistant Crops

To limit crop losses due to insect attack, farmers have either traditionally planted certain varieties bred to be resistant to herbivores or employed cultural practices such as crop rotation to prevent the buildup of injurious levels of pest populations. However, since the 1940s the main line of defense to control or eliminate pest insects in many crops has been the application of synthetic organic insecticides. In 1993, 1.6 billion pounds of insecticide (active ingredient) were applied worldwide for agricultural, industrial, government, and home garden uses at a cost of $7.9 billion (Aspelin 1994). In the United States, 247 million pounds of insecticide were applied, with 69 percent devoted to the agricultural sector. This means that 4.5 percent of the world's population uses 15 percent of the insecticides. Some U.S. insecticides go for food exported to other nations.

Initially hailed as a miraculous technology that would eliminate one of humankind's most persistent and noxious pest problems, the widespread use of insecticides has resulted in several significant environmental hazards. These include acute and chronic toxicity to humans, wildlife, and domesticated animals; secondary pest outbreaks resulting from the elimination of beneficial insects; the development of pests resistant to insecticides; and the persistence of these chemicals in soil and water that contaminate the environment (Edwards 1993; NRC 1989).

Traditionally, plant breeders have selected crops that have shown resistance to insect damage without knowing the mechanism of resistance. With genetic engineering scientists have identified the genes for resistance in plants and microorganisms and have transferred those genes to crop plants. One approach has been to transfer a protease inhibitor gene from cowpea to reduce the nutritional value of crops to insects (Boulter, Gatehouse, and Hilder 1990; Hilder et al. 1987). Transferring a gene that expresses a protein that inhibits starch digestion from common bean to pea seeds confers high levels of resistance to seed-feeding beetles (Shade et al. 1994). The strategy that has proved most successful and effective—and the only one being commercially developed—involves transferring gene(s) from *Bacillus thuringiensis* (*Bt*) to crop plants. The potential for developing new applied uses for *Bt*, including transgenic plants as well as recombinant and nonrecombinant microbial products, has resulted in an explosion of activity among companies to discover new isolates with different host specificities and increased virulence. There has also been a marked increase in research to determine the mode of action of the *Bt* toxins.

Bacillus thuringiensis is a widespread soil bacterium that produces a crystalline particle during sporulation that contains proteins called δ-endotoxins. Many of the proteins have highly specific insecticidal activity. More than forty *Bt* crystal protein genes have been sequenced and fourteen distinct genes identified and classified into six major groups based on the similarity of their amino acid sequence and range of insecticidal activity (Feitelson, Payne, and Kim 1992; Höfte and Whiteley 1989). One group of proteins is toxic only to caterpillars, another group to caterpillars and dipteran (fly) larvae, a third to coleopteran (beetle) larvae, a fourth is specific to dipteran larvae, and the fifth and sixth groups are toxic to nematodes. A single crystal may contain one or more related proteins. Individual insect species show different susceptibilities to each crystal protein (MacIntosh et al. 1990). For example, cabbage butterflies are highly sensitive to several but not all caterpillar δ-endotoxins, whereas armyworms are generally insensitive to them (Höfte and Whiteley 1989, 246).

Upon ingestion, the *Bt* crystal dissolves in the insect midgut, releasing the δ-endotoxins. These proteins are broken down by midgut enzymes into smaller toxic polypeptides. Intact *Bt* δ-endotoxins are termed "protoxins" because they only become active toxins after ingestion and processing (Gill, Cowles, and Pietrantonio 1992; Honée and Visser 1993; Lambert and Peferoen 1992; Whiteley and Schnepf 1986; Van Rie et al. 1990). The activated polypeptides bind with midgut epithelial cells, causing pores to develop and disrupting osmotic balance (Gill, Cowles, and Pietrantonio 1992; Honée and Visser 1993). A susceptible insect that ingests the crystal protein soon stops feeding and dies within a few days.

Bt δ-endotoxins are not stable in the acid environment of vertebrate guts, and thus the toxic polypeptides do not form. Even if the toxic polypeptides were present in a vertebrate, they would probably be harmless unless the animal also had the proper epithelial binding site for the protein.

Bacillus thuringiensis was first identified in 1902 in Japan as a pathogen of the silk moth. Beginning in the 1920s, entomologists began experiments to exploit *Bt*'s insecticidal properties for pest control. It was not until the 1950s that the crystalline proteins produced by the bacteria during sporulation were identified as the cause of toxicity to insects (Angus 1956; Hannay and Fitz-James 1955). Since 1958 *Bt* has been commercially available in the United States (Andrews et al. 1987). Several *Bt* powders are even available at home gardening centers. *Bt*-based formulations are widely used and considered the most effective microbial insecticide (Lambert and Peferoen 1992). However, worldwide sales of *Bt* in 1991 were only $105 million (Lambert and Peferoen 1992) compared to worldwide synthetic insecticide sales of $7.6 billion the same year (Aspelin, Grube, and Torla 1992).

One major advantage of *Bt* over synthetic insecticides is that the latter are nonselective, whereas the former is toxic to certain classes of herbivorous insects. Insecticides are toxic not only to the insects that feed on crops but also to the predators and parasites (natural enemies) of the pests. Crops are hosts to a variety of herbivorous insect species, but only some of these cause economic problems and are known as "primary pests." Populations of "secondary pests" are ordinarily kept under control by their natural enemies. When fields are sprayed with insecticides to control the primary pests, the natural enemies are killed, and resurgence of primary and eruptions of secondary pests sometimes occur. *Bt* δ-endotoxin must be ingested for it to act, so only herbivorous insects are affected and natural enemies are conserved. In most uses *Bt* will not be toxic to the natural enemies that ingest it, therefore, they can continue to exert control over the secondary pests and even help control resurgences of the primary pest (table 3). A second important advantage of *Bt* over most synthetic insecticides is that δ-endotoxins are not acutely toxic to mammals, birds, and fish, and no long-term effects have been identified.

A third advantage is that *Bt* can be applied just before harvest. Because of lack of toxicity to humans and rapid degradation, workers can enter a *Bt*-sprayed field for harvest without the delay required after treatment with synthetic insecticides. Finally, *Bt* has been used for more than thirty years without incident, and regulators are convinced of its safety.

Although the *Bt* δ-endotoxin has several advantages over synthet-

Table 3. The Advantages and Disadvantages of *Bacillus Thuringiensis* for Insect Control

---

Advantages
- Ingestion is required for insecticidal activity so only herbivores are affected and natural enemies are conserved.
- Not toxic to mammals (humans), birds, and fish.
- Degrades rapidly so it can be used just before harvest if necessary.
- Long history of safe use.

Disadvantages
- Narrow spectrum of activity limits usefulness if crop is attacked by a variety of pests.
- Degrades rapidly in sunlight, so effectiveness is limited in time; multiple applications may be required.
- Slow-acting compared to synthetic chemical insecticides.
- Timing of applications is important; early instars are susceptible while later instars may be tolerant.
- Formulations are not considered as reliable as synthetic chemicals.

---

ic insecticides, its drawbacks have so far limited its use (table 3 and section B). The narrow selectivity of *Bt* for some herbivores can be a disadvantage because crops are usually attacked by a variety of insects. A *Bt* application may control caterpillars but have no effect on other insects feeding on the crop. In contrast, synthetic insecticides provide broad-spectrum control. Another drawback is that *Bt* δ-endotoxins degrade rapidly in sunlight. In many situations *Bt* must be applied frequently to be effective. The timing of *Bt* applications is also important because early instars (young larvae) are often much more susceptible than later instars. Finally, most farmers do not regard *Bt* formulations as being as effective as synthetic insecticides. This may be because farmers do not apply them correctly, but *Bt* formulations have a reputation for inconsistent performance.

A. Genetic Engineering of Insect Resistant Crops

Scientists have transferred *Bt* genes to crops in an effort to create plants that would produce an insect toxin so that any susceptible insect consuming the plant would be eliminated or disabled. Using rDNA techniques, δ-endotoxin genes have been identified, cloned, sometimes modified, and then transferred to a number of dicot and monocot crops including tomato (Fischhoff et al. 1987), cotton (Perlak et al. 1990), tobacco (Vaeck et al. 1987), rice (Fujimoto et al. 1993), and corn (Koziel et al. 1993). Because the toxin could be produced at all times within the plant, degradation of δ-endotoxin exposed to sunlight would no longer be a problem. By using fragments of the δ-endotoxin genes rather than the entire wild-type gene (Fischhoff et al. 1987; Vaeck et al. 1987) and by altering the DNA sequence of the gene fragment without altering the amino acid sequence (Fujimoto et al. 1993; Koziel et al. 1993; Perlak et al. 1991), higher levels of expression of the insect toxin have been obtained. Research is now concentrated on developing commercial varieties of insect resistant corn, cotton, potatoes, and tomatoes (table 4).

Table 4. Transgenic Insect Resistant Crops, with *Bt* δ-Endotoxins, Approved for Field Tests in the United States from 1987 to July 1995

Crop	Research Organization
Alfalfa	Mycogen
Apples	Dry Creek
	University of California, Davis
Corn	Asgrow
	Cargill
	Ciba-Geigy
	Dow
	Genetic Enterprises
	Holdens
	Hunt-Wesson
	Monsanto
	Mycogen
	NC+ Hybrids
	Northrup King
	Pioneer Hi-Bred
	Rogers NK Seed
Cotton	Calgene
	Delta and Pineland
	Jacob Hartz
	Monsanto
	Mycogen
	Northrup King
Cranberry	University of Wisconsin
Eggplant	Rutgers University
Poplar	University of Wisconsin

Table 4, continued

Crop	Research Organization
Potatoes	USDA
	Calgene
	Frito-Lay
	Michigan State University
	Monsanto
	Montana State University
	New Mexico State University
	University of Idaho
Rice	Louisiana State University
Spruce	University of Wisconsin
Tobacco	Auburn University
	Calgene
	Ciba-Geigy
	EPA
	Mycogen
	North Carolina State University
	Rohm & Haas
Tomatoes	Campbell
	EPA
	Monsanto
	Ohio State
	PetoSeeds
	Rogers NK Seed
Walnuts	University of California, Davis
	USDA

Source: Compiled by authors from USDA data.

B. The State of Development

In May 1995 the EPA approved the first commercial release of a transgenic crop containing an insecticide—*Bt*-potatoes created by Monsanto for control of the Colorado potato beetle. In August 1995 commercial approval was given to *Bt*-corn developed by a partnership of Ciba Seeds and Mycogen Plant Sciences for control of European corn borer. Several more crop varieties containing *Bt*-derived insecticidal genes are likely to reach the marketplace soon. This comes after seven years of small-scale field tests by several companies, the USDA, and university research groups (table 4).

Field tests have shown the effectiveness of this strategy for insect control. Caterpillar damage to cotton bolls at several locations in the Southeast and Southwest averaged about 4 percent compared to 30 percent in nontransgenic controls not treated with insecticides (Fischhoff 1991). The level of protection provided by transgenic cotton was about the same as using synthetic insecticides. The varieties tested reportedly provided control of a wide spectrum of caterpillar pests of cotton. Perlak et al. (1993) report high levels of control of Colorado potato beetle in field tests on transgenic Russet Burbank potatoes expressing a δ-endotoxin gene. Yields of the transgenic plants were equivalent to potato plants treated with insecticides.

Research to develop insect resistant cereal crops initially lagged behind the development of other transgenic crops because of the difficulty in transforming cells and regenerating fertile plants from cell protoplasts. A newly developed technique called microprojectile bombardment has been used to transfer genes to corn and other cereal crops (Gordon-Kamm et al. 1990; figure 6). Meanwhile, other research groups have developed techniques to regenerate cereal cells from protoplasts. Because of these two breakthroughs, transgenic corn, including varieties containing δ-endotoxin genes, are being field-tested by several companies (e.g., Koziel et al. 1993; table 4). Ciba-Geigy predicts that within ten years of introduction, the majority of corn acreage in the United States will be planted with Bt-corn (Gene Exchange 1995).

Research on insect resistant tomatoes has proceeded slowly. Monsanto's first field trial in 1988 was on a Bt tomato. However, the company views this market as less attractive than either cotton or potatoes because relatively little insecticide is used on tomatoes. More than $100 million is spent annually on caterpillar control in cotton compared to $10–15 million on control in tomatoes (Hebblethwaite 1991). Thus, market considerations and not technological problems have delayed progress of this product.

C. The Use of Insect Resistant Crops in Pest Management Programs

The most obvious advantage of using transgenic plants producing insect toxins is the replacement of synthetic insecticides now used to control pests. Monsanto estimates that a transgenic plant that could effectively control caterpillar pests in cotton could result in a four-to-five-million-pound reduction or more than 35 percent of insecticides applied each year to the crop (Hebblethwaite 1991).

Some observers question how easily insect resistant transgenic plants will fit into many pest management systems (Goodman 1990). The narrow spectrum of activity of *Bt* is a disadvantage for the many crops that have a diversity of insect pests (table 3). Insecticides might still have to be applied to control other pests not susceptible to the δ-endotoxin expressed by the crop. The elimination of a susceptible caterpillar might open opportunities for the expansion of populations of resistant competing pests such as beetles (Chilton 1991). The overall benefit to the farmers of insect resistant plants would then be reduced.

Fred Gould, an entomologist at North Carolina State University, observes (1991), however, that some crops such as cotton have a single major pest, which requires many treatments with insecticides, as well as a number of minor pests. Gould believes that if the primary pest could be controlled without using broadly toxic insecticides (i.e., with a *Bt*-type product), other pests could then be controlled by naturally occurring predators and parasites, cultural controls, and biological control techniques. In this way transgenic crops with *Bt* genes would fit into and enhance an integrated pest management approach to overall pest control of crops. Significant reductions in the use of insecticides would then be realized.

Gould argues that insect resistant transgenic plants may not result in decreased insecticide use in all crops. In corn, for example, the European corn borer (ECB) is a major pest and limits production in some regions of the United States. Insecticide treatments for this pest are usually limited because they are not very effective. Corn plants producing *Bt* insect toxins that are effective in controlling the corn borer would have little effect on insecticide use because not much is applied for this pest. Gould believes, therefore, that the major impact of corn resistant to the ECB would be social and economic rather than environmental. For example, protection from the corn borer might increase U.S. corn production affecting corn prices and the viability of some farm operations (section E).

Rebecca Goldburg (1991), a senior scientist with the Environmental Defense Fund, questions the economic reasoning of companies that develop *Bt* crops. She contends that they may have trouble marketing an insect resistant transgenic plant to most U.S. farmers unless the toxin has biological activity over a wide range of insect pests. Goldburg argues that the greatest appeal of narrow-spectrum *Bt* crop plants may be to small farmers who use multiple methods of pest control. This narrow market niche would not justify the capital investments of companies in developing transgenic insect resistant varieties.

Researchers have discussed broadening the spectrum of activity of Bt plants by engineering multiple δ-endotoxin genes into a single crop variety. A crop could then be protected from both beetle and caterpillar pests, for instance. One might imagine a repository of insect toxin genes that could be engineered into seeds of desirable varieties to be called into use when major insect pest outbreaks would be expected. By only using the toxin genes occasionally when they are essential to maintain crop production, the onset of resistance could be prevented or delayed (section D).

In certain instances, transgenic crops expressing insect toxins could be more effective in controlling pests than synthetic chemicals. Some insects feed inside the crop plant, for example, within leaves, stems, or buds. Contact insecticides are not very effective in controlling these insects. As a result, higher doses of insecticide are often applied than is the case for treating surface-feeding insects. Plants internally producing their own pest control substances would have the insect toxin available where the insect is feeding.

Agrichemical companies that are also developing bioengineered insect resistant crops can find themselves in a difficult position. They justify the environmental benefits of switching to the transgenic plants to reduce insecticide use while also defending insecticides as not being harmful to the environment. For example, representatives of Monsanto, a large pesticide manufacturer as well as a leading investor in agricultural biotechnology, consider the reduction in insecticide use associated with using transgenic crops producing Bt δ-endotoxin as a strong selling point for farmers (Hebblethwaite 1991). Company officials have stated that environmental friendliness is a primary consideration in Monsanto's choice of new products to develop for agriculture (Fischhoff 1991). But they also defend the use of insecticides as environmentally safe.

D. The Evolution of Insect Resistance to Bt δ-Endotoxins

The widespread use of large quantities of synthetic insecticides has resulted in strong selection pressure for the evolution of insecticide resistance in pest populations. It is estimated that more than five hundred species of insects are resistant to at least one major insecticide, and cross-resistance to several insecticides is common (Georghiou and Lagunes-Tejeda 1991). Resistance to Bt δ-endotoxin has not been a problem, probably because Bt sprays have generally been used sporadically and degrade rapidly. Both factors, limited use and rapid degradation, act to decrease selection pressure for the emergence of resistance. Will the continuous expression of δ-endotoxin genes in transgenic plants, even when insect populations are below the economic threshold, provide strong selection pressure for the evolution of pest resistance?

Without empirical data, it is difficult to predict whether or how quickly an insect species will develop resistance to a selective agent (Gould 1989; Gould 1991). No studies on the development of resistance in populations of pest insects exposed to transgenic plants producing δ-endotoxin have been reported, although some are planned (Gould 1991). Although it is not known how natural populations of pest insects will respond to transgenic plants producing *Bt* toxins (Goodman 1990; Gould 1991), there is mounting evidence that diverse groups of insects can develop resistance if selection pressure is strong. Resistance has been reported in field populations of a lepidopteran pest of stored grain (McGaughey 1985) and the leaf-feeding diamondback moth in the United States and Asia exposed to intensive *Bt* sprays (references in Tabashnik 1994). More than a thousandfold increase in resistance to δ-endotoxin has been reported for laboratory-selected strains of pest caterpillars (Tabashnik 1994). After twelve generations of selection a laboratory strain of Colorado potato beetle, compared to an unselected strain, was fifty-nine times more resistant to δ-endotoxin (Whalon et al. 1993). The authors state that "resistance in Colorado potato beetle could progress rapidly (3–5 years) when resistant alleles are present in the population and if selection pressure is maintained" (Whalon et al. 1993, 232).

Richard Roush (1992, 2) of Cornell University is an expert on the evolution of resistance. He cautions in a letter to the *Gene Exchange* that "it is a widely held but unproven hypothesis that transgenic plants will always cause resistance more quickly than sprays." He points out that the evolution of resistance is a complex phenomenon and dependent on a number of factors, including the persistence and decay rate of the pesticide, expression of resistant genotypes in pests, and the fraction of the population that escapes exposure. Transgenic plants, Roush argues, might delay resistance more effectively than sprays by producing a high toxic dose consistently throughout the plant without decaying over time. Thus, transgenic crops might be able to eliminate all pests that feed on it and avoid pest adaptation.

Marvin Harris (1991, 1075) an entomologist at Texas A&M University, has a decidedly more pessimistic view of the impact of transgenic plants with *Bt* δ-endotoxins on pest management. He observes that "transgenic *Bt* endotoxins will suffer the same fate (as insecticides) if they are used to protect plant populations over wide areas. This and related genetic engineering technologies that rely on confrontational prophylactic tactics pose a significant threat to the stability of production agriculture." Harris predicts that within three to nine years after widespread adoption of *Bt* transgenic plants the evolution of pest resistance will render "the technology useless." Once resistance is common, he argues, conventional *Bt* sprays will also become worthless. Transgenic plants with *Bt*, in Harris's view, will "stifle competition" so that many conventional insecticides will be removed from the market and new technologies will not be developed. When resistance to *Bt* δ-endotoxin becomes critical there will be few alternatives to which to turn.

The biotechnology industry is concerned about resistance and has formed a working group to discuss strategies and to fund research on insect resistance to *Bt* δ-endotoxins. A number of strategies have been suggested to limit the development of resistance (McGaughey and Whalon 1992; Tabashnik 1994). Genetic engineers could create transgenic plants with two or more forms of the *Bt* δ-endotoxin gene that affect different active sites in the target pest. A plant containing multiple-resistance factors under the control of several genes would probably prevent or delay the evolution of resistance compared to single resistance factors (Gould 1988a). Some laboratory studies have found that insects selected for resistance to one form of δ-endotoxin were not resistant to other forms (Ferré et al. 1991; Van Rie et al. 1990). Recent studies, however, indicate that mixtures of δ-endotoxins may be of limited value in slowing the development of resistance. Tabashnik et al. (1991) report that field populations of the diamondback moth in Hawaii have developed resistance to spray formulations of *Bt* containing mixtures of toxins. Similarly, resistance to mixtures of *Bt* strains are reported for the Indianmeal moth (McGaughey and Johnson 1992). Gould et al. (1992) found cross-resistance to δ-endotoxins differing in structure and site of activity (different binding sites within the insect gut) in a laboratory-selected strain of the lepidopteran pest *Heliothis virescens*.

Resistance in pest populations could be managed with planting strategies that reduce selection favoring resistant pest genotypes. This could be accomplished by planting mixtures of insect resistant and susceptible seeds in the same field or by planting adjoining fields: one with crops expressing δ-endotoxin and one toxin-free (Gould 1988a; Mallet 1989).These management techniques are unlikely to be implemented voluntarily by farmers who desire maximum crop protection. A company could market premixed seeds as the farmer's only choice of δ-endotoxin-containing varieties. One simulation model suggests, however, that planting mixtures of insect resistant and susceptible crops may be counterproductive for mobile insect pests and actually speed the evolution of pest resistance (Mallet and Porter 1992).

Alstad and Andow (1995), using computer models that incorporated the plant preferences and movement patterns of the pest insect, devised a planting strategy to delay the evolution of resistance in the European corn borer. Early planting of corn protected with insecticidal genes were used to reduce the first generation of pests attacking the crop. Much of the late corn plantings could then be left unprotected because the second pest generation is small. This planting strategy reduces selection pressure for resistance while minimizing crop damage.

Another strategy proposed to avoid or delay the evolution of resistance involves engineering plants with insect resistant genes that are only turned on during part of the plant's life-cycle (Gould 1988b). This would create temporal refugia, allowing some susceptible insects to survive and thus reducing selection for resistance. Field tests have been conducted of transgenic tobacco in which the δ-endotoxin genes are only activated when an externally applied chemical inducer is used (Williams et al. 1992). Alternatively, within-plant spatial refugia could be created by limiting expression of the δ-endotoxin gene to the most vulnerable plant tissues that have to be protected from insect damage (Chilton 1991; Goodman 1990; Gould 1991; Tabashnik 1994). For example, tomato fruits would express the insect toxin while leaves would be left unprotected. The key to all of these resistance management schemes is to prevent the eradication of susceptible individuals, thus conserving susceptible genes in the pest population. However, tissue-specific expression would reduce the overall effectiveness of insect control and crop yield, making it unattractive in the market place (Fischhoff 1991). This technique might also encourage the same resistance problems for certain types of insects as the seed mixtures discussed earlier (Mallet and Porter 1992).

Whatever resistance management plan is adopted for a particular crop, it will require careful forethought, planning, and cooperation among companies, farmers, and extension agents. Critics assert that the profit motivations of the first companies marketing plants with *Bt* genes will result in widespread unmanaged use (Rissler 1991). They claim that the EPA is under pressure from industry to commercialize products without adequate resistance management planning (Mellon 1995). The first commercially available insect resistant transgenic plants will produce the δ-endotoxin constitutively in all tissues at all times.

If pest resistance to δ-endotoxin evolves rapidly, the success of this product and the environmental benefit of reduced synthetic insecticide use will be compromised. However, it is the organic and alternative farmers who will be severely and unjustly impacted (Rissler and Mellon 1993). Many of these farmers now rely on microbial preparations of *Bt*, which could be rendered useless by unwise use of insecticidal plants.

Our earlier suggestion—that is, for the restrained use of *Bt* toxin genes limited to times when they were really needed to prevent widespread crop damage—probably would be considered unrealistic because it restricts a firm's ability to use products for maximum profitability. This dilemma highlights a general problem for pesticides that was discussed for herbicides in chapter 2. All pesticides select for pests resistant to the control agent. Resistance evolves most rapidly to the most effective control agents that are used most frequently or are the most persistent. Agriculture would be best served by a policy of well-thought-out restrained use of environmentally compatible control agents to conserve their effectiveness. This is in direct conflict with the competitive structure of the agrichemical and, in this case, biotechnology industries (Kennedy and Whalon 1995). Their purpose is to sell as much product as quickly as possible to recover investment in research and development. Our analysis reveals, however, that one cannot separate the problem of pest control from the problem of pest resistance.

Industry may now be convinced that proactive resistance management is in its best interest. A research report on transgenic potatoes by a team of industry and university scientists (Perlak et al. 1993, 318) includes the following qualifier: "For these insect-protected potato plants to become an integral part of potato pest management, additional studies of both the plants and insect populations is required. The goal . . . is to develop an integrated pest management (IPM) program that effectively utilizes these genetically modified plants, while at the same time protecting their durability as an insect control system."

E. δ-endotoxin Residues in Plants and Food

The crystalline protein produced by *Bt* is a protoxin because it only becomes an activated toxin *after* alteration in the alkaline environment of the insect midgut. Humans do not normally ingest δ-endo-toxin that is applied to crops because it degrades rapidly in sunlight. However, the endotoxins expressed within crops are not exposed to degrading radiation, and residues may remain and make human consumption more of a concern. It is assumed that the instability of the δ-endotoxin in acid environments would protect humans and other mammals even if the protoxin was ingested. No acute or chronic health effects have been noted in toxicological tests conduct-ed on mammals, including human volunteers (Fischer and Rosner 1959; Hadley et al. 1987; references in Drobniewski 1994). In these tests Bt formulations consisting of spores and crystal proteins were ingested. A few infections may be attributable to human exposure to microbial preparations of Bts (chapter 6).

To our knowledge, the results of toxicological tests using the types and levels of expression of δ-endotoxins produced by transgenic plants have yet to be published. Goldburg and Tjaden (1990) claim that the synthetic protein produced in transgenic plants is an acti-vated form of the toxin. This implies that at least one of the pro-tections from the toxin afforded vertebrates has been eliminated: the alkaline gut pH required to alter and activate the protoxin proper-ly. Jepson, Croft, and Pratt (1994) suggest that consumption of cat-erpillars poisoned by feeding on an endotoxin-producing transgenic plant might present a health risk to wildlife and humans. Even if the synthetic protein is in the activated form, vertebrates would still be protected if the toxin is rapidly degraded under acid conditions or if vertebrates do not possess an active site to which the protein can bind. Because toxicological data based on naturally occurring forms of δ-endotoxin may not apply to the toxins being produced by transgenic plants, Goldburg and Tjaden (1990) call for new and ex-tensive testing to assess the safety of foods containing δ-endotoxin.

Monsanto has set standards for itself to prove the safety of trans-genic plants producing δ-endotoxin. First, the company must show that the transgenic plant is "substantially equivalent" to the non-transformed plant (Fuchs 1993). The transgenic crop must be com-parable to the nontransformed variety in terms of "composition, nutritional quality, morphology, and in all other aspects that could impact the use, value, and the environmental, food, and feed safety of this product" (Fuchs 1993, 58). The only difference can be that the transgenic plant, compared to nontransformed plants, produces one or more proteins derived from its additional genes.

Second, there must be substantial evidence demonstrating that the novel proteins being expressed by the transformed plant are harmless to humans, the environment, and nontarget animals.

For the *Bt* potato, Monsanto claims to have developed data to satisfy regulators that (1) there is substantial equivalence to non-transformed potatoes (Fuchs 1993); (2) the amino acid sequence of the endotoxin protein produced by the transgenic potato is identical to that produced by naturally occurring *Bt* (McPherson et al. 1988); (3) laboratory experiments show no evidence of disease or mortality impacts on mice and beneficial insects (ladybugs, honey bees, lacewings, and parasitic wasps) from *Bt* δ-endotoxin (Fuchs 1993); and (4) the NPTII protein, expressed in transgenic potatoes and other transgenic plants as an antibiotic resistance marker permitting the selection of plant cells containing the recombinant gene of interest, has no adverse health effects on tube-fed laboratory mice and is degraded rapidly (within twenty seconds) in a simulated mammalian gastric system (Flavell et al. 1992; Fuchs et al. 1993).

The full registration granted Monsanto's *Bt*-potato indicates that both the EPA and the FDA agree that the δ-endotoxin expressed in that crop does not constitute a human health hazard. However, the acceptance of this transgenic plant has not assuaged the concerns of critics who point out that many modified forms of the δ-endotoxin gene are used in engineered plants. Thus, they contend that each *Bt* crop with its modified form of the toxin gene needs to be evaluated individually (*Gene Exchange* 1995).

F. Economics of Insect Resistant Crops

The insecticide market for agricultural uses in the United States in 1993 was $1.2 billion (Aspelin 1994). Significant percentages of several large-acreage crops receive insecticide treatment each year, including cotton (65 percent of ten million acres; corn (30 percent of seventy-five million acres); and potatoes (90 percent of one million acres) (USDA 1993a). Control of Colorado potato beetle in potatoes is estimated at $75–$100 million per year (Perlak et al. 1993). A substantial market exists for insect resistant crops that could reduce the cost incurred by farmers. A market analysis by Decision Resources, Inc. (DRI 1992, 85) projects that "seed of insect resistant corn, cotton, soybeans, and tobacco will probably claim sales of $1 billion by 2000. Insect resistant tomato and potato . . . will have $150 million in sales by 2000." However, the same report includes a significant caveat: "If resistant insect populations develop quickly in response to cultivation of transgenic crop plants, the market potential of such varieties will certainly be diminished."

The potential emergence of resistance among target insects to *Bt* δ-endotoxin makes it difficult to offer reliable market figures. Another confounding variable in evaluating *Bt* is that it may be used along with the same synthetic chemical treatments now being applied as an additional insect control rather than as a replacement product.

The economic gain of increasing agricultural yields are complicated by the price control system in the United States. Thus, if insect resistant crops were environmentally benign and widely adopted, there could be a differential economic impact on farmers. For example, this country produces a surplus of corn, and farmers are given monetary incentives from the government to decrease corn acreage. The introduction of corn plants protected from the corn borer would allow increased corn production in parts of the country where production is now limited by corn-borer infestation not controlled by chemical insecticides. The average corn yield per acre in the United States would increase because of the decreased impact of the corn borer. To deal with the new surplus of corn, either the taxpayer would have to subsidize greater decreases in total corn acreage or the price of corn would drop. Although some farmers would benefit by being able to increase corn production, those who already grow large quantities of corn would be harmed if prices fell. A similar scenario has been developed for the impacts of the adoption of recombinant bovine somatotropin in milk production (chapter 9).

G. Conclusions

Transgenic crop plants expressing *Bt* δ-endotoxins offer the direct environmental benefit of reducing the amount of synthetic insecticides now used to protect crops. Although this is a product whose development was clearly science-driven, the investment community had to take a serious look at whether a research program that would reduce chemical insecticides had a good chance of success. The need has existed for more effective biological insect control products to replace the highly toxic insecticides now widely used. Thus, the development of transgenic insect resistant plants conforms both to the diffusion model and induced model of innovation (chapter 1).

The early tests for insect resistant crops used a toxin that was very effective and fairly well known. The government has been supportive in expanding the use of *Bt*, and the USDA and EPA see it as a win-win situation. The economics make sense for companies that are already involved in seed production. This innovation is well suited to research programs for breeding plants for resistance; it also fits with the chemical paradigm in which one uses a toxin for quick action against a pest. This innovation is easy to sell to the user who wishes to avoid expensive, time-consuming, and potentially hazardous insecticide applications and responds to existing needs to reduce insecticide use while maintaining yields.

Decisions of the U.S. Patent and Trademark Office can have a significant impact on innovation of transgenic crops. Broad patent control of a technology by one company can stifle multiple applications of a technique within a competitive market. For example, a PTO decision, which it later reversed, granted a species-wide patent for all genetically engineered cotton to Agracetus, Inc., a subsidiary of the multinational chemical company W. R. Grace. The patent would give the company exclusive rights over all genetically engineered cotton, regardless of the method of gene transfer used or the trait modified. Had the decision stood, it can easily be seen how a large company could protect its chemical markets from innovations in biotechnology that would engineer insect resistance into crops.

Insect resistant plant technology is progressing rapidly toward commercialization in several large-acreage crops. However, the major uncertainty associated with the widespread use of insect resistant plants is the possibility that insects, in relatively short time, will evolve resistance to Bt δ-endotoxins.

Farmers and regulators have more than thirty years of experience using microbial formulations of Bt. It is considered a safe and, with certain limitations, a relatively effective alternative to synthetic insecticides. As such it has been adopted by farmers who eschew the use of synthetic insecticides. Bt is also been widely used for control of forest pests such as gypsy moth and for abatement of mosquitoes.

Insect resistant transgenic plants are ideally suited for use in integrated pest management programs because δ-endotoxins do not harm the predators and parasites of pest insects. Thus, the wise use of insect resistant transgenic plants would conserve beneficial insects and avoid the primary pest resurgence and secondary outbreak sometimes observed after treatment with synthetic broad-spectrum insecticides.

Because of the danger of pest resistance it is imperative that industry move cautiously and strictly control commercial use of these products. Substantial laboratory and field data suggest that many herbivorous insect species can evolve resistance to δ-endotoxins under constant selection pressure. Large plantings of crops that express δ-endotoxin in all plant parts throughout the growing season could provide sufficient selection pressure for the rapid evolution of resistance. Widespread resistance to δ-endotoxins would not only render insect resistant transgenic plants useless but also adversely impact conventional microbial applications, thus eliminating the most effective biological alternate to synthetic insecticides. Various resistance management strategies based on models have been proposed to prevent or delay the onset of resistance to δ-endotoxins. Field experiments using transgenic plants should now be required to determine the proper application strategy for a given crop and pest species.

Our fear is that companies seeking to gain an advantage over competitors will release commercial insect resistant varieties that produce δ-endotoxin constitutively. Although companies may encourage farmers to follow resistance management strategies, there is no assurance farmers will comply. Researchers do not have time to remediate the problem before it gets out of hand if predictions hold true that resistance could evolve in as few as three years after *Bt* transgenic crops are adopted widely. If resistance evolves, it will severely diminish the usefulness of insect resistant transgenic plants with δ-endotoxin genes and eliminate an effective alternative to synthetic insecticides for pest control. For this technology to be effective and durable, proactive resistance management programs must be initiated and insect resistant transgenic plants must be viewed as a tool for use in a larger integrated pest management program rather than the single solution to insect pest problems.

4   Disease Resistant Crops

Plant pathogens (viruses, bacteria, and fungi) are responsible for significant crop losses estimated at 12 percent, or nine hundred million tons of preharvest yield worldwide (Cramer 1967). Losses range from 9 percent in rice to 22 percent in potatoes. Estimated losses to plant diseases in the major acreage crops in the United States for 1951 to 1960 were 12 percent for corn and cotton and 14 percent for soybeans and wheat (James, Teng, and Nutter 1991).* Yield penalties of more than 15 percent occur in beans, sugar beets, sugar cane, oats, and peanuts in the United States (James, Teng, and Nutter 1991).

All crops are susceptible to at least several pathogens. In most cases pathogens infect crops at low levels. Attributing crop losses to low levels of disease is difficult and confounded by variability in weather, which can exacerbate pathogen impacts. Because of chronic disease conditions indigenous to certain locales, farmers may be prevented from growing susceptible crops.

Viral diseases cannot be treated effectively once they occur. Very few antibacterial chemicals are available to control bacterial diseases (Schroth and McCain 1991). The main defense for these pathogens is to prevent their establishment or to limit their spread once they occur. Prevention includes planting disease-free stock and using disease resistant strains. Another line of defense is sanitation, the removal of diseased plants once they are discovered to prevent the spread of disease.

Plant pathogenic fungi are the only plant disease organisms directly amenable to treatment with chemical pesticides. Fungicide use in the United States (including agricultural, industrial, and home use) has nearly doubled since 1979. In 1993, 131 million pounds of

*There has not been a comprehensive accounting of losses for all crops in the United States since 1965 (James, Teng, and Nutter 1991, 18).

active ingredient was applied at a cost of $584 million (Aspelin 1994, 8). Pesticide treatments are used indirectly to control populations of insects, mites, nematodes, and fungi that are vectors of plant pathogens, especially viruses.

Since the end of the nineteenth century, selecting and breeding plants resistant to pathogens has been the main strategy used to minimize yield losses from disease. Breeding programs tend to be expensive, time-consuming, and labor-intensive. Plant breeding for resistance has usually been a trial-and-error endeavor. Moreover, pathogens have been very adaptable in overcoming resistances. The mechanisms of resistance in crops are rarely known. Thus, breeding programs focus on individual crops rather than on generalizable mechanisms that can be applied across crops or pathogens.

Plants are exposed to myriads of potential pathogens, but only a few actually cause disease symptoms. Thus, all plants are already resistant to almost all microbes they encounter. Molecular techniques are employed widely to discover and explicate the processes and interactions between plants and pathogens that result in disease resistance or virulence (e.g., de Wit 1992; Walton and Panaccione 1993). Using recombinant DNA technology coupled with tissue culture and traditional plant breeding, researchers hope to develop new varieties incorporating longer-lasting disease resistance mechanisms and to discover more generalizable strategies for plant protection (Moffat 1992; Moffat 1994).

More than 350 field tests of genetically engineered disease resistant plants have been approved in the United States since 1987 (figure 5). The most interest, discussion, research, and success in creating disease resistant transgenic crops has focused on viral resistance. About three times as many field tests of plants incorporating viral resistance genes have been approved, compared to the tests for fungal and bacterial resistance (figure 8).

In this chapter we describe the most recent research approaches for developing transgenic plants that have fungal, bacterial, and viral resistance. We also examine the environmental, ecological, and economic issues associated with the use of plant genetic engineering for developing and enhancing disease resistance.

A. The Current State of Development

1. Protection from Fungal and Bacterial Diseases: Inducible Defenses

Upon invasion by pathogens, plants can mount a number of defenses, including the thickening of cell walls to entrap the pathogen,

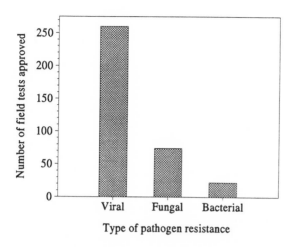

Figure 8. Disease Resistant Transgenic Plant Varieties Approved for Field Tests in the United States from 1987 to July 1995. *Source:* Compiled by the authors from USDA data

rapid death of invaded cells (hypersensitive response) to deny the pathogen adequate resources to survive and spread, production of small antimicrobial molecules known as phytoalexins, or production of larger antimicrobial proteins. Because plant responses are activated after pathogen attack, these types of protective mechanisms are known as "inducible defenses." Some of the plant responses may be localized in the invaded plant cells and/or be specific for particular pathogens. Other responses may be generalized over the entire plant, may be effective against a broad range of pathogens, and may last weeks or months after the initial response to infection (Kuc 1982). For example, a leaf not in direct contact with the pathogen might have elevated levels of antimicrobial chemicals after a leaf in another part of the plant is invaded by a pathogen. This type of inducible defense, which can be generalized throughout the plant, is known as systemic acquired resistance (SAR) (Ross 1961; Ryals, Ward, and Métraux 1992).

Inducible antimicrobial proteins are called "pathogenesis related proteins" (PR proteins) and vary in type and function (Bol, Linthorst, and Cornelissen 1990). PR proteins can operate locally within an individual cell, limiting infections of the initial invading organism, and/or they can act widely and make the entire plant less susceptible to subsequent infection by a variety of organisms. PR proteins include chitinases and B-1,3–glucanases, which are believed to hydrolyze the cell walls of some fungi (Mauch, Mauch-Mani, and Boller 1988; Schlumbaum et al. 1986); osmotin, isolated from tobacco and tomato, which in vitro destroys fungal sporangia and inhibits fungal growth (Woloshuk et al. 1991); and other antimicrobial proteins of unknown function (e.g., Alexander et al. 1993).

Plants succumb to disease when they fail to recognize or respond to a pathogen, when they respond too late or inadequately, or when the pathogen is able to negate or overcome the defense. Research has been directed at identifying the genes that control production of PR proteins. The practical application of this work is to engineer plants genetically to produce protective proteins constitutively, in all plant parts all the time, or to be able to activate the defense systems quickly before pathogens cause much damage. Most research on using PR proteins for plant protection has been limited to laboratory and greenhouse experiments, with very few field tests conducted or in progress. No results of field tests have been published in the scientific literature, so it is difficult to assess the efficacy of such approaches.

Strategies to create fungal resistance in plants through genetic engineering have involved introducing plant-derived chitinases and B-1,3–glucanases intended to break down the cell walls of chitinous fungi (Broglie et al. 1991; Neuhaus et al. 1991) or other PR proteins that have antifungal properties (Alexander 1993; Woloshuk et al. 1991). Chitinases are found in some plant cells at low levels, and their expression increases or is induced following pathogen attack. By creating plants that express chitinases constitutively and at elevated levels, researchers hope to prevent or severely limit the establishment and spread of fungal infections. Transgenic tobacco plants with a chitinase gene from beans produced elevated levels of chitinase in roots and leaves compared to control plants in greenhouse experiments (Broglie et al. 1991). Transgenic and control plants were grown in soil inoculated with the fungal pathogen *Rhizoctonia solani*. More than half of the control plants died, whereas mortality of transgenic plants ranged from 23 to 37 percent. A positive association was found between the level of chitinase expressed in experimental plants and survival. Of the surviving plants, the transgenics were larger and hardier than the controls. Broglie et al. (1991) and Lin et al. (1995) report similar results for transgenic canola and rice, respectively, expressing chitinase genes.

In contrast, Neuhaus et al. (1991), while reporting success in the transformation of tobacco plants with chitinase genes expressed at elevated levels, found no beneficial effect on resistance to infection by the fungal pathogen *Cercospora nicotinae.*

The results from these experiments may indicate that chitinase is not a generalizable defense for all fungal pathogens. There may be other plant or environmental factors required for chitinase to prevent disease establishment. For instance, Mauch, Mauch-Mani, and Boller (1988) discovered a synergism between chitinase and B-1,3–glucanase. A mixture of the two enzymes extracted from fungus-infected pea pods was applied to paper discs on which fungal cells were growing. The cell walls of the fungi were destroyed, and fungal growth was halted. Purified extracts of either enzyme tested separately did not inhibit fungal growth.

The Oomycetes are a group of fungi whose cell walls contain no or very little chitin. Members of this fungal group include the downy mildews, *Phytophthora* spp., and *Pythium* spp., which cause significant economic loss. Growth of some of the species of Oomycetes is not inhibited by treatments with chitinases and B-1,3–glucanases separately or in mixture (Mauch, Mauch-Mani, and Boller 1988). However, other PR proteins can inhibit the growth of *Phytophthora infestans* (late blight of potato) in vitro (Woloshuk et al. 1991) or increase tolerance to infection by two Oomycete species in transgenic plants grown in greenhouses (Alexander 1993). Field tests of these types of PR proteins are in progress (Ryals 1994).

PR proteins in plants may not be turned on at once when a plant is invaded. The activation of PR proteins in uninfected tissues may be dependent on the biosynthesis and release of plant chemicals from pathogen-infected cells. These compounds are thought to act as chemical messengers or signals that move through the plant and turn on the genes controlling PR protein production but have no direct toxic effect on the pathogens themselves. The hypersensitive response of plant cells to invasion by pathogens may be involved with the production and release of these messenger chemicals.

Evidence from several experiments indicates that salicylic acid, an endogenous plant chemical, may be a chemical messenger inducing PR proteins. Salicylic acid is associated with the activation of SAR genes and the accumulation of PR proteins (Van Loon and Antoniw 1982; Ward et al. 1991). Transgenic tobacco plants expressing a gene that prevents salicylic acid from accumulating were unable to develop systemic resistance following infection with tobacco mosaic virus (TMV) (Gaffney et al. 1993). Transgenic and nontransgenic control plants that did accumulate salicylic acid became resistant to subsequent TMV infection. A synthetic chemical has also been used to induce SAR (Métraux et al. 1991; Uknes et al. 1992; Ward et al. 1991; Zessman et al. 1994).

How would a chemical inducer be used to protect crops from disease? When low levels of plant disease symptoms are identified in the field, a chemical inducer, applied as a spray, would quickly turn on SAR genes in the crop, increasing the level of PR proteins throughout the plant. Infection would be halted, with the added benefit of reducing selection pressure for resistant pathogens that might occur if high levels of plant defense chemicals were expressed in crops throughout the season. Such an inducing chemical has been used to turn on *Bt* genes in transgenic plants for insect resistance (chapter 3; Williams et al. 1992).

Most approaches for creating transgenic plants to inhibit fungal and bacterial plant pathogens involve increasing expression of a single antimicrobial substance in the plant. A strategy that seeks to control disease by using a single plant defense mechanism may be basically flawed and may explain the slow progress of this strategy. Individual plants under pathogen attack respond in a variety of ways. A number of different mechanisms, some involving several PR proteins, might be activated in a plant after microbial invasion. The activation of a single defense mechanism in genetically engineered plants could be insufficient to prevent infection or reduce pathogenicity, especially under field conditions. In addition, the ability of a single PR protein strategy to control a broad range of pathogens may be limited. For example, Alexander et al. (1993) found that a highly expressed PR (PR-1a) provided no resistance against a variety of plant viruses but did limit disease severity caused by two species of pathogenic fungi. Finally, reliance on a single protective chemical, whether endogenously produced or exogenously applied, may increase the likelihood of selection of resistant pathogens.

2. Protection from Viral Diseases: Pathogen-Derived Resistance

After a virus infects a plant, there are no curative treatments. Avoidance of virus infection has been the only defense. Farmers have relied on classically bred crops, when available, with some level of resistance to particular viruses. The mechanisms underlying virus resistance in plants are almost never known, so breeding for resistance is empirically based (trial and error) for each plant-virus system. Other disease management techniques include planting virus-free stock, eradicating diseased plants, applying pesticides to control or eliminate virus vectors, and eliminating weeds that may be reservoirs for crop-plant viruses. These techniques have had limited success, whereas selecting and breeding virus resistant varieties by traditional methods tend to be expensive and time-consuming.

Since the 1930s plant pathologists have known that plants infected with a virus sometimes show resistance to subsequent infection by different strains of the same, closely related, or occasionally unrelated virus species (Fulton 1986). New infections are prevented or disease symptoms are suppressed or delayed compared to infections of virus-free plants. These observations have been applied by inoculating plants with mild strains of virus to prevent ensuing severe infection (Fulton 1986; references in Powell-Abel 1986). This seemingly immune response of the plant is known as cross-protection or pathogen-derived resistance. The mechanism(s) of cross-protection is not known, but several hypotheses have been proposed to explain the phenomenon. Scholthof, Scholthof, and Jackson (1993, 7) summarized the hypothesis first proposed by Sandford and Johnston (1985): "The expression of certain genes of a pathogen . . . in a host would disrupt the normal balance of viral components and thereby interfere with the virus life cycle. In the most successful instances, such disruptions would prevent the replication and/or movement of the virus beyond the initially infected cell."

Although plant viruses differ in morphology and the type of genetic material they carry, several common steps in the virus infection cycle are vulnerable to disruption (figure 9). But before the infection cycle begins, all viruses must find some way to enter the plant cell by penetrating the cell wall. The plant cell wall may be damaged by physical forces such as wind-blown sand or herbivore feeding. Wind-borne virus particles passively landing on wounded plant tissue may gain entry to plant cells, although this is still unconfirmed. Many viruses are associated with plant-feeding organisms, including insects, fungi, and nematodes. These herbivores act as vectors, moving the virus to the host plant and also damaging plant cells so viruses can gain entrance. More than two hundred viruses have been identified that are transmitted to plants by herbivorous insects (Carter 1973).

Insect transmission of plant viruses may be viewed as either mechanical or biological. In mechanical (also called nonpersistent) transmission, viruses adhere to the mouthparts of an insect while it feeds on an infected plant. When the insect moves to another plant and begins feeding, the virus is transmitted to the new host. Infectivity is maintained only as long as there are viable virus particles clinging to the insect's mouth parts. The biological (also known as

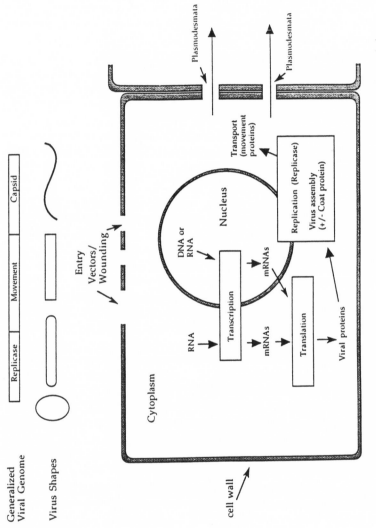

Figure 9. Typical Plant Pathogenic Virus Infection Cycle. *Source:* Adapted from Scholthof, Scholthof, and Jackson 1993

persistent) transmission cycle starts with the virus entering the insect's gut during feeding. The virus then moves about within the insect and sometimes propagates. After a latent period the plant-feeding insect can transmit the virus to new hosts. In propagative biological transmission, after an insect becomes infective it usually remains that way for its entire life. Aphids and leafhoppers, both members of the insect order Homoptera, are the most common and widespread insect vectors of viruses. Both aphids and leafhoppers have styletlike mouthparts adapted to pierce plant tissue and suck plant fluids. This type of feeding mechanism has proven very efficient at transmitting viruses among plants.

Once the virus gains entry into a plant cell, there are five critical steps in the infection cycle (figure 9). Disruption in any one of these steps can hamper the success of the virus pathogen. First, the virus particle, which usually consists of simply a protein coat surrounding a strand of RNA (most often) or DNA, disassembles or "uncoats," exposing the genetic material within to the plant cell. Second, the virus RNA or DNA acts as a template for the transcription of messenger RNA (mRNA). Most plant viruses contain mRNA as their genomic material, and the transcription step is bypassed. Third, mRNA is translated to virus-specific proteins involved in replication, encapsidation (the virus RNA enclosed within its protein coat), and mobility. Fourth, the virus genetic material must be properly replicated. Fifth, replicated and sometimes encapsidated virus progeny bound to mobile protein complexes are transported to other plant cells through cytoplasmic connections known as plasmodesmata (figure 9). The infection cycle can be interrupted at any of these critical steps: uncoating, transcription, translation, replication, and transport.

The use of a mild strain of a viral pathogen for cross-protection has several disadvantages that limit its usefulness (Fulton 1986; Powell-Abel et al. 1986). The mild strain may mutate to a more virulent form, may cause undesirable yield losses itself, or may interact synergistically with unrelated viruses to cause severe yield losses. A virus strain that exhibits low levels of virulence for one crop may also have more severe effects on other crops, which would make it undesirable to spread it in the environment.

Experiments demonstrating that transferring a single gene (rather than the whole pathogen) from a virus to a crop can prevent, delay, or limit disease while avoiding the undesirable effects of mild strain infections have led to a flourishing of research activity around pathogen-derived virus resistance (Fitchen and Beachy 1993;

Scholthof, Scholthof, and Jackson 1993; Wilson 1993). As Wilson (1993, 3134) notes,

> The ability to confer resistance against an otherwise devastating virus by introducing a pathogen-derived or virus targeted sequence into the DNA of a potential host plant has had a marked influence on much of the research effort, focus, and short-term objectives of plant virologists throughout the world. . . . attests to our fascination for unravelling fundamental molecular mechanism(s), our (vain) search for a unifying hypothesis, and our pragmatic interest in commercially exploitable opportunities for crop protection.

Thus, the rise of molecular techniques in plant genetics has led to a new research focus: controlling the mechanisms of viral replication as a means to developing disease resistant crops.

a. Protection Using Viral Coat Proteins.   The first, most successful, and widely tested strategy for conferring pathogen-derived viral resistance on a plant using recombinant DNA technology has been the transfer of the gene that expresses the coat protein (capsid or *CP* gene) of the pathogenic virus to the crop. The coat protein protects the viral genome from degradation in the environment and is involved in virus replication and movement inside the plant cell. In addition, the coat protein in many viruses acts as the site of recognition for virus vectors and is thus essential for transmission. The coat protein is considered innocuous in itself. The only potential adverse impact would arise if a foreign virus were encapsidated by a coat protein produced in a transgenic plant (section C-2).

In 1986 the first such experiments were reported in which the *CP* gene of tobacco mosaic virus was transferred to tobacco plants (Powell-Abel et al. 1986). The recombinant tobacco exhibited high levels of resistance to the pathogen. Many of the transformed plants did not develop disease symptoms after exposure to TMV throughout the experiment. In those transgenic plants developing the disease, symptoms were delayed compared to controls.*

The first field tests of plants transformed with *CP* genes were conducted in 1987 on tomato plants (Nelson et al. 1988). When inoculated with TMV, only 5 percent of the plants expressing coat

---

*Many of the early disease resistant (as well as herbicide and insect resistant) transgenic plant experiments used tobacco as a model system because its cells are easily transformed and regenerated. It is also susceptible to a number of viral diseases.

protein developed disease symptoms compared to 99 percent of the control plants. Yield was reduced by 26 to 36 percent in unprotected plants, while plants expressing coat protein had no yield loss compared to nontransformed disease-free plants. Some have argued that the addition of genes to a plant, leading to the diversion of plant resources and energy to produce supplemental proteins, would reduce the yield of transgenic plants compared to nontransgenic plants. At least in this experiment the inclusion and expression of the virus-derived *CP* gene had no adverse impact on yield. This may be due to the small amount of the coat protein produced in transgenic plants compared to virus-infected plants.

The use of *CP* genes to confer virus resistance as been demonstrated across many crops for a variety of RNA viruses under field conditions (e.g., Gonsalves et al. 1992; Kaniewski et al. 1990; Ling et al. 1991; Nelson et al. 1988). DNA viruses have appeared less amenable to *CP*-mediated protection (Wilson 1993). However, Kunik et al. (1994) demonstrated effective resistance in tomatoes due to expression of the coat protein of a DNA virus. Crops transformed with *CP* genes and field-tested in the United States since 1990 are shown in table 5.

Plants with *CP* transgenes have reduced numbers of infection sites, decreased accumulation of virus in plant parts, delayed or reduced spread of infection throughout the plant, and/or delayed or diminished symptoms compared to control plants (Fitchen and Beachy 1993). Often for transformed plants to develop disease symptoms they must be challenged by virus concentrations hundreds to thousands of times greater than control plants. While complete prevention of disease may seem most desirable, delay of symptoms can allow the plant enough time to produce a full harvest of fruits or seeds (Wilson 1993). Reducing the amount or spread of a virus within a plant can also diminish the efficiency with which vectors spread the disease to other plants.

Evidence from the experiments involving plants with *CP* genes has not revealed a unifying hypothesis to explain pathogen-derived resistance (Fitchen and Beachy 1993; Wilson 1993). It is likely that several mechanisms are involved and that more than a single mechanism may operate for even one plant-virus system (Fitchen and Beachy 1993).

In the most studied system, TMV introduced into tobacco plants possessing TMV-*CP* transgenes appeared unable to remove its protein coat, an initial step necessary for the infection cycle to progress. This seems to explain why the transformed plants have greatly re-

Table 5. Transgenic Plants, with Virus Coat Protein Genes, Approved for Field Tests in the United States from 1987 to July 1995

Crop	Disease(s)	Research Organization
Alfalfa	alfalfa mosaic virus, tobacco mosaic virus (TMV), cucumber mosaic virus (CMV)	Pioneer Hi-Bred
Barley	barley yellow dwarf virus (BYDV)	USDA
Beets	beet necrotic yellow vein virus	Betaseed
Cantaloupe and/or Squash	CMV, papaya ringspot virus (PRV), zucchini yellow mosaic virus (ZYMV), watermelon mosaic virus II (WMVII)	UpJohn
	CMV	Harris Moran Seed
	ZYMV	Michigan State University
	ZYMV	Rogers NK Seed
	soybean mosaic virus (SMV)	Cornell University
	SMV, CMV	New York State Experiment Station
Corn	maize dwarf mosaic virus (MDMV), maize chlorotic mottle virus (MCMV), maize chlorotic dwarf virus (MCDV)	Pioneer Hi-Bred
	MDMV	Northrup King
	MDMV	DeKalb
	MDMV	Rogers NK Seed
Cucumbers	CMV	New York State Experiment Station
Lettuce	tomato spotted wilt virus (TSWV)	UpJohn
Papayas	PRV	University of Hawaii
Peanuts	TSWV	Agracetus

Crop	Virus	Organization
Plum trees	PRV, plum pox virus	USDA
Potatoes	potato leaf roll virus (PLRV), potato virus x (PVX), potato virus y (PVY)	Monsanto
	PLRV, PVY, late blight of potatoes	Frito-Lay
	PLRV	Calgene
	PLRV, PVY	University of Idaho
	PLRV, PVY	USDA
	PVY	Oregon State University
Soybeans	SMV	Pioneer Hi-Bred
Tobacco	ALMV, tobacco vein mottling virus, tobacco etch virus (TEV)	University of Kentucky
	TEV, PVY	University of Florida
	TEV, PVY	North Carolina State University
	TMV	Oklahoma State University
	TEV	USDA
Tomatoes	TMV, tomato mosaic virus (ToMV), CMV, tomato yellow leafcurl virus	Monsanto
	TMV, ToMV	
	ToMV	UpJohn
	CMV	Rogers NK Seed
	CMV	PetoSeed
	CMV	Asgrow
	CMV	Harris Moran Seeds
	CMV	Cornell University
	CMV	New York State Experiment Station
	CMV	USDA

Source: Compiled by the authors from USDA data.

duced numbers of infection sites compared to controls, although other mechanisms probably contribute to the virus resistance as well (Fitchen and Beachy 1993).

The breadth of resistance appears to be associated with the taxonomic relatedness of the virus from which the *CP* gene was taken and the new invading species. For example, tobacco plants resistant to a strain of TMV were also resistant to some other closely related viruses but not to more distant relatives (Nejidat and Beachy 1990). A narrow range of resistance would limit the usefulness of *CP* genes to protect against a range of virus pathogens. However, broader resistance has sometimes been observed. For example, a corn plant expressing a *CP* gene for one virus also gives protection against another unrelated virus (Murry et al. 1993). At this point, more research is needed to determine whether any general rules can be applied to predict the range of *CP*-conferred resistance or whether each case must be evaluated independently.

One company, Asgrow Seed Company, has received regulatory approval to market squash seed incorporating coat-protein mediated resistance for two viruses. The company plans to market the seed primarily in Georgia and Florida, where squash yield can be reduced 50 to 80 percent by viral diseases (Quemada 1994).

b. Other Plant-Derived Viral Resistances. Several other types of plant-derived virus resistance, including antisense RNA, satellite RNA, defective interfering viruses, and replicase-mediated resistance, have been demonstrated in laboratory experiments, although field tests have yet to be reported. It appears that *CP*-derived resistance has a broader range than other plant-derived resistances, making it of more agronomic interest. However, because of the possibility of virus adaptation overcoming any single resistance tactic (section C-2), the discovery of additional gene sequences that protect plants from infection is important. We will discuss one such strategy, replicase-mediated resistance, that is furthest along in development and holds some commercial promise. Detailed descriptions and explanations of the other approaches can be found in Fitchen and Beachy (1993), Scholthof, Scholthof, and Jackson (1993), Tepfer (1993), and Wilson (1993).

Viral replicase genes encode proteins for making copies of the virus genome in a host. Results from experiments on several plant viruses confirm that transfer of part of what appears to be the replicase gene to plants confers protection from the viral strain from which the gene was derived and sometimes from closely related strains (Anderson, Palukaitis, and Zaitlin 1992; Braun and Hemenway 1992; Carr et al. 1992; MacFarlane and Davies 1992). Resistance seems to be due in some cases to inhibition of virus replication, which prevents systemic spread of the virus, or in one case to inhibition of protein translation (Fitchen and Beachy 1993). Although the protein product of the presumed replicase gene has not been detected in transgenic plants there is evidence that the protein is the active component required for the acquisition of virus resistance (Carr et al. 1992; McFarlane and Davies 1992). Scholthof, Scholthof, and Jackson (1993) have observed that "these recently developed replicase-based strategies offer new possibilities for protecting plants from the deleterious effects of virus infection . . . , and they will also increase our understanding of strategies utilized by viruses for replication in plant cells."

c. Animal-Derived Virus Resistance. In a novel effort to obtain broad protection against plant pathogenic viruses, Truve et al. (1993) report transferring a mammalian gene from the rat interferon immuno-response system to potato plants. Interferons are proteins that are expressed in animal cells following virus attack. They activate expression of other proteins that have antiviral properties. The gene transferred to potato expresses oligoadenylate synthetase, one of the animal antiviral proteins. The transgenic plants expressing oligoadenylate synthetase were protected from potato virus X under field conditions. In addition, some of the clones of the transformed plants, challenged with PVX, had fewer virus particles in leaves and tubers than transgenic potato plants expressing the coat protein of PVX. The researchers (Truve et al. 1993) claimed to have, although they did not present, preliminary data indicating that expression of the mammalian antiviral gene confers protection for a broad spectrum of plant viruses.

B. The Economics of Disease Resistant Crops

The costs of seeds incorporating disease resistance(s) is unknown, so any economic analysis is speculative. Annual monetary losses from plant disease are estimated at $90 billion worldwide (James, Teng, and Nutter 1991). In the United States losses to disease in corn, wheat, cotton, and soybeans are estimated at $1.3 billion. Losses in fruit and vegetable crops are estimated at $500 million (James, Teng, and Nutter 1991). Thus, the market for effective disease resistant crops would appear robust. Disease resistant crops fit easily into the current agricultural system. Farmers need not adopt new practices to use this technology. Seed is chosen, in part, based on traditionally bred resistance(s) to pathogens that are problems in specific growing regions. Thus, selecting and growing transgenic disease resistant seed will be a familiar practice.

Moses and Cape (1991, 436), however, are skeptical about genetically engineered disease resistant products becoming viable economically:

> Despite the large loss numbers and the imperfect control afforded by current preparations the benefit of a specific disease control product is likely to be limited. Unlike herbicides and insecticides, for which a few major crops and a few major pests account for large expenditures for agrichemicals, plant disease problems are spread widely among many crops and over many disease pathogens in each crop. The significance of any one of them is minor in comparison to the significance . . . of cotton bollworms to cotton or maize rootworm to maize.

Moses and Cape emphasize the fragmentation of the disease resistance market because of the diversity of crops and pathogens. Indeed, the research on viruses so far shows that, generally, resistances are limited in breadth. However, there is nothing to prevent resistance to several diseases being incorporated in a single seed. The types of field tests that companies are conducting (USDA 1993b) indicate that crops are being engineered with resistance to multiple pathogens. However, this approach would not be commercially viable if it turns out that plants expressing multiple coat protein genes, for example, suffer reduced yield. Moses and Cape are probably correct; the market for a single disease resistant product will never equal the markets for herbicide and insect resistances. However, there would appear to be substantial niche markets that could support specialized products.

If the pathogen-derived resistances turn out to be applicable to many crops and many viruses, as appears to be the case with coat protein-derived resistance, the technical difficulty of creating many products would be substantially reduced and the problem of market fragmentation minimized.

Economic benefits to farmers will vary depending on the severity of their disease problems. Because virus resistant seed is likely to be the first pathogen-protection product to reach the market, only farmers suffering economic losses due to virus diseases will be affected. They would see savings if the cost of virus-free planting stock were greater than the cost of transgenic disease resistant seed. Farmers would also save if using disease resistant seed reduced applications of pesticides used for disease vector control. However, farmers may continue to use chemical inputs to control insect, weed, fungal, or nematode pests, even if protection from disease transmission is no longer needed. Reduction in expenses associated with fungicide applications would be the most direct economic benefit if fungus resistant transgenic crops were available. However, the efficacy of plants resistant to fungal pathogens has yet to be proven in the field.

C. Environmental Benefits and Risks of Disease Resistant Crops

1. Benefits

The most direct environmental benefit of disease resistant plants would be reductions in chemical usage. Any reductions in fungicide use are dependent on the success of research programs now in the early stages of development. Insecticide reductions based on eliminating the need for vector control are harder to predict. Vectors often present a direct pest problem that farmers may want to control in the absence of a disease problem. The elimination or significant reduction of yield losses to disease might result in fewer acres being planted each year, with the associated benefits of reduced erosion and other adverse environmental impacts of agriculture. Increased yields in third world countries would help achieve food self-sufficiency and improve the standard of living, gaining many indirect environmental benefits.

2. Environmental Risks

Several scenarios involving adverse ecological effects from transgenic plants incorporating pathogen-derived genes for virus resistance have been theorized. These schemes describe the creation of "new diseases" when invading viruses replicate in transgenic plants; they also describe the possibility of increased rather than diminished disease severity in transgenic plants.

a. Transencapsidation. When the replicated genes of an invading virus become enclosed in the coat protein of a virus of a different strain or species that had previously infected the plant, the process is called transencapsidation (figure 10). This could alter the host range and vector relationships of a plant virus. Coat protein is im-

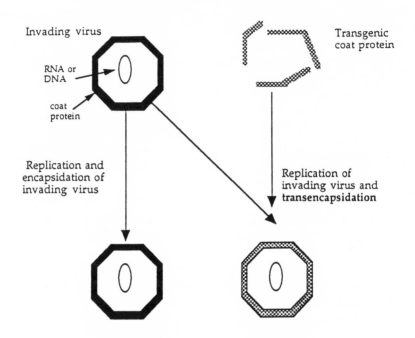

Figure 10. Transencapsidation. *Source:* Adapted from de Zoeten 1991

portant in determining the host range of viruses in two ways. First, plants use coat protein to recognize invading viruses and to activate defenses. The fact that plants are not susceptible to most viruses may depend on the host's recognition of the coat protein of the invader. Second, coat protein allows specific vectors to transmit specific viruses. There is a risk that the coat protein expressed in transgenic plants might result in transencapsidation of an invading virus, allowing a formerly noninsect vectored virus, for example, to be transported to and infect new plant hosts (de Zoeten 1991; Palukaitis 1991; Rissler and Mellon 1993; Tepfer 1993). In this way a nearby crop plant could be damaged severely by a pathogen that previously had never been a problem.

Transencapsidation is known to occur between different strains of the same virus in nature (Rochow 1977) and in greenhouse experiments with transgenic plants (Farinelli, Malnoe, and Collet 1992; Osborne, Sarkar, and Wilson 1990). Candelier-Harvey and Hull (1993) demonstrated high levels (eleven of thirty-three transgenic plants tested) of interspecific transencapsidation of cucumber mosaic virus (CMV) by alfalfa mosaic virus (AMV) coat protein expressed by transgenic tobacco. Lecoq et al. (1993) showed that transencapsidation of plum pox virus coat protein expressed in a transgenic plant allowed aphids to transmit a nontransmissible virus (i.e., a virus not capable of being vectored by an insect) to a host plant. This result demonstrates that transencapsidation may lead to changes in vector transmission and possibly to changes in virus host range. Note that if the transencapsidated virus does make it to a new plant the virus must still be able to replicate and move systemically through the potential new host to be pathogenic. Simply exposing a plant to a new virus does not mean that a pathogenic infection will occur.

There are some differences of opinion among plant virologists about the risks of transencapsidation. The following scenario illustrates the points in contention. Suppose a plant virus A in plant S takes on a coat protein of plant virus B (transencapsidized). Insect P, which normally does not carry A in plant S, is now able to transmit A (because of its new protein coat) to a new host, plant T. Wilson (1993) argues that this will only be a problem for one generation because virus A, once it reproduces in its new host, T, will regain its original protein coat and will resist transmission by insect P. One the other hand, de Zoeten (1991) argues that, while in its new host, virus A may come in contact with a new insect vector Q that can transmit virus A with its original protein coat. Q is only active in plant T, therefore any process that brings A to a new plant will introduce new risks of spreading plant virus A. In summary, critics contend that by genetically modifying plants to produce coat proteins there will be an increase in transencapsidation, which could result in the expansion of the host range of plant viruses, for example, viruses will infect more types of plants in wider regions. Others counter by citing the one generation effect described above and by pointing out that transencapsidation already occurs in nature without causing epidemics. Against this background, they predict that human engineering of plants with virus genes will have no appreciable impact.

In Tepfer's (1993) estimation, it is difficult to determine the risks from transencapsidation for transgenic crops planted in large scale. However, he points out an interesting case of a little-known family of pathogenic viruses, the umbraviruses, which require transencapsidation with coat protein from another family, the luteoviruses, for their transmission to be possible. Some of the luteoviruses are common, and transgenic crops expressing luteovirus coat protein have been field-tested (e.g., potato leaf roll virus and barley yellow mosaic virus). The population increase of umbraviruses may now be limited by low levels of infection by luteoviruses. A large-scale release of transgenic plants expressing luteovirus coat protein could increase the population size and dispersal of umbraviruses. Because some umbraviruses can cause serious plant diseases, Tepfer recommends an extensive search for umbraviruses before any large-scale release of transgenic plants expressing luteovirus *CP* genes.

Tepfer (1993) also suggests that in some cases of transencapsidation certain technical solutions could be employed to prevent insect transmission. In one example, deletion of segments of a coat protein gene still conferred virus resistance but prevented the transmission of the virus particle by a vector.

Transencapsidation continues to be an area of concern for the spread of plant viruses. Empirical studies are needed to distinguish among the competing risk scenarios.

b. Recombination.   Recombination of viral genetic material could occur between an invading virus and viral transgenes incorporated in a plant for virus resistance. After recombination, a new virus containing some of the plant-derived viral genetic material would be created that may be more virulent or have an expanded host range compared to the original invading virus (Chassan 1993; de Zoeten 1991; Falk and Bruening 1994; Tepfer 1993). Recombination of plant viruses does occur at low frequency in nature and probably has contributed to virus evolution (Falk and Bruening 1994). In laboratory experiments recombination has been demonstrated between co-infecting viral RNAs and between viral and transgenic RNAs (references in Chassan 1993; references in Falk and Bruening 1994; Gal et al. 1992; Greene and Allison 1994; Schoelz and Wintermantel 1993). In all laboratory experiments different strains of the same virus species were involved. Thus, the likelihood of interspecific recombination remains unknown.

Mixed viral infections of plants are common in nature, so viral genomes are often in close contact, leading to innumerable opportunities for recombination (Chassan 1993; Falk and Bruening 1994). Falk and Bruening (1994, 1396) take the position that there is little risk of adverse effects from recombination: "Even though ordinary infections in agricultural and natural settings continuously provide viruses with multiple opportunities to interact, new viral diseases are usually due to minor variants of already known viruses and not to new viruses of recombinant origin."

Natural rates of recombination are low, possibly because of the physical separation of viruses within plant cells (compartmentalization) (Gibbs 1994; Hull 1994). Physical separation of invading viruses may limit contact during virus replication such that recombination does not occur. Recombination might occur at higher rates in transgenic plants if transgenes were not similarly compartmentalized.

Greene and Allison (1994) provide experimental evidence that under strong selection pressure recombination among viruses does occur in transgenic plants. Because recombination may be involved in the rapid evolution of new virus strains with altered host range and vector specificities, they conclude that recombination is an important consideration when analyzing the risks posed by virus-resistant transgenic plants.

c. *Synergistic Infections.* The co-occurrence of two viruses can cause a more severe plant infection than the additive effects of either virus alone. However, mechanisms to explain this synergism are unknown. Palukaitis (1991) speculates that transgenic plants expressing a virus *CP* gene could cause agronomic difficulties not experienced with nontransgenic plants if coat proteins are involved in increasing the pathogenicity of secondarily invading viruses.

d. *Evolution of Pest Resistance to Pathogen-Derived Plant Protection.* The probability that viruses would evolve to overcome pathogen-derived resistance is unknown. When mild strains have been used for cross-protection, resistance has not been reported, although viruses have overcome traditionally bred resistance in a number of cases (Tolin 1991). Scholthof, Scholthof, and Jackson (1993, 10) point out that the evolution of resistant strains would not be "unexpected, since viruses are rapidly replicating entities. Thus, it is highly likely that strains able to circumvent resistance will evolve, particularly as such genes become widely used in crop protection, and it can be expected that multiple forms of protection will be necessary to realize the maximum potential for virus-free transgenic crops when they are subjected to field conditions."

e. *Implications for Risk Assessment.* What are the potential risks of a large-scale release of transgenic plants containing viral genes, how do those risks compare to the risks from any naturally co-occurring plant viruses, and what policy actions should be taken? De Zoeten (1991, 586) concludes, "It is clearly possible that a combination of heterologous encapsidation and template switching* in released *CP*-transgenic plants could lead to the formation of new viruses with altered vectors and host ranges and new combinations of genes." De Zoeten cautions against being blinded by the success and power of the new technology and ignoring the pertinent risk issues that require resolution.

Chassan (1993, 1490) downplays the level of risk by comparing it to natural recombinations: "Mixed viral infections are widespread in nature, and they offer the same kinds of opportunities for recombination as do cross-protected plants that are infected with a virus. There is no reason to believe that the recombinants that arise in infected transgenic plants will be qualitatively different than those that arise 'naturally.'" Such reasoning could be extended to include transencapsidated viruses.

Bruening and Falk (1994) argue that in some cases traditionally bred virus protection has led to the outbreak of virulent viral strains due to selection for resistance. Because of the overall benefit gained, there has been no call for a cessation of the breeding of virus resistant cultivars. Likewise, Ryals (1994) contends that the critics of biotechnology have failed to appreciate the benefits of transgenic disease resistant plants, which must be understood to properly evaluate the risks.

A key factor in determining if transencapsidation, or recombination, results in a disease problem is understanding whether the "new viruses" created have any selective advantage. The new strain will die out if the phenotypic change resulting from recombination or transencapsidation does not result in more competitive organisms compared to existing viruses. In Bruening and Falk's (1994, 1396) view, there is little risk because "it . . . is unlikely that any given new virus will be more viable than competing viruses throughout the infection cycle: transmission to a new host, uncoating and gene expression, replication, assembly of new virions, and possibly infection of alternative hosts."

De Zoeten (1991) contends, however, that the experimental evidence on the frequency and the ecological and evolutionary importance of transencapsidation and recombination, needed for proper risk assessment, are lacking. De Zoeten asserts that risk assessment is now based on "popular opinion" rather than on scientifically val-

*Template switching is one mechanism to account for recombination.

idated information and recommends increased experimentation to address risk issues versus relying on undocumented opinion and uninformed risk assessment.

Apparently, the Environmental Protection Agency does not regard the risks associated with the development of genetically engineered crops resistant to viruses as significant, and it has proposed that they be exempted from government oversight (Schneider 1994a).

The only long-term study evaluating the environmental impact of genetically engineered, virus resistant plants is by Asakawa et al. (1993). Tomato plants transformed with the coat protein gene of tobacco mosaic virus were studied in field plots over a three-year period. The evaluation included comparisons between transgenic and nontransformed plants for plant height and vigor, pollen dispersion and fertilization success, production of unusual allelochemicals, effects on soil microorganisms, overwintering ability, and weediness. No harmful effects were identified, resistance to TMV was maintained in the progeny of the transgenic plants, and a recommendation was made for open cultivation of the transgenic plants. Note that the molecular-level risks of transencapsidation and recombination discussed previously were not evaluated in this study.

D. Conclusions

The power of molecular biology in providing long-term solutions for plant disease problems lies in its ability to augment our understanding of the basic biological processes involved in plant resistance to pathogens as posed by Chassan (1994, 461), "Learning about the nature of plant resistance mechanisms also promises insights into some very basic questions about plant cell function: How do plant cells recognize pathogens? By what biochemical steps does recognition signal the initiation of a resistance response? . . . which events are actually necessary for resistance, and what is the biochemical basis for the resistance response?"

Molecular techniques provide the tools to discover the underlying structure and functional relationships that can then be used to create strategies for pathogen resistance (e.g., Staskawicz et al. 1995). Successful methods of plant protection have already been uncovered and are being developed commercially while other promising avenues are being pursued. Some of the strategies being developed appear to have broad applicability. For example, virus resistance derived from viral coat protein genes seems to be effective for a number of different types of viruses infecting a variety of crops. Resistance based on the expression of virus coat protein also appears to be relatively broad, affecting the donor virus and at least some closely related strains. Research toward discovering mechanisms of systemic acquired resistance may provide plant protection against a diversity of pathogens. However, we should be cautious in implementing protection strategies that rely on single substances or mechanisms and that ignore the ability of pathogens to evolve to overcome resistances. Disease resistant plants created through classical breeding or genetic engineering are best viewed as tools in an integrated pest management system rather than as the single solution to disease problems.

The quest to develop viable commercial products within a relatively short period means that companies are trying to exploit technologies without a complete understanding of how they work at the molecular and whole-plant levels. The most controversy surrounds the possible problems associated with large-scale use of pathogen-derived virus resistance. None of the experts suggests that there are no risks. However, large differences in opinion revolve around the probability and cost of adverse effects and the extent of our confidence in risk predictions based on experience with natural systems. Some scientists believe that experience with natural pathogens and plant populations is sufficient to assure that any risk is minimal and greatly outweighed by the benefit from disease resistant crops. Others are not so sanguine and call for more research now to quantify the risk from large-scale plantings of virus resistant transgenic crops.

Regulatory officials appear to agree with those who argue that the benefits of the technology in reducing crop loss outweigh the risk of adverse effects, the probability of which they deemed as slight. Thus, unless small-scale field tests raise unexpected questions, genetically engineered crops containing disease resistant genes will enter the marketplace following the successful commercialization of disease resistant squash.

Genetically engineering plants for resistance to viral and other diseases is an innovation that fits nicely into the established practice of classically selecting crops for resistance to pathogens. Farmers accustomed to choosing seed varieties with resistance to multiple diseases can benefit from this innovation without having to change any practices. These products also fill an agricultural need; viral plant pathogens continue to cause significant yield losses in many crops and thus the introduction of disease resistance into commercial crops fits into the induced innovation model (chapter 1). It is fortuitous that viral coat protein—a factor easily transferable with recombinant techniques and seemingly innocuous to nontarget organisms—has been effective in protecting a range of crops. The flourishing of activity into the basic molecular biology of plant response to pathogens, brought about by the breakthroughs in molecular techniques, may create a window through which a series of new, innovative disease resistant plant protection products will emerge.

Some social criticism over this research strategy involved concerns over the spread of disease resistance to weedy plants. Yet the research has been promoted by some public groups as an innovation that is easily transferable to third world countries to solve a serious yield-reducing problem. From a farmer's standpoint, the more one can breed into the seed, the less troublesome the adoption of innovations will be unless something stigmatizing is in the product.

5 Transgenic Plant Products: Foods and Pharmaceuticals

Plants are being genetically transformed to produce improved foods and new nonfood substances such as industrial oils, polymers, vaccines, and pharmaceuticals. Transgenic plant products are a subcategory of genetically modified plants that also include plants resistant to herbicides, insects, and diseases. Transgenic food products have a genetically modified locus on their edible parts. According to our nomenclature, a transgenic food product is one in which foreign genes have been introduced into the plant or have been altered. In either case, the genetic changes modify the edible portion of the plant consumed directly or used in processed food. The putative function of the genetic modification is to improve the quality of the food specifically designed for human consumption. Other genetic modifications for the production of nonfood substances for industrial and medicinal uses may be in any plant part, because it is usually intended for such substances to be extracted and processed before use.

A. Technical Developments

1. Transgenic Food Products (TFP)

Among the many innovations proposed in TFPs are potatoes with increased starch content; coffee with lower caffeine; tomatoes with a higher solid to liquid ratio, plants such as corn, soybeans, and rice with altered amino acid composition; and oilseed crops (rapeseed and soybean) with altered saturated fat content. The most publicized and controversial of the TFPs is the Flavr Savr tomato introduced by Calgene, a Davis, California, plant biotechnology company formed in 1980.

The incentive for producing a transgenic tomato comes from the fact that modern tomatoes have been bred for transport, not taste. Thus, most winter tomatoes lack the flavor, color, and sweetness of a fresh-ripened garden grown variety. According to Roberts (1988, 1290), "What makes store-bought tomatoes so pale, mealy, and generally flavorless is that they are picked green, refrigerated, and then gassed with ethylene to bring on the red color." If the tomatoes were picked ripened on the vine, they would retain their flavor but become too soft for shipping.

a. Genes and Ripening. The chemical ethylene is essential to many plant developmental processes, including fruit ripening. At the molecular level, the appearance of ethylene activates genes involved in the ripening process. Therefore, scientists, to delay ripening, have sought ways to reduce ethylene synthesis. According to Klee et al. (1991, 1189), plants that produce significantly lower levels of ethylene exhibit no differences in the fruit's phenotype compared to controls, with the exception of the ripening time of the fruit.

Several approaches have been taken to reduce ethylene production in the fruit. A bacterial protein has been identified that degrades a chemical in the ethylene synthesis pathway. The isolated gene introduced into tomato plants has been shown to reduce ethylene production.

In test studies, transgenic plants with delayed ethylene synthesis were shown to remain firm as much as six weeks longer than nontransgenic controls. This time period is a highly significant factor in the application of the technology to a diverse group of fruits. The time period for the viability of the fruit—when it is picked in the field to when it is selected in the market—is key to its success. A superior-tasting fruit that overripens when it reaches the consumer loses its commercial value.

A second approach involves the use of antisense gene technology. In this process a reverse copy of the gene is produced and introduced into the organism. The antisense technology can reduce the production of an endogenous enzyme PG (polygalacturonase) required for the synthesis of ethylene, which is essential for the degradation of pectin and the initiation of ripening (Sheehy, Kramer, and Hiatt 1988). Slowing down the rate of ripening may always be reversed, because externally applied ethylene can result in a normal ripening process.

The antisense or reverse-order gene is incorporated into the seed, which also contains the correct order gene. Both sense and antisense genes encode messenger RNA molecules that bind together and thus inhibit the role of the sense mRNA in the enzymatic process that initiates ripening. Leemans (1993, S25) maintains that the goal of this and other approaches is to develop fruits with enhanced shelf-life, delayed spoilage, and better processing characteristics that might ultimately improve flavor and texture.

One uncertainty associated with antisense technology is that it might inadvertently result in other undesirable traits. Scientists at Calgene evaluated genetically modified tomatoes that had PG levels reduced by more than 99 percent after modification by the incorporation of antisense DNA.

> We have demonstrated that a reduction in PG activity through expression of an antisense gene results in processed fruit products with improved serum viscosity. In addition, we have demonstrated that fresh tomato fruit with dramatically reduced levels of PG activity exhibit improved quality due to enhanced firmness and increased resistance to fungal diseases. This may benefit commercial producers of fresh market tomatoes by reducing losses due to disease and rot, and by allowing for the harvest of greater proportion of fruit with color while avoiding the usual losses attributed to the packing and shipping of vine-ripe fruit. (Kramer et al. 1992, 253)

In its public relations literature, Calgene claims that its genetically modified tomatoes have the same nutritional value and vitamin content as any other fresh tomato. The benefit of the Flavr Savr to tomato producers will be to encourage that 25 percent of the population who does not purchase tomatoes during the winter to be drawn back into the market. The off-season tomato market is further complicated by the appearance of European greenhouse varieties that are competitive with the Flavr Savr.

In May 1994, following an evaluation of the Flavr Savr tomato, the FDA issued a finding that the transgenic variety was as safe as traditionally bred varieties (*HHS News* 1994). The FDA also approved as a food additive the marker enzyme for resistance to the antibiotic kanamycin that is produced in the Flavr Savr tomato. A bacterial gene encoding the marker enzyme was placed in the tomato for easy identification of the trait of interest that prevents fruit-softening during vine-ripening. The FDA did not require any special labeling of the tomato because it held that the Flavr Savr "maintains the essential characteristics of traditionally developed tomatoes." Calgene quickly began shipping the Flavr Savr to test markets in California and Illinois. It became the first transgenic whole-food product to be available to consumers.

Recombinant DNA molecular technology defined as the in vitro transfer of genes is the latest in a number of techniques that have been used to add hundreds of new varieties of food plants into commerce each year (Kessler et al. 1992, 1747). These techniques include hybridization between plants of the same or different species, chemical and physical mutagenesis, protoplast fusion (combining the cytoplasm of two different plant cells), and somaclonal variation. In the latter technique, which began to be used in the mid-1980s, small segments of tissue from adult plants are placed in a glass vessel with nutrients and plant hormones. Within several days, a lump of tissue (a callus) is formed. The callus consists of undifferentiated cells. Each callus is capable of generating an entirely new plant. Some small percentage of these plants will exhibit new traits at a frequency much higher than what can be expected by spontaneous mutations. Somaclonal variation offers a more accelerated approach to discovering new varieties than the tedious process of selecting from the natural variations in seed strains from breeding experiments. The one-to-two-year time frame for obtaining results using rDNA techniques is considerably faster than conventional breeding, which may take seven to ten years to develop a desired strain.

One of the central public policy debates that arose during the development of the Flavr Savr tomato was whether food products produced by recombinant DNA molecule technology should be treated any differently than the other techniques used to create novel varieties. Recombinant DNA is certainly not the only technique in which foreign genes, even genes from two species of different genera, can be combined in a viable organism. It has been frequently argued that rDNA techniques are as safe or safer than traditional breeding techniques because of their specificity. According to this argument, the traits introduced by the foreign genes can be controlled more easily. As Kessler et al. (1992, 1747) note, "First, any single-gene trait (and potentially, multi-gene traits) whose chromosomal location or molecular identity is known can be transferred to another organism irrespective of mating barriers. Second, this transfer can be accomplished without simultaneously introducing undesirable traits that are chromosomally linked to the desirable trait in the donor organism. Thus, the techniques have great power and precision." A discussion of the relationship between the predictive power of genetic engineering and the control over nature is found in chapter 11.

2. Transgenic Nonfood Plant Products

In addition to engineering plant-derived foods, several companies are creating plants that produce new products. For example, Calgene has an oils division that is developing genetically engineered rapeseed (canola) to produce several different types of specialty oils. Genes from the California bay (*Umbellularia californica*) have been genetically engineered into rapeseed to produce large quantities of laurate, an oil that is a primary component in many soaps, detergents, and cosmetics and is also found in nondairy coffee whitener and whipped toppings (Voelker et al. 1992). Rapeseed does not normally produce laurate, which is now obtained from palm kernel oil and coconut oil. In October 1994 Calgene was granted regulatory approval to commercialize its laurate-producing canola. Worldwide production of laurate is 9 billion pounds a year. Consumption in the United States is 1.2 billion pounds, worth $350 million (Salameh 1994). If successful, this product would shift some production of laurate from the Philippines, Malaysia, and Indonesia to North America.

Other genetically engineered strains of rapeseed undergoing development at Calgene include high stearic oil for margarine, edible canola oil with reduced saturated fat content, and other fatty acids to be used as biodegradable lubricants for high-performance engines, in cosmetics and shampoos, and as mild cleaning fluids.

There has been growing interest in genetically engineering plants to produce polymers for use as biodegradable plastics and packaging materials (Wrage 1993a). Many biopolymers are now produced by fermentation, which is a relatively expensive process compared to lipids and starches obtained from plants. The goal is to expand production while decreasing costs of biopolymers to make them more competitive with petrochemical-derived materials. Unlike oil-based products, biopolymers have the added environmental benefit of biodegradability.

Polyhydroxyalkanoates (PHA) are a family of polyesters that are produced by a wide range of bacteria. Polymers of PHAs vary in properties from elastic to hard and brittle. Because many PHAs are completely biodegradable, there has been interest in them as an alternative to petroleum-based plastics. One class of PHAs is produced commercially by fermentation for speciality applications. Producing PHAs in plants would significantly reduce the expense of manufacture, compared to fermentation, and make these biopolymers competitive with petroleum-based plastics for low-cost uses (Poirier, Nawrath, and Somerville 1995).

Efforts to produce PHAs in plants have met with some success. Three bacterial genes necessary to synthesize polyhydroxybutyrate (PHB), a type of PHA, were transferred to *Arabidopsis thaliana* plants (Nawrath, Poirier, and Somerville 1994). The transgenic plants accumulated up to 14 percent dry weight of PHB without any dele-terious effect on plant growth or fertility. That level of polymer yield is considered commercially practical, and several companies are pursuing development of PHA-producing transgenic oilseed crops (Poirier, Nawrath, and Somerville 1995; Wrage 1995). Ideally, a crop such as rapeseed would be engineered to yield 10 to 15 percent cano-la oil, allowing a double harvest from a single plant (Wrage 1995).

Once the primary source of human medicines, the role of plants in drug production was replaced in the mid-twentieth century by the introduction of fermentation and synthetic chemical processes. Because of advances in rDNA technology, plants are now being re-considered not only as a source of medicinal substances but also as a site of production of pharmaceuticals (Moffat 1995).

Agracetus, Inc. the biotechnology subsidiary of W. R. Grace Inc., is promoting the use of transgenic plants as bioreactors for drug manufacture (Wrage 1993b). Like biopolymers, some drugs obtained through fermentation could probably be produced at a reduced cost in plants. Lee (1993, 230) reports on the enormous potential for human protein production in plants.

> In 1989 researchers at Plant Genetic Systems and at the Rijks University, both in Ghent, genetically engineered the oilseed plant and *Arabidopsis*, a plant which has become favored for many genetic studies, to produce seeds which contained leuen-kephalin, a human brain chemical. Another group at Morgan International in Leiden, the Netherlands, induced the growth of human serum albumin in potatoes and tobacco. . . . In 1992 Agricultural Genetics Co., Ltd., in Cambridge, U.K., revealed that it had devised a way to produce large quantities of animal vaccines in plants.

Haq et al. (1995) report the creation of transgenic tobacco and potato plants expressing a protein antigen derived from a strain of *E. coli* that causes enteric diseases such as cholera. Mice fed tobac-co leaf extracts or potatoes produced antibodies that neutralized the enterotoxin in vitro, thus demonstrating the potential of using trans-genic plants to produce and deliver oral vaccines.

Plants are being genetically engineered with genes to produce vaccines to protect livestock from diseases. Agristar Inc., a biotech-nology firm in Texas, is creating transgenic plants with bacterial and viral genes as edible vaccines for cattle and pigs under an agreement with a manufacturer of oral livestock vaccines (*Biotech Reporter* 1993).

Plants may someday be used as factories for the production of transgenic viral vaccines. HIV genes have been transferred to cowpea mosaic virus (CPMV), a plant pathogen, so that some of the amino acid sequence of HIV was expressed in the virus coat protein (Stone, ed. 1994). The transgenic virus was then injected into cowpea plants, where it replicated. It has been hypothesized that mice treated with the viruses harvested from the plants produce antibodies that might deactivate the HIV virus. If successful, this technology would have widespread application for producing vaccines for many viral pathogens. The research, although promising, is still in its nascent development stages.

B. Economics of Transgenic Plant Products

The fresh tomato market in the United States is estimated to be somewhere between $2.5 and $4 billion annually (McMurray 1993, B1; Seabrook 1993, 32). If the Flavr Savr tomato succeeds in capturing even 1 percent of the market, that would amount to $25 to $40 million in annual sales. This is only one product among hundreds being testing in the laboratory and the field. Estimates of the financial growth of the biotechnology industry have targeted $30 billion by 2000. Pharmaceuticals have been primarily responsible for biotechnology sales. The revenues from biotechnology in 1989 were $1.5 billion, almost entirely from pharmaceuticals and diagnostics (Browning 1992, 47). By 1992 the revenues of agricultural biotechnology products grew to about $184 million (Hodgson and Barlow 1993).

The benefits of the antisense technology for improving fruit quality have been questioned in a *Wall Street Journal* story (McMurray 1993, B6). Ironically, the article quoted a scientist from Calgene, the company that stood to gain the most from the technology. The scientist stated that "the altered gene makes a 'subtle, statistical difference' during the earlier stage of ripening." Moreover, McMurray noted that PG (polygalacturonase) actually is not solely responsible for softening, but is instead regulated as part of a more complex process that occurs during normal ripening. The article cited reports that nongenetically engineered tomatoes are available that have equivalent shelf-life and that taste as good or better than the Flavr Savr. According to this view, the key to taste is breeding, marketing, and special handling rather than biotechnology.

Calgene's financial success has been linked to the Flavr Savr tomato. McMurray (1993) reported that the company has lost $83 million since it was formed in the early 1980s by a University of California tomato scientist. Calgene has purportedly expended $25 million on research and development for its antisense tomato.

Because most transgenic nonfood plant products are still in early stages of development, any predictions of market size would be highly speculative. However, farmers should benefit by the prospect of expanding the types of products that could be produced and by the likelihood that some of these products would be high-value crops. Success in developing plants that produce new products, such as industrial oils, biopolymers, and pharmaceuticals, expands the types of substances that could be harvested from plants, thereby expanding agricultural demand. Farmers would have additional options and flexibility in choosing which crops to grow each season. Small-acreage plantings of several different high-value crops could increase crop diversity, a goal of sustainable agriculture and a practice that reduces the risk associated with monocultural crop production.

In some cases, new plant products may shift production to one region at the expense of another. For example, Calgene's rapeseed variety that produces laurate in North America might adversely impact the palm and coconut oil industries of Southeast Asia. An ample supply of laurate close to processing plants could reduce demand for these tropical oils. However, laurate has been suggested as a replacement of some petrochemically derived oils. Some experts claim that laurate is biodegradable and therefore more environmentally sound than petrochemical-based oils. Greater availability of laurate might have the effect of increasing demand if new uses are found.

C. Social and Environmental Impacts

Calgene's genetically modified tomato was the catalyst for a national debate on TFPs just as ice minus prompted the first international debate over the release into the environment of a genetically modified microorganism a decade ago (chapter 8). Much of the debate over the Flavr Savr tomato focused on safety, nutrition, and labeling. The tomato, however, was a symbol of a new system of food production that began with the germ line and ended as part of the consumer's diet. Some groups opposed the products because of their view that genetic modification of food defiles it. No satisfactory moral distinctions were offered between more traditional techniques of genetic modification and rDNA-based techniques. The opposition to rDNA-modified food was similar in form to consumer opposition to irradiated food.

Like irradiation, the controversy over the Flavr Savr tomato is emblematic of a pure food strategy in which some people view genetic modification of an edible crop as a form of contamination or defilement. It does not represent the public's repudiation of recombinant DNA techniques themselves, or even its use in food manufacture. Rennet, an enzyme used in the manufacture of cheese, was traditionally extracted from the stomachs of four-to-ten-day-old calves. Rennet is now manufactured by an rDNA method that does not require calves' stomachs, and it has not been a target of controversy. The use of a microbially produced enzyme is a favored alternative to vegetarians, animal protectionists, and certain religious groups.

The Food and Drug Administration issued a policy statement pertaining to "foods derived from new plant varieties" in May 1992 to clarify the agency's regulatory oversight of transgenic food products. According to the ruling, all foods derived from plant varieties developed by "new methods of genetic modification" will be regulated in the same manner as foods developed by traditional plant breeding. The FDA was emphatic about its risk-based approach to TFPs, according to which the characteristics of the product and not the method by which it is produced or developed are the key to evaluating its safety and nutritional value. Following this line of reasoning, the FDA's policy did not require labeling of genetically modified food other than in special circumstances, such as when a gene from a known allergin is introduced into a new food (a peanut gene introduced into a tomato). The agency's policy statement maintained that the use of rDNA techniques to modify plants increases the potential for safer, better-characterized, and more predictable foods.

FDA's statutory framework for regulating genetically modified food derives substantially from section 402(a)(1) of the Food, Drug and Cosmetic Act. Under this section, it is the responsibility of the producer of the new food product to evaluate its safety and ensure that the requirements of the section are met. If the new gene and its protein product were considered a food additive, then section 409 would be brought into play by the FDA and, in most cases, the agency would be obliged to undertake a lengthy premarket approval process.

Spurred by its report titled *A Mutable Feast: Assuring Food Safety in an Era of Genetic Engineering*, the Environmental Defense Fund (EDF) petitioned the FDA to regulate as food additives or as additives "generally regarded as safe" (GRAS) most expression products of interspecific and synthetic genetic material added to food products (Hopkins, Goldburg, and Hirsch 1991). Included in EDF's petition were proposals for labeling transgenic food and for a premarket notification program.

The EDF argued that the FDA should regulate foods modified by genetic engineering in the same manner it regulates processed food to which chemical substances have been added. The EDF cited the FDA for failing to follow established law and policy by applying new definitions of food additive and GRAS when regulating genetically engineered foods. Specifically, the EDF stated that the FDA substantially relaxed the definition of "generally regarded as safe (GRAS)" to make it much easier for producers of foods containing new substances added through genetic engineering to avoid having to submit food additive petitions (Goldburg and Hopkins 1992).

If transgenic food were regulated like food additives, manufacturers would have a strong burden of proof to demonstrate safe uses of the ingredients. At a time when the biotechnology industry struggled to gain approval for its first major agricultural product, defeating any labeling provisions is the signal that the industry sought to reinforce investor confidence.

Another source of social criticism toward the biotechnology industry is encapsulated by the term *bio-imperialism*, which some analysts use to describe biotechnology's contribution to the economic subordination of farmers in the developing world. According to a special report, "Biotech Bondage," published in the *New Statesmen and Society*, "The greatest danger to the South is through displacement of traditional farmers and commodities by genetically engineered laboratory-made substitutes" (Seabrook 1991, 19). Artificial sweeteners depress sugar production; laboratory-made vanilla threatens the future of seventy thousand vanilla farmers in Madagascar; and clonal production of oil palms or cocoa butter adversely affects small farmers in Africa and South America.

Henk Hobbelink has been keeping track of the socioeconomic impacts of biotechnology on the developing world. In *Biotechnology and the Future of World Agriculture* (1991) he contends that biotechnology will have a tremendous impact on the agriculture of the developing world and that the prospects for small farmers in the third world are not bright. The problem is not unique; it is simply the acceleration of a deepening crisis.

Rapid product displacement from one region to another has always affected the poor at the very beginning of the production chain: the small farmers and the landless wage workers.

The disastrous situation for the laborers employed in indigo production in Asia, after indigo was replaced by aniline dyes from Germany at the end of the 19th century, is one example of how product displacement affected the poor. The tremendous recession in whole regions of South America after rubber production was first transferred to Asia, and later shifted to synthetic rubber produced in the North, is another. (96)

Hobbelink cites the displacement of sugar production from the South as a result of new biotechnologies but cannot find any examples that illustrate avoidance of such economic tragedies. "Preoccupied by a determination to stay ahead in the biotech race," he concludes, "industrialized countries advocate policies that will further eliminate the need for imports from the South, regardless of the implications for the poor and resourceless" (96).

Not all analysts have as pessimistic an outlook on the impact of biotechnology on developing countries. Persely (1990) outlines the potential assets and liabilities. He sees biotechnology's major benefit as the potential to increase crop productivity and food production to meet expanding population needs in the developing world. Brenner (1991) views biotechnology as an important vehicle for improving maize production, particularly through genetically modified germ plasm that could be beneficial to global producers if proprietary interests and seed ownership do not thwart the transfer of the benefits to the developing world. Walgate (1990) describes the development of edible oils from flax as a way to reduce large deficits in oil production experienced by China and India.

The creation of seed for specialty foods and other plant products may cause a shift in the structure of agriculture in the United States. Biotechnology companies that have created "value-added" seed may be unwilling to relinquish control over production by selling seeds to the general market. Instead, some companies plan to contract with farmers to grow the specialty seeds and then contract with processors to turn the plants into marketable products. Calgene's production and marketing of the Flavr Savr tomato follows this pattern, as do their plans for developing specialty oil seed crops.

D. Health Issues: Allergenicity

The strongest argument for regulating transgenic food as food additives concerns the spread of allergenicity throughout the food supply. The prevalence of food allergies in the population is 4 to 6 percent in infants, 1 to 2 percent in young children, and less than 1 percent in adults. A minority of those with food allergies experience life-threatening reactions (Taylor 1993) such as breathing difficulty, low blood pressure, and loss of consciousness (anaphylactic shock). Critics of the FDA's bioengineered food policy contend that it fails to protect consumers against the spread of new food allergens among food groups. The agency will, of course, pay attention to known protein allergens when they are transferred to new foods. But how will the regulations address the emergence of new allergens or the reintroduction of lesser-known allergens? There is, after all, no complete inventory of food proteins that induce allergic reactions. Moreover, the introduction of new foods (kiwi fruit, for example) can produce novel allergenic affects.

It is most common for people with allergies to determine from personal experience the foods they must avoid, although they are often aided by testing. Unlabeled and unregulated genetically engineered food could undercut the self-protective knowledge people who have food allergies have gained from experience. EDF spokespersons (Goldburg and Hopkins 1992, 13–14) noted that "proteins that have no history of human consumption (e.g., certain insect proteins) may turn out to be allergenic when food organisms are genetically engineered to express them. . . . We know of no *a priori* reason why novel proteins introduced to foods via genetic engineering could not be allergenic."

Thus, the role of biotechnology in the spread of allergens remains unresolved. Moreover, even if labeling were adopted, there is no assurance that it would provide protection to those people who, although sensitive or allergenic to certain food types, would not be inclined to read labels and be warned by them. One of the most understated benefits of labels is that they make possible post hoc epidemiological studies of consumers who are aware of their consumption of transgenic varieties should untoward effects result in the population.

E. Public Perceptions of Transgenic Food

The public's sensitivity to changes in the manufacture or makeup of food is no surprise. There is sufficient evidence from prior controversies over fumigants such as EDB, pesticides such as DDT, and growth regulators like Alar (the trade name of daminozide) to demonstrate the volatility of public attitudes toward food products. Thomas Hoban of the Department of Sociology and Anthropology at North Carolina State University and Patricia Kendall of the Department of Food Science and Human Nutrition at Colorado State University conducted a USDA-funded national survey of consumer reactions to the use of biotechnology in agriculture and food production (Hoban and Kendall 1992). Drawing from a random sample of U.S. households, the investigators conducted 1,228 telephone interviews. Most respondents believed that they would benefit from research in biotechnology and expressed an overall positive viewpoint about the technology. Respondents were given different examples of transgenic organisms and asked to express their approval or disapproval of the products. Sixty-six percent indicated that plant-to-plant gene transfers were acceptable; 25 percent found animal-to-plant gene exchanges acceptable; 40 percent found transfers of genes from one animal to another acceptable; and only 10 percent approved of human-to-animal gene transfers.

The survey team also sought to learn about the public's general attitude toward biotechnology. Almost two-thirds of all respondents answered affirmatively to the following question: Overall, would you say you support or oppose the use of biotechnology in agriculture and food production? The most common reasons for opposition to biotechnology concerned threats to the balance of nature or serious impacts to the natural environment.

Some results of the Hoban-Kendall study illustrate the differences between general public opinion and the perspective of environmental groups. More than 60 percent of the survey's respondents believed that biotechnology would produce positive environmental effects and judged herbicide resistant crops to be acceptable. A poll of environmentalists would likely show a complete reversal.

In Europe, public attitudes toward transgenic food appear less favorable than in the United States. German citizen activists won strong support from consumers to ban most genetically engineered food products (Schmickle 1993). Strict regulations require scientists to obtain government permission before genetically modifying plants and animals. Given the pressures for harmonization of regulations within the European Community, most observers doubt that the strong German restrictions on transgenic food products will be retained.

A survey of public attitudes toward biotechnology in the United Kingdom was carried out by Sam Martin and Joyce Tait of the Open University. The investigators distributed questionnaires between November 1991 and February 1992 to members of several different organizations. They received 484 responses. According to the authors:

A large proportion said they would accept genetically manipulated foodstuffs provided they were confident about testing and that the product looked and tasted the same or better. . . . There was a widespread call for genetically-manipulated products, and those which use genetic manipulation in the processing, to be labelled (Martin and Tait 1992, 15–16). One half of the respondents felt it would be a good thing to use genetic manipulation "to attempt to solve the third world's food problems." . . . Relatively few people felt it would be good to use genetic manipulation "to attempt to provide more food for the Western world" (16 percent) or "to improve food for the Western world" (25 percent) . . . with 79 percent of respondents of the opinion that it would be a bad thing "if genetic manipulation was used for products which [they] think we don't need." (Martin and Tait 1992, 55)

In the United States, local and state laws have in some instances been enacted to augment federal biotechnology regulations. The first rDNA law in the United States was passed by the city council in Cambridge, Massachusetts, in 1977. Its purpose was to establish local review of the research activities and to require private-sector compliance with NIH guidelines.

State and local jurisdictions have also debated the need for additional legislation that responds to the commercialization of biotechnology products. A Minnesota law requires an environmental impact statement and a permit before a genetically engineered organism can be released into the environment. Under this law, Calgene would be required to obtain a permit to grow and sell its Flavr Savr tomatoes. Vermont has passed a BST labeling act, and other states are looking into similar legislation. Labeling transgenic food would enable consumers to express social values in their food preferences, which is consistent with the trend toward "green consumerism."

F. Conclusions

The use of genetic engineering for creating plant foods and other plant products is an example of innovation that has largely been science-driven rather than need-driven and thus fits well with the diffusion model (chapter 1). Although the companies developing transgenic delayed-ripening tomatoes may argue that there is a market demand for high-quality tomatoes in winter, we would classify this "need" as a marketing opportunity. For those willing to pay a premium, off-season tomatoes can be obtained from the increasing availability of greenhouse-grown produce imported from Europe. Plant products like laurate extracted from transgenic canola are available from other plant sources, and the transgenic product may take market share from current producers.

Many of the proposed new uses for transgenic plants, such as the production of biopolymers and pharmaceuticals, are attempts at increasing the efficiency of production rather than filling a product need that is not now met. As such these innovations also fit well into the diffusion model. This is another clear example of technology push. This technology addresses no obvious unmet need. For canola, the transgenic plant provides reduced factor costs and yields increasing efficiency of edible and industrial oil production.

A strong public reaction anticipated the marketing of the first product. That reaction extended the regulatory review and brought a great deal of media publicity to the issue of genetically engineered food. The innovation grew directly out of a particular scientific breakthrough with antisense genes. The success of the Flavr Savr in gaining regulatory approval provided an incentive for other companies, and it also set the stage for the deregulation of transgenic food products. By January 1995 the DNA Plant Technology Corporation (DNAP) received notification from the USDA and the FDA that its genetically engineered, delayed-ripening tomato had been granted nonregulated status. The company was then free to grow, ship, and sell its tomato throughout the United States without having to meet a burden of safety assessment. DNAP and Calgene began applying genetic technologies to other varieties of tomatoes as well as to other fruits and vegetables in cases where modification of the ripening process can extend the product's shelf-life and provide commercial advantages in harvesting and shipping that can reduce the costs of production. Large multinational agricultural companies such as Monsanto and Zeneca are also entering these markets.

That there is a powerful imagery associated with genetic engineering cannot be denied in light of the public's response to surveys and transgenic food products. This is particularly striking when the term *genetically engineered food* is introduced into popular discourse. The public is responding with caution, but it does not appear to be a caution based on strict forbiddance. Surveys indicate quite a spread of attitudes, from those individuals who are more experimental to those who would prefer to avoid food products that have been genetically altered.

To say that the science of food modification is precise is an overstatement. The introduction of a new protein or new DNA noncoding sequences may or may not alter the product or adversely affect some subgroup in the population. Once it has been decided that genetically modifying food is not intrinsically unmanageable from a health or nutritional standpoint (and that may remain questionable for some time to come), the next logical step is to set up evaluative procedures and disclosure mechanisms. Labeling products is as sensible for those who are comfortable trying out new technologies as it is for those who choose to wait until others have cleared the way.

The new synthesis between crop breeding and molecular genetics is clearly indicated by the rapid growth in food and other plant products subject to genetic engineering. This partnership will serve some interests well. Genetically engineered seeds will be more easily patentable. Innovations in this sector will foster shifts in seed ownership. Among the most far-reaching innovations is the commercial development of plants with foreign genes that may be used in the production of industrial chemicals and pharmaceuticals. Although there are some hopeful signs of success, these applications of transgenic plants have not yet been put to the test of efficacy, efficiency, and cost-effectiveness.

6 Microbial Pesticides

Predators and pathogens are important in controlling the numbers of herbivorous insects in natural ecosystems (Hairston, Smith, and Slobodkin 1960). Applying this model of nature to managed habitats in the United States, entomologists since the 1880s have released parasites and predators into agricultural ecosystems for the biological control of insects. Insect pathogens, including bacteria, viruses, fungi, and nematodes, have also been used for biological control in agriculture to a more limited degree. Farmers and foresters of the last century released viruses that are pathogenic to insects in an effort to create human-induced epidemics within pest insect populations. Several insect-pathogenic viruses are commercially available for control of caterpillars such as *Heliothis virescens* (tobacco budworm), *Helicoverpa zea* (cotton bollworm), and *Lymantria dispar* (gypsy moth). Bacterially produced insect toxins derived from *Bacillus thuringiensis* (*Bt*) are widely used by organic farmers (chapter 3). However, the acceptance of microbial insecticides has been limited and represents less than 1 percent of the total insecticide market. This is largely because these bioinsecticides are not as fast-acting, lose effectiveness more rapidly, have a narrower host spectrum, and require more knowledge to use efficiently than the synthetic chemical insecticides with which they compete (table 3). The new methods of biotechnology have created opportunities for developing and marketing the next generation of microbial pest control products. The primary reason for this optimism is twofold. First, there is continuing pressure from regulatory, environmental, and consumer groups to reduce the use of synthetic chemicals (e.g., Schneider 1991; K. Schneider 1992). Second, researchers believe they can improve the effectiveness of microbial products to the point where farmers would be willing to replace their current pest control products with biological ones.

There are a number of disadvantages in developing, marketing, and using synthetic chemicals, and the developers of microbial pest control products hope to gain a share of the market by exploiting these weaknesses. Microbial pest control products have a sizable advantage over synthetic chemicals with respect to the time and expense it takes for the EPA to approve products for commercial use. As a result of environmental concerns and public anxiety about the health effects of synthetic chemical residues in food, the EPA requires extensive and stringent toxicological testing before new synthetic chemicals are registered for use in crops. It can cost up to $40 million and take about four years to develop and register a new chemical insecticide (Panetta 1992). In contrast, the EPA has had a program in place since the 1970s that allows microbial pesticides to be registered relatively quickly and at low cost (W. Schneider 1992). Mycogen Corporation estimates the cost of bringing each of its recombinant microbial products to market at $1 million (Panetta 1992), and the average period to obtain registration of a microbial insecticide is about one year (Gallagher 1992; Marrone 1992).

The amendments to the Federal Insecticide, Fungicide, and Rodenticide Act (1988) require most synthetic chemical pesticides already on the market to be reregistered. Some older chemical pesticides are being withdrawn from the market because the costs of reregistration are not justified by potential sales and profits. This is especially the case for pesticides used mainly on small-acreage crops. Other pesticides have been withdrawn because of the discovery of toxic effects on nontarget organisms (W. Schneider 1992). Some synthetic chemical insecticides have become less effective over time because insects have developed resistance to them. Herbivorous insects possess very efficient detoxification and sequestration systems, probably evolved to deal with the myriad of plant chemicals encountered in nature (Brattsten 1979; Duffey 1980). Insecticides provide a strong selective advantage for herbivores that can overcome the chemical's toxicity. So far, agrichemical manufacturers have been able to do little to combat this natural process other than cautioning farmers against overusing insecticides, integrating insecticide use with other control methods, and developing new insecticides to replace those with diminished efficacy. The net effect of reregistration requirements and the evolution of insect resistance is to reduce the number of synthetic chemicals available for particular crops.

The unacceptably broad chemical toxicity of synthetic insecticides, regulatory considerations, economics, and pest resistance have led to a marked decline in the number of chemical options available to growers for insect control. Microbial pesticide producers view this as an opportunity to promote the advantageous qualities of their products to farmers. In the wake of intensified public concern over the environment, these companies believe there is a long-term trend toward moving away from heavy reliance on synthetic chemicals and to increasing market demand for alternative technologies, including microbial pesticides (Gelernter 1992; Hess 1992a; Miller 1992; Sandmeier 1992).

The major companies developing and marketing microbial insecticides have targeted larger, mainstream farms for their products rather than smaller, organic operations. Mainstream farmers are required by food processors, grocery chains, and consumers to maintain high cosmetic and other quality standards that have only been achievable with chemical insecticides. Some have argued that many of these standards do not contribute to the nutritional quality of food and should be eliminated to obviate the need for many chemical pesticides (Pimentel et al. 1977). However, rather than attempting to change market tastes or demands, many companies promoting microbial insecticides are trying to fit their products into the existing food and fiber production system. Almost uniformly the company representatives we interviewed for this book reported that environmental, health, and safety arguments do not sell insect control products to most farmers. Rather, they relate, the primary selling factor is to prove that microbials are as effective as the chemicals they would replace. The bottom line for most farmers is how well the new products work, how easy they are to use, and how much they cost (Gallagher 1992; Marrone 1992).

Given the incentives to reduce reliance on chemical insecticides, why have microbial insecticides not had more market success? Microbials may be environmentally preferable to chemicals, but how does that affect a farmer's decision to use them? Farmers employing pesticide-free methods are often compensated by consumers willing to pay higher prices and accept somewhat lower cosmetic standards for organically grown produce. However, there are now indications that demand for organically grown foods is weakening (Kong 1992). A survey of consumers found fewer than 10 percent of those interviewed willing to pay 10 percent more than current supermarket prices for pesticide-free produce (Ott 1990). In the same study, more than 60 percent of respondents were unwilling to accept additional cosmetic defects for pesticide-free produce. Thus, farmers may be loath to switch to alternate pest control methods if they feel they will be at a competitive disadvantage in the marketplace. If microbial pesticides prove effective and economically efficient, farmers will be able to meet consumer demand for low food prices and high cosmetic standards and claim a synthetic chemical-free product as well.

A. The Development of Bacteria for Insect Control

All recombinant bacterial insecticides with commercial prospects for agriculture involve the use of Bt in some form. Bt has been produced in bacterial culture and has been available as a biological insecticide since 1958 (Andrews et al. 1987) Bt-based formulations are the most widely used and most effective microbial insecticides (Lambert and Peferoen 1992). Sales, which account for 80 to 90 percent of the biological pest control market worldwide (Carlton, Gawron-Burke, and Johnson 1990), have more than quadrupled since the 1980s (Feitelson, Payne, and Kim 1992).*

Formulations containing Bt spores and/or δ-endotoxin crystals are sprayed on the surfaces of leaves or fruits; for mosquito and black fly control Bt is dispersed in water where larvae of these flies develop. Because the endotoxin crystals must be ingested to be toxic, beneficial insects (predators and parasites) are conserved, making Bt an ideal candidate for inclusion in integrated pest management (IPM) programs. The δ-endotoxin has no known toxicity to animals (other than target insects), humans, or plants. It degrades rapidly in the environment so that food-contaminating residues are not a problem. Farm workers can enter a field immediately after spraying, which they cannot do when synthetic insecticides are used, so that Bt can be applied just before harvest.

Even with these advantages Bt still accounts for less than 1 percent of insecticide sales worldwide. Narrow host range limits the usefulness of the δ-endotoxin if a crop is attacked by a diverse group of pests, which is often the case. Because Bt δ-endotoxin is applied to above-ground plant surfaces and not taken up systemically, it is not an effective control agent for internally feeding, fluid sucking, and root feeding pests.

The δ-endotoxin crystals have low residual activity, losing effectiveness within about four days after exposure to UV light. Rainfall can also wash the crystals from plant surfaces. Thus, frequent spraying is required if pests are emerging over a period of time. The timing of application is important to its effectiveness; the early larval stages are much more sensitive to the toxin than older larvae. *Ba-*

*See chapter 3 for discussion of the characteristics and mode of action of Bt.

cillus thuringiensis is often used prophylactically and is usually not effective against established pest populations (Lambert and Peferoen 1992).

1. Free-Living Plant Colonizing Bacteria

One of the early ideas for creating more effective biological insecticides involved transferring a gene for a protein toxin, such as the *Bt* δ-endotoxin, to a bacteria that colonizes plant leaves or roots. Unlike synthetic chemicals, free-living bacteria could reproduce and move among crop plants. Pests would be eliminated as the infection spread through the field after an initial inoculation. The leaf or root colonizing bacteria could deliver the biological insecticide directly to the plant part vulnerable to insect attack.

In 1985 Monsanto applied to the EPA for a permit to field test just such a product. Monsanto had created a recombinant bacteria, *P. fluorescens*, which contained δ-endotoxin genes effective against caterpillars (Obukowicz et al. 1986). The bacteria colonized the roots of corn plants. The EPA reviewed the request and had a number of concerns (Akçakaya and Ginzburg 1991). Tests had shown that bacteria isolated from infected insects were capable of infecting other insects. This would be a desirable characteristic in a pest control agent, because the infection could spread through the pest population. However, it raised the possibility that the recombinant bacteria would colonize wild plant species and kill nontarget insects, leading to unintended and undesirable ecological effects. There was also concern that the recombinant bacteria would be able to colonize above-ground plant parts as well as plant roots, with the risk of uncontrolled spread of the organism. Monsanto was required to repeat some of its experiments and provide additional information on the biological and ecological characteristics of the recombinant bacteria.

The field test of this *P. fluorescens*/δ-endotoxin organism was never conducted. Eventually, Monsanto dropped all work on recombinant microorganisms. Some commentators assert that the difficulty in getting regulatory approval for this field test, as well as the prospect of encountering opposition from public interest and community groups similar to that which accompanied the field tests of the ice-minus bacteria (chapter 8), caused Monsanto to cut back its agricultural biotechnology program (Miller 1994; Stewart et al. 1991). Company officials paint a slightly different picture, however, stating that the microbial biotechnology program was eliminated so that the company could concentrate on development of transgenic plants, which appeared to be a more profitable market (Stonard 1992).

2. Endophytic Bacteria

Endophytic bacteria occur naturally and inhabit the vascular systems of plants. Many endophytic bacteria have no known effects, although research shows that they can be both beneficial and deleterious to plant functioning.

Beginning in 1985, Crop Genetics International (CGI) of Hanover, Maryland, worked to develop the bacterial endophyte *Clavibacter xyli*, which is naturally found in the vascular system of Bermuda grass (*Cynodon dactylon*), as a carrier for *Bt* δ-endotoxin genes.[*] The idea was to infect crop plants with the transgenic bacteria, which would provide protection from insect pests feeding on the plants. The company devoted a significant part of its early research effort to developing basic biological and ecological information about the little-known *C. xyli*. This was essential; before allowing field tests the USDA and the EPA would demand assurance that the transgenic organism did not present a plant pest risk (Carlson 1992). Experiments carried out by CGI, in which *C. xyli* were injected into plants, revealed that the bacteria survives, reproduces, and spreads in several plant species besides its primary host, Bermuda grass. CGI determined that, unlike free-living bacteria, *C. xyli* can only survive inside its host plant and cannot be transmitted to other plants by insect vectors, pollen, or through the seed (Carlson 1992). Thus, the company felt able to allay any regulatory concerns over any unintended environmental impacts of the recombinant bacteria. Between 1988 and 1993, CGI conducted annual small-scale field tests of *C. xyli*/*Bt* δ-endotoxin in corn and rice (table 6).

CGI put its greatest effort into developing a recombinant *C. xyli* bacteria to protect corn from damage from the European corn borer (ECB). The pest feeds for most of its larval life within the corn husk. Contact insecticides and *Bt* sprayed on the plant surface are largely ineffective control methods. *C. xyli*/δ-endotoxin-infected corn plants provided what the company deemed excellent control of ECB. However, infected plants had lower yields than uninfected plants in the absence of ECB infestation (Carlson 1992). Thus, the product probably would only be economically attractive to farmers in areas where ECB infestation is severe. However, disappointing field results during the 1993 season may have doomed the product. Although corn protected with *C. xyli*/δ-endotoxin experienced only 20 percent ECB infestation compared to untreated corn, yields were equivalent

[*]Crop Genetics International was merged into biosys Inc. in 1995.

Table 6. Genetically Engineered Microbial Insecticides Field-Tested in the United States from 1988 to July 1995

Organism	Date	Type of Genetic Modification	Purpose of Modification	Organization	Current Status
Bacteria *Clavibacter xyli cynodontis* (endophytic bacteria)	1988–93	insertion of δ-endotoxin gene from *Bacillus thuringiensis kurstaki*	control of European corn borer (*Ostrinia nubilalis*) and evaluation of effect of endophyte on crop characteristics	Crop Genetics International and USDA	research halted in 1994 after inability to demonstrate positive yield effects in corn
Bacillus thuringiensis kurstaki (soil bacteria)	1990–93	insertion of δ-endotoxin gene from *B. thuringiensis wuhanensis*	improve efficacy for control of caterpillars	Sandoz Agro Inc.	research continuing with goal of commercialization
Bacillus thuringiensis kurstaki	1992–94	insertion of δ-endotoxin gene from *B. thuringiensis tenebrionis*	improve efficacy for control of Colorado potato beetle	Ecogen Inc.	commercialized in February 1995
Viruses *Autographa californica* nuclear polyhedrosis virus (lepidopteran pathogen)	1989	deletion of polyhedrosis gene	determine persistence in environment	Boyce Thompson Institute for Plant Research	technology licensed to Agrivirion Inc.

Organism	Date	Modification	Purpose	Institution	Status
Lymantria dispar nuclear polyhedrosis virus (gypsy moth pathogen)	1993	deletion of polyhedrosis gene; insertion of *lacZ* gene	determine persistence in environment; track movement in environment	Boyce Thompson Institute for Plant Research	research continuing; no plans for commercial product
Autographa californica nuclear polyhedrosis virus	1993–94	deletion of polyhedrosis gene (this is the same organism tested by BTI in 1989)	determine infectivity and persistence of mutant virus against *Trichoplusia ni* (cabbage looper) larvae	Agrivirion Inc.	research continuing; commercialization potential to be determined
Autographa californica nuclear polyhedrosis virus	1993	deletion of *egt* gene of virus (this gene prevents host insect from molting and pupating)	improve efficacy for control of caterpillars	American Cyanamid	research continuing with addition of other genes (see below)
Autographa californica nuclear polyhedrosis virus	1995	deletion of *egt* gene of virus and insertion of scorpion venom gene	improve performance of virus as bioinsecticide by reducing the time taken to kill its caterpillar host	American Cyanamid	research continuing with goal to develop a commercial product

Source: Compiled by the authors from various sources.

(Davis 1994). The 20 percent of corn borers remaining, the endophyte itself, or some combination of factors was responsible for the yield losses in the protected crop. In any case, CGI has no plans for further field tests or commercialization of the product.

3. *Killed Bacteria*

Mycogen Corporation of San Diego, California, has developed a method of encapsulating active δ-endotoxin protein within another bacterial species that is killed before application. Because the recombinant bacteria is dead when released, the company was able to get regulatory approval quickly for products, without controversy or objection from environmental groups. *Bacillus thuringiensis* δ-endotoxin genes are inserted into *P. fluorescens* cells. The cells with the δ-endotoxin genes are grown in fermentation tanks and produce levels of δ-endotoxin greater than 60 percent of total protein (Kim 1992). Before the *P. fluorescens* lyse, they are chemically cured; the cells are killed and stabilized by strengthening the cells walls and inactivating proteolytic enzymes (Feitelson, Payne, and Kim 1992). The δ-endotoxin remains active within the bacterial skeleton. Encapsulated δ-endotoxin has two times the residual activity of nonencapsulated δ-endotoxin (Gelernter 1992; Gelernter 1990).

Small-scale field tests on these killed *P. fluorescens/Bt* δ-endotoxin transgenic organisms were conducted from 1985 to 1989. In 1990 Mycogen received permission from the EPA to go to large-scale testing. In July 1991 Mycogen received EPA approval to market two of the recombinant bacterial insecticides, M-Trak (active against Colorado potato beetle) and MVP (active against caterpillars). Mycogen has since commercialized a third *Bt*-encapsulated product, M-Peril, for control of European corn borer. These were the first agricultural pest control products to be commercialized using recombinant organisms.

The technology of transferring genes of interest into microbes, having the microbe produce the gene product at high levels and then killing the recombinant organisms, has been patented by Mycogen as the CellCap® encapsulation system (Kim 1992). Company officials indicate that they are no longer pursuing development of live recombinant organisms because they believe that the CellCap system can be adapted for a myriad of products.

4. *Improving* Bacillus Thuringiensis

A number of companies have focused on improving *Bt* in various ways other than transferring δ-endotoxin genes to other species.

Researchers at Sandoz Agro in Palo Alto, California, have used recombinant techniques to transfer δ-endotoxin genes between *Bt* strains. The aim of this research is to increase the specific activity of the *Bt* product against a target pest. To accomplish this, genes from particularly virulent *Bt* strains are transferred to *Bt* strains that have the capacity to produce high yields of δ-endotoxin and other desirable commercial characteristics. Sandoz has been conducting yearly field tests of these strains since 1991 and conducted one in California in 1994 (table 6).

Sandoz is also using molecular techniques to identify the receptor sites for δ-endotoxin in target insects as well as working to identify the shape of the different δ-endotoxin molecules. The long-term goal of this research is to learn how to alter the structure of δ-endotoxin to increase efficacy.

Ecogen Inc., a biopesticide developer in Langehorne, Pennsylvania, has genetically engineered *Bt kurstaki* with a δ-endotoxin gene from *Bt tenebrionis*. The genetically engineered organism was registered by the EPA in February 1995 for control of Colorado potato beetle (Olson 1995).

5. *Improving* Bacillus Thuringiensis *without Genetic Engineering*

Nonrecombinant research on improving *Bt* has focused first on isolating new strains that have superior activity against target insect pests or are effective against pests not susceptible to known δ-endotoxins; second, on improving fermentation processes so that the yield of δ-endotoxin is increased; third, on altering formulations to get better plant coverage and increased protection from UV radiation; and fourth, on genetically manipulating and selecting strains for increased virulence and persistence (Carlton, Gawron-Burke, and Johnson 1990; Gallagher 1992; Kim 1992; Marrone 1992).

Nonrecombinant genetic manipulation includes creating mutant strains for subsequent selection by exposing organisms to a mutagenic substance and promoting the exchange of δ-endotoxin genes between *Bt* strains using techniques that occur in nature. For example, Novo Nordisk Entotech, a biotechnology company in Davis, California, has selected mutant strains of *Bt* that produced especially large δ-endotoxin crystals, which are more potent than the wild type (Marrone 1992). Novo Nordisk also markets a *Bt* product called Novodor for control of Colorado potato beetle. Novodor was created by mutagenesis followed by selection for strains producing large amounts of δ-endotoxin. Ecogen has used two naturally occurring bacterial processes, plasmid curing and conjugation, to construct new *Bt* strains with favorable attributes. Plasmid curing exploits the tendency of plasmids to be lost from bacteria during cell division. Strains can be selected that have lost the δ-endotoxin genes that are not effective insecticides. The remaining genes produce larger amounts of the more effective δ-endotoxins. "Conjugation" refers to the transfer of genetic material from a donor bacterium to a recipient bacterium while the two organisms are temporarily connected by a tubelike structure. Using conjugation, Ecogen has constructed a single strain of *Bt* that produces both caterpillar and beetle δ-endotoxins (Carlton, Gawron-Burke, and Johnson 1990). Ecogen markets three conjugation-improved *Bt* products for insect pests of potatoes, leafy vegetables, soybeans, and trees.

6. Health and Safety Issues

Bacillus thuringiensis is generally considered not to present any human health risk. As Meadows (1992, 125) noted, "The safety record of *Bacillus thuringiensis* is impeccable. . . . There have been no reports of harm associated with its use for pest control. It has proved totally safe for use even on food crops harvested the same day for human consumption. No problems have been reported in the food industry, and it has been absent from cases of food poisoning. There have been no reports of *B. thuringiensis* having any effect on nontarget organisms in the field."

However, Dixon (1994, 435) cautions that although "any organism that has been disseminated throughout the world for several decades as a biological control agent is likely to be relatively safe . . . there are a few worrying features, which at least imply that closer monitoring of its application would be prudent."

The reason for Dixon's caveat is that there has been but a single epidemiologic study of a human population exposed to *Bt* spraying, and several human infections may have been caused by *Bt*. *Bt* is morphologically similar to all of the *Bacillus* species that cause human disease and is probably closely related (Drobniewski 1994). Toxicological tests show that the ingestion of *Bt*, *Bt* spores, or δ-endotoxin by mammals, including humans, is safe. However, one case of a corneal ulcer was attributed to *Bt* being splashed in a farmer's eye (Samples and Buettner 1983). Green et al. (1990) studied infections in the population of Lane County, Oregon. For two successive seasons *Bt* had been aerially sprayed in the county for gypsy moth control. Eighty thousand people were exposed to *Bt* in the first year and forty thousand the second year. Routine cultures processed by clinical laboratories were screened for the presence of *Bt* isolates. In three cases *Bt* could not be ruled in or out as the causative agent of infection. All three patients had other medical conditions, and Green et al. suggest that *Bt*, acting as an opportunist, may exacerbate existing disease. They also suggest that immunocompromised patients may be vulnerable to infection from *Bt* and need to be protected. Even though the reported cases of disease attributable to *Bt* is extremely small, Drobniewski (1994, 106) recommends that "new varieties and toxin mixtures, such as those derived from recombinant techniques, should not be assumed safe . . . and should be carefully evaluated."

B. Viruses for Insect Control

Baculoviruses are the most common family of insect-pathogenic viruses (Maeda 1989). Since the last century farmers and foresters have used them to control insect pests. Most of the insect-pathogenic viruses that are available commercially are for control of caterpillars, such as tobacco budworm, cotton bollworm, and gypsy moth. However, these products have had a hard time competing against chemical insecticides. For example, Elcar, a virus marketed by Sandoz Agro and considered relatively effective for control of certain caterpillar pests of cotton, was withdrawn from the market in 1984 under competitive pressure from pyrethrum insecticides (Gallagher 1992). There has also been renewed interest in improving the effectiveness of insect-pathogenic viruses as alternatives to synthetic insecticides (Hoyle 1992).

1. Mode of Action of Baculoviruses

After an insect ingests baculovirus particles, gut enzymes dissolve the protein coat or occlusion body surrounding the virus. The occlusion body protects the virus from inactivating agents in the environment. The released virus invades the midgut cells, where more virus particles are produced and spread through the insect. Thirty percent of the dry weight of infected dead caterpillars may be attributable to the virus (Bonning, Merryweather, and Possee 1991). Horizontal (nonsexual) transfer of the virus to other caterpillars is accomplished by the release into the environment of occluded virions from decaying caterpillar corpses.

2. Characteristics of Baculoviruses

Insect-pathogenic baculoviruses are highly specific to single or narrow groups of insect species. Baculoviruses are not pathogenic to vertebrates or plants (Maeda 1989). Thus, nontarget insects (predators, parasites, and pollinators) and other nontarget taxa are generally not susceptible, making these viruses well suited for integrated pest management programs. However, Altmann (1992) has raised questions concerning the possible host-range expansion of baculoviruses resulting from exchange of DNA when two virus species infect the same insect. He cautions that viruses now restricted to infecting pest species might become pathogens of beneficial insects and other organisms. Evidence presented by Kondo and Maeda (1991) supports the contention that recombination of viral DNA between species can occur in coinfected insect cell lines, resulting in wider virus host-range among insect cell lines and larvae. Issues pertaining to host-range specificity will have to be considered before recombinant viruses, which contain genes to increase virulence, can be used widely for insect pest control.

The main disadvantage of baculovirus bioinsecticides is that they are slow-acting compared to chemical insecticides. An insect infected with a virus may continue to eat for a number of days before death. Host specificity can be another disadvantage if the crop is attacked by an array of insects, some of which are not susceptible to the virus.

3. Research on Baculoviruses

Scientists have tried to improve virus performance by screening and selecting more virulent strains. It is also possible to find better ways to use viruses by improving formulation, delivery methods, and timing of application (*Agrichemical Age* 1990). In December 1991 CGI and Du Pont announced a joint venture to develop, formulate, and market naturally occurring viruses for insect control (Feder 1991; Hoyle 1992). The joint venture has targeted high-value vegetable and orchard crops, where effective insecticides are unavailable, perhaps due to insect resistance or where insecticide residues are problematic (Carlson 1992). CGI has developed a method to produce low-cost, high-quality viruses, making them attractive to farmers (Carlson 1992). Initial plans at CGI call for use of naturally occurring viral strains and traditional selection methods.

Other research teams have attempted to improve virus performance by engineering foreign genes into baculoviruses. Their goal is to create viruses that have faster kill rates or cause insects to cease feeding after infection. The main strategies to improve virus performance with rDNA techniques have focused on transferring three components to viruses: (1) insect neurohormone associated genes to disrupt insect physiology (Hammock et al. 1990; Maeda 1989); (2) genes producing insect-sensitive neurotoxins found in scorpions (McCutchen et al. 1991; Stewart et al. 1991) and mites (Tomalski and Miller 1991); and (3) δ-endotoxin genes from *Bacillus thuringiensis* (Merryweather et al. 1990).

Sandoz Agro had been one of most active companies in isolating and synthesizing insect neurohormone genes and cloning them into baculoviruses. However, the production of insect neurohormones in baculoviruses did not significantly reduce the kill time or insect feeding rates after infection (Hess 1992a). Research efforts at Sandoz were refocused on transferring neurotoxin genes to baculoviruses. In 1992, however, Sandoz Agro terminated its in-house research program on genetically engineered and wild-type baculoviruses. Instead, the company has entered into a research and development agreement with biosys of Columbia, Maryland, for the development of insect-specific, naturally occurring baculovirus-based insecticides (*Ag Biotechnology News* 1993). Sandoz Agro will continue to support university research on genetically engineered baculoviruses (Hess 1992b).

Baculoviruses produce proteins that inhibit insect molting. Changes in insect hormone ratios associated with molting normally signal the insect to stop feeding one to two days before each molt. By inhibiting molting, the virus causes the insect to continue feeding and live longer. This increases the number of virus particles that can be produced in an insect before death. Promotion of insect feeding, however, runs counter to the definition of an effective bioinsecticide. O'Reilly and Miller (1991) employed a novel approach by deleting the gene in the baculovirus *Autographa californica* that encodes a protein responsible for inhibiting insect molting. Larvae infected by baculoviruses with a nonfunctional molting-inhibition gene ate less and died sooner than larvae infected with wild-type virus.

4. State of Development

Recombinant insect-pathogenic viruses are still in their early development. Several lines of research have not been able to demonstrate improvements in the speed and efficacy of transgenic insect-pathogenic viruses over wild-type viruses. Researchers at the Boyce Thompson Institute for Plant Research and Agrivirion, both in Ithaca, New York, have been working to alter baculoviruses to limit their persistence in the environment (table 6). Other genes could then be transferred to the viruses to improve their insect control properties without fear that a recombinant virus would spread out of control once released (Wood 1993). American Cyanamid has been conducting field tests of baculoviruses with the molting-inhibitor *egt* gene deleted and a scorpion venom gene inserted (table 6). The goal is to increase efficacy by speeding the time it takes for the virus to kill its caterpillar host.

C. Economics of Microbial Pesticides

The world market for insecticides is about $6 billion, with the U.S. market accounting for $1 billion. The world sales of biological insecticides total about $120 million annually, with *Bt*-based products accounting for more than 90 percent. Increased sales of bioinsecticides should be expected as more products reach the market. Bioinsecticides, especially *Bt*-based products, will have to compete with genetically engineered plants containing δ-endotoxin genes in the near future, and this may hurt sales.

Cost differences between synthetic chemicals and biological insecticides do not appear to be significant impediments to the sale of microbial products. The cost of microbials has historically been higher than synthetic chemicals because of the difficulties of dealing with live organisms in manufacturing processes. The cost advantage of synthetic chemicals, however, is rapidly disappearing as improvements are being made in microbial fermentation and formulation processes to increase the efficiency of production and the effectiveness of the product (Marrone 1992).

The major impediment to market penetration by biological insecticides is that many lack equivalent effectiveness compared to synthetic chemicals. Synthetic chemicals are relatively cheap and effective, and farmers are unlikely to give them up voluntarily unless microbial insecticides provide similar performance (Marrone 1992). Farmers who expect biological pest control to work exactly like synthetic chemicals are often disappointed. Thus, the principal challenges confronting companies that market microbial insecticides are to demonstrate equivalent effectiveness with synthetics, to educate farmers on the correct methods of using biological products for maximum effectiveness, and to communicate realistic performance expectations (Gallagher 1992; Gelernter 1992; Marrone 1992; Panetta 1992; section D).

Industry remains optimistic because it sees the social, legal, and political pressure to replace chemicals continuing, as evidenced by the federal appellate court ruling that instructed the EPA to ban all potentially carcinogenic pesticides that leave residues in food (K. Schneider 1992) and the Clinton administration's plan to expedite the removal of pesticides that are health and environmental risks. Industry believes that the technology exists to improve biological products significantly while maintaining their beneficial environmental characteristics (Sandmeier 1992). Available *Bt*-based insecticides are much more effective than those of the 1980s (Gallagher 1992; Marrone 1992). Sales increased from $24 million in 1988 to $107 million in 1991. Developers predict continued improvement and that genetic engineering will play an increasingly important role (Carlton 1992)

Some microbial products created through advanced techniques are being advertised as having similar control abilities compared to synthetic chemicals. Novo Nordisk markets two *Bt*-based products, Foray (for gypsy moth control in forests, e.g., Dubois, Reardon, and Mierzejewski [1993]) and Novodor (for control of Colorado potato beetle in potatoes). The company claims that if properly used these two products are as effective as the leading synthetic chemicals on the market. In company-run field tests under ideal conditions Novodor has reportedly achieved 98 percent control of Colorado potato beetle (Marrone 1992). However, sales of these products, which at first were encouraging, have lagged. One company official reported that farmers who were initially impressed with the results from the improved *Bt*-based product may have become disappointed in the following year due to suboptimal performance. The same official attributed the poor performance to inadequate technical support (Marrone 1995; section F).

D. Product Development Choices

A number of factors have influenced decisions by companies to pursue development of certain types of microbial insecticides while avoiding development of other possible products. A company's ability to make a profit from the product is, of course, the primary concern, but other factors also come into play.

1. Regulation and Public Opinion

The regulatory environment is often cited as a principal factor in explaining why the development and commercialization of genetically engineered products for agriculture have been slower than some had predicted (Alper 1987). Some view the regulations and guidelines, and the delays in putting EPA regulations in place (Betz 1992), as inhibiting the development of genetically engineered products for agriculture without providing any added protection for the environment or public health (Brill 1985; Brill 1991; Miller 1993). Environmental releases of genetically engineered microorganisms (GEMs) have caused more controversy than the release of transgenic plants even though both may have similar adverse environmental impacts. The number of field tests of transgenic plants dwarfs the number of field tests of genetically engineered microbes that have been released (figure 11). Two factors may help explain this. First, our understanding of the biology and ecology of microorganisms is limited, especially when compared to higher plants and animals. Therefore, more uncertainty is associated with predicting the probability of untoward effects associated with environmental release of microorganisms. Second, unlike field tests of transgenic plants, even small-scale field releases of GEMs are difficult to contain. Once released, GEMs are nearly impossible to retrieve. Whereas the first attempts to field test GEMs were met with great public fear and caution on the part of regulatory agencies (Krimsky 1991), the first field tests of transgenic plants proceeded without much public concern. These explanations do not fully account for the vastly disproportionate progress toward commercial development between GEMs and transgenic plants.

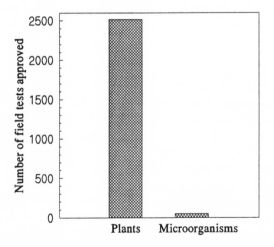

Figure 11. U.S. Field Tests of Transgenic Plants and Microorganisms from 1987 to July 1995. *Source:* Compiled by the authors from USDA and EPA data

The regulatory environment had been a factor in some companies' decisions to develop particular microbial insecticide products and in their progress toward testing and commercializing those products. However, the extent of the regulatory environment's influence on the pace of development is not clear. Small companies may have been deterred from entering the field for fear that the time and costs of the initial experimental work needed to gain regulatory approval for field tests would be too great (Tiedje 1992). Technical problems, rather than government regulation, are probably the most important factor in explaining the relatively slow progress of the industry (Wrubel, Krimsky, and Anderson 1995). For example, Sandoz Agro has had little trouble gaining government approval to field test its genetically engineered microbial products. Company representatives are confident that they will not encounter regulatory opposition to commercialization (Gallagher 1992; Sandmeier 1992). They contend that the time-limiting factor in product development has been obtaining sufficiently impressive field data to convince the marketing people in the company that the product would sell. In 1992 Ecogen received a blanket approval from the EPA to field test an improved *Bt* product that combined genes from two different strains. Subsequent field tests were automatically approved for the same recombinant strain, and Ecogen has petitioned the EPA to market this product as its Raven Bioinsecticide.

In the early 1980s the first attempts were made to test genetically engineered bacteria in the environment. Monsanto's problems in getting permission to field test a recombinant *P. fluorescens* bacteria has been discussed. Advanced Genetic Sciences (AGS), however, did receive approval for field testing the ice-minus recombinant *P. syringae* bacteria during the same period.* Tests were only allowed to go forward after protracted legal conflicts and public debate, and under highly regulated circumstances (chapter 8; Krimsky and Plough 1988). Companies developing, or considering developing, similar products were aware of the difficulties Monsanto and AGS experienced in field testing their recombinant free-living bacteria. This awareness affected subsequent decisions on how to proceed with other research programs.

Some companies chose to wait for the regulatory road to be paved before traveling on it. For example, these controversies directly affected decisions made by CGI, which was then developing its recom-

---

* Advanced Genetic Sciences was merged into DNA Plant Technology Corporation in 1989.

binant endophytic bacterium *C. xyli/Bt* δ-endotoxin. Rather than pushing ahead with its own application to field test the recombinant *C. xyli*, CGI altered its strategy and decided first to examine the safety of using the endophytic bacteria as an insecticide carrier (Carlson 1992). Company officials report that they were very concerned that the public have trust in the studies and decided to cooperate with the Agricultural Research Service (ARS) of the USDA in conducting the field trials. In 1985, at the USDA Beltsville, Maryland, facility, CGI along with ARS researchers began small-scale experiments with wild-type *C. xyli*. Information on the ecology and behavior of the bacterium was gathered that would later be used to justify the safety of a field test of the recombinant *C. xyli/δ*-endotoxin construct. In 1988, using data obtained from the initial field studies, CGI applied and received approval from both the USDA and the EPA to conduct field tests of the recombinant bacteria. Those field tests continued each year until 1993 without incident. In this case it appears that the regulatory environment was a factor in the decision by CGI officials to delay field tests of the recombinant bacteria. Nevertheless, the company was able to adjust and pursue its research and development program. The company's decision to halt development of *C. xyli/δ*-endotoxin was based on the efficacy of the product, not regulatory considerations.

Another company whose research agenda was affected by the regulatory context was Mycogen Corporation. In 1983–84 Mycogen was developing live *P. fluorescens/Bt* δ-endotoxin transgenic bacteria intended for environmental release. The feeling within the company was that it would be a tremendous undertaking to get a live recombinant *P. fluorescens/Bt* product tested and registered (Panetta 1992). The company made a strategic decision not to pursue field testing of the live recombinant organism. Discussion of how the product might be made more acceptable from a regulatory standpoint led to the idea of killing the recombinant cells and then applying the dead cells as an insecticide. Mycogen has commercialized three of these products without regulatory delays. Had the regulatory situation been more encouraging early on, company officials believe they would have pursued development of the live recombinant product (Panetta 1992). Now the company sees no need to develop a live recombinant product and is not attempting to do so. Mycogen believes that the CellCap system can be adapted successfully to exploit the large diversity of *Bt* strains the company is discovering (Kim 1992).

We are not aware of any company that is now developing an intergeneric recombinant bacterial insect control product that combines δ-endotoxin genes in a free-living bacteria that could colonize plants and spread once released. Two other biotechnology companies, Ecogen and Novo Nordisk Entotech, delayed using genetic engineering to develop microbial products. Both companies felt that it would take significantly longer to develop and win regulatory approval for recombinant *Bt*-based products and chose first to develop products using nonrecombinant techniques, which could be more quickly commercialized. Ecogen commercialized a recombinant bioinsectcide in 1995, while Novo Nordisk abandoned rDNA research. Novo Nordisk's decision was based on European opposition to field tests of recombinant organisms and on uneasiness within the company concerning release of microbes with antibiotic resistance genes into the environment (Marrone 1995).

Several companies are trying to improve the performance of *Bt*-based insecticides by using genetic engineering to combine genes from two or more *Bt* strains into a single *Bt* organism. These companies believe that it will be easier for people to accept environmental release of a *Bt/Bt* recombinant organism rather than putting a novel toxin into another species (Gallagher 1992; Marrone 1992). The companies are banking that *Bt/Bt* recombinant products will receive the same expeditious registration treatment accorded nonengineered *Bt* products by the EPA (Gallagher 1992).

Avoidance of public and government controversy, however, was only one reason given for developing *Bt* transgenic bacteria. Researchers stated that because *Bt* was already known to be an efficient producer of δ-endotoxin it made little sense to begin work by moving δ-endotoxin genes to foreign organisms (Gallagher 1992; Marrone 1992). There is also doubt about the ability of a recombinant bacteria carrying a foreign gene to compete with indigenous bacteria and effectively survive to colonize plants under field conditions (Hankinson 1992; Marrone 1992; Tiedje 1992).

In summary, the regulatory environment has affected the decisions of some companies to pursue specific research and development paths and avoid others, but we have found little evidence that government regulation or regulatory uncertainty have significantly slowed the development and commercialization of most microbial products.

2. Patentability

Many companies require that the products they develop be patentable. One company indicated that it withdrew from breeding tropical crops with tissue culture techniques for the South American market because patent protection was not available. The company decided to focus on U.S. crop improvement through genetic engineering even though it was believed that the need for new crop varieties was greater in the third world (Carlson 1992). Patentability of microorganisms was settled by the Supreme Court in *Diamond v. Chakrabarty* (477 U.S. 303) in 1980.

3. Replacement Products versus Unmet Market Needs

Insecticide markets are considered mature because there are products, usually synthetic chemicals, available to meet almost all market needs. Thus, biotechnology companies are primarily trying to replace chemical insecticides with improved microbial ones and must compete directly against those chemicals. Most of the microbial products are employed in ways that are similar to the synthetic chemicals they are designed to replace. Some type of spray applicator is used to deposit the toxic formulation on the crop plant. One exception was CGI's endophytic bacteria, which acted as a systemic insecticide but has since been abandoned.

4. Crop Markets

Biotechnology companies have chosen niche markets that they think represent the best opportunities for microbial products to succeed (Gelernter 1992). Companies developing transgenic plants, where seeds will be the product sold to farmers, have targeted the large-acreage crops like corn, soybeans, and cotton. In contrast, companies developing microbial insecticides see their greatest opportunities in high-value, small-acreage crops such as fruits and vegetables. Synthetic chemical insecticides are registered for use on the large-acreage crops first, where profit potential is greatest. Only secondarily are some of these insecticides registered on smaller crops that have more limited profit potential. Thus, fewer chemical products are available for each small-acreage crop (Kim 1992). Market needs for additional insect control methods may develop in these fresh-food crops as consumers become more concerned about toxic residues and more chemicals are withdrawn from the market during the reregistration process. Farmers who grow high-value crops have a large investment in each plant and are likely to invest the time and energy necessary to learn proper methods for getting the best results from microbial products.

Other companies indicate that although they are first trying to gain a foothold in the high-value crops they are still considering ways to use microbial products in the more lucrative larger crop markets (Gelernter 1992). Mycogen is targeting one of its *Bt*-based products to control European corn borer, a market estimated at between $150 and $400 million annually. CGI has identified corn as its target market because of the size of that market.

E. Microbial Insecticides and the Agricultural Chemical Industry

Most companies developing recombinant microbial insecticides view themselves as part of the larger pest control industry, which includes the companies producing synthetic organic insecticides. They do not see themselves as a radical or alternative industry trying to displace all synthetics. Some of the companies developing microbials also sell synthetic chemicals and therefore would not be expected to speak out strongly against chemical products. However, even companies without connections to the chemical producers are not, with few exceptions, outspoken antichemical environmentalists. Company personnel do not see chemicals as necessarily "bad" but rather believe that market opportunities and niches exist for biological pesticides. The leaders of these companies are not environmental idealists but sophisticated entrepreneurs. Companies do not see their products as displacing most chemicals but as being used for specific insect problems in certain crops where chemicals have been withdrawn or insects are resistant to the chemicals. Because of the specificity of the microbials, companies envision their products being used to complement broader-spectrum synthetic chemicals. For companies trying to appeal to mainstream farmers, "green qualities" are less important in product promotion than efficacy.

F. Farmer Education and Insect Resistance: Two Factors Influencing the Success of Microbial Insecticides

1. Education

To maximize performance of a microbial insecticide requires more knowledge of the crop-pest environment and perhaps greater care and labor in application compared with synthetic chemicals. The effectiveness of some microbial insecticides may be equivalent to chemical alternatives, but their usefulness is not optimized because of mistakes in application. For example, because most microbial insecticides have to be ingested by the target insect and also tend to degrade relatively quickly once put into the environment, the timing of application and placement on the host plant are very important for product performance.

Farmers' expectations of how bioinsecticides will perform may not match reality. Those who expect the results of treatment with microbial insecticides to be identical to that of chemicals are usually disappointed. For example, after spraying a synthetic chemical that is a nerve toxin, a farmer can expect to see dead insects in the field immediately. Microbial insecticides are slower-acting than chemical insecticides. Consequently, to a farmer it may appear that the microbial treatment is ineffective when it just takes longer to work.

Thus, companies selling microbial insecticides, in order to succeed, must induce farmers to change the way they think about pest management and disseminate information on the proper use of biological pest control products. Biologicals might be as effective as synthetic insecticides, but to reach that level of efficacy requires added information, especially about the proper timing of treatments. The companies we interviewed all appeared to be aware of this need and described conducting support sessions to inform extension personnel and farmers about the correct methods for using microbial insecticides. However, they must continue to offer product support in order for microbial insecticides to continue to provide good results. This is an investment not required when promoting synthetic chemicals. With proper advice, farmers might get good results the first year, but results may suffer if support is not available in subsequent years. Farmers are then likely to return to the synthetic insecticides for more consistent results.

2. Insect Resistance to Microbial Insecticides

There is no reason to believe that insects will not be able to adapt and become resistant to microbial insecticides if the microbial insecticides are used to the same extent as the synthetic chemicals they would replace (Fox 1991; Stevens 1992). Growing evidence suggests that a variety of insect pest species can become resistant to *Bt* δ-endotoxin (Ferré et al. 1991; Gould et al. 1992; McGaughey and Whalon 1992; Tabashnik 1994; Tabashnik et al. 1990; Tabashnik, Finson, and Johnson 1991; chapter 3).

Transgenic plants that produce δ-endotoxin continuously in all plant parts are thought more likely to encourage pest resistance than those sprayed with δ-endotoxin, which degrades relatively quickly (in about four days) in sunlight. However, foliar applications of *Bt*-based insecticides can be as frequent as every three days during the

rapid growth stages of vegetable crops (Gallagher 1992). The evolution of resistance to Bt after intensive spraying has been documented
for the diamondback moth (*Plutella xylostella*), a pest of cole (e.g.,
cabbage, broccoli) crops. This intensive spraying followed the failure of synthetic insecticides to provide control because of pest resistance (Tabashnik 1994). Thus, repeated spraying may select for
resistant pest biotypes, and the possibility of resistance to Bt-based
insecticide sprays should not be underestimated (Roush 1992).

It has been suggested that genetic engineering can be used to delay the onset of resistance by creating a single Bt strain that produces
several types of δ-endotoxin (Kim 1992). If each type of δ-endotoxin
has a different site of activity, the insect would have to adapt at more
than one gene locus to develop resistance. In theory, this would
decrease the probability of resistance—or at least delay its onset.
Research has shown that insects can be cross-resistant to two struc-
turally unrelated δ-endotoxins (Gould et al. 1992) and that mixtures
of toxins may not prevent or delay resistance (McGaughey and
Johnson 1992; Tabashnik, Finson, and Johnson 1991). These results
appear to cast doubt on the advantage of engineering multiple δ-
endotoxins to avoid resistance.

G. Conclusions

The general level of research activity as reflected in the number of
applications approved for field tests of genetically engineered microorganisms has greatly lagged transgenic plants (figure 11). Similarly, research to develop transgenic microbial insecticides has not
matched that in plant biotechnology to develop insect resistant
crops. Efforts to use genetic engineering to improve viruses as biological insecticides has just begun to move from the laboratory to
the field. Genetically engineered bacteria, specifically Bt-based insecticides, are now commercially available.

The major impediment to biological insecticides' market success
has been their lack of effectiveness compared to synthetic chemicals. Farmers will not rely on biological insecticides voluntarily,
although they have many environmental advantages, unless they are
as effective as the chemicals they would replace. Companies are
putting research efforts into developing new biological insecticides
because they believe that there will be continuing pressure to replace
synthetic pesticides for environmental and health reasons and that
the performance of biologicals can be improved significantly. It is
unlikely that microbial products will reduce chemical usage signifi-

cantly during the next decade, although inroads are possible in the longer term.

The regulatory environment has affected the decisions of some companies to pursue specific research and development paths and avoid others, but we did not find evidence that government regulation or regulatory uncertainty have slowed significantly or prevented the development and commercialization of microbial products. Rather technical problems, especially lack of efficacy, are probably more important than any government constraints in explaining the relatively slow progress of the industry.

Companies developing biological insecticides see themselves as part of the larger pest control industry and not as an alternative industry seeking to replace conventional chemically based management techniques. They believe that microbial products can fill certain niche markets now opening due to some of the short-comings of synthetic chemicals. Although biologicals will certainly replace some of the synthetic chemicals now being used, they will generally be used along with other synthetic chemicals. We are not witnessing a competitive struggle between innovation sectors, as was the case when transistors replaced vacuum tubes. This is a case of co-evolution.

Manufacturers want to appeal to large, mainstream farmers rather than to small organic operations that traditionally have been the consumers of biological pest control products. The success of microbial insecticides will be determined by the ability of manufacturers to improve the efficacy and consistency of their products and to provide consistent support to farmers and extension personnel on the techniques needed to maximize effectiveness and avoid the insect resistance problems that have reduced the usefulness of many synthetic chemicals.

7   Nitrogen-Fixing Bacteria

Improvement of nitrogen fixation was one of the earliest anticipated applications for genetic engineering in agriculture (Barton and Brill 1983). Nitrogen is part of amino acid molecules, which are the building blocks of proteins and are required by all organisms. For plants to use nitrogen it must be converted from the diatomic form found in the atmosphere (N_2) to a reduced form such as ammonia (NH_3). The process of nitrogen reduction is called nitrogen fixation. Plants obtain reduced nitrogen from the soil, where it has been liberated by bacterial and fungal degradation of dead plants and animals, fixed by free-living nitrogen-fixing bacteria, or added to the soil as fertilizers by farmers (figure 12). Inorganic fertilizers are commonly applied to many crops each year. These additives are expensive and create pollution problems due to run-off and leaching into streams and groundwater.

Some plants, including the legumes (e.g., peas, beans, alfalfa, soybeans, clover, peanuts), form mutualistic associations with soil bacteria that can fix atmospheric nitrogen (figure 13). These plants have a source of nitrogen unavailable to non-nitrogen-fixing plants.

The ancient Greek and Roman agriculturalists were well aware that legumes possess special properties that make them productive on poor soils (soils low in nitrogen) and are also able to improve the yields of nonleguminous crops. Nothing was known about the basis of legumes' capabilities until 1838, when Jean Baptiste Boussingault, a French chemist, provided the first experimental evidence that these plants use nitrogen from the air as a source of nitrogen for plant growth. Boussingault's results were not accepted by the scientific community, and eventually he himself repudiated them (Wilson 1940).[*] There followed fifty years of experimentation and

---

[*]See Wilson (1940, chapter 2) for an engrossing historical view of the quest to resolve the nitrogen-fixation controversy.

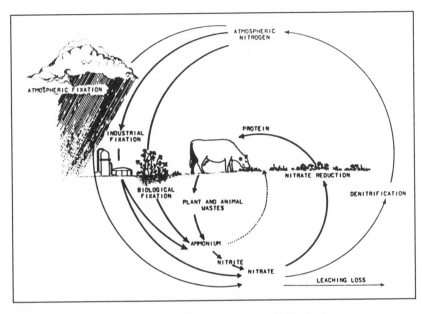

Figure 12. The Nitrogen Cycle. *Source:* Research Seeds, Inc.

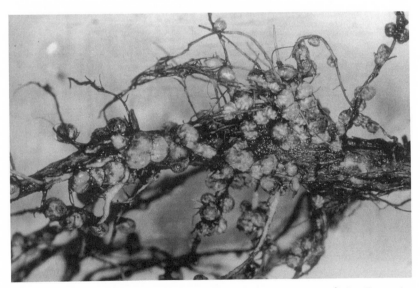

Figure 13. Root Nodules on Soybeans Containing Nitrogen-fixing Bacteria. Soybean roots with bumps called nodules. Nodules are masses of root tissue containing many nitrogen-fixing bacteria. In a mutualistic association the plant provides nutrients to the bacteria, which fix nitrogen for use by the plant. *Source:* Research Seeds, Inc.

controversy. In 1886 Hellriegel and Wilfarth, two German chemists, discovered that root nodules (the small tubercles on the roots of legumes) contained bacteria that converted atmospheric nitrogen to ammonia. In 1888 the bacteria were isolated and identified as "rhizobia," or root-inhabiting bacteria. By the first decade of the twentieth century farmers were applying rhizobia to fields where beans and peas were grown to ensure adequate nitrogen fixation (Brill 1991).

Free-living and symbiotic bacteria and free-living blue-green algae (cyanobacteria), all prokaryotes, are the only organisms discovered that can biologically fix nitrogen (Burris and Roberts 1993). The free-living microbes found in soil and water include *Klebsiella spp.*, *Azotobacter chroococcum*, *Clostridium pasteurianum*, and *Anabaena spp.* Bacterial symbionts reside in nodules on the roots of a variety of plants. Leguminous plants are of most interest because they provide major sources of protein nutrition around the world. Nonleguminous symbionts have also been identified, such as *Frankia spp.* associated with the roots of alders, and are probably widespread. But none of these are significant food sources for humans, and thus they have received much less attention (Burris and Roberts 1993).

Nitrogen-fixing bacteria associated with legumes are in the genera *Rhizobium* and *Bradyrhizobium*, which are often referred to collectively as "rhizobia." Particular species of rhizobia colonize either a single or a narrow range of plant species. Thus, *R. meliloti* is associated with the roots of alfalfa, *B. japonicum* with soybean, and various strains of *R. leguminosarum* with clover, peas, and beans. The association between legumes and rhizobia is a mutualism, allowing the plants to grow on nitrogen-poor soils while the bacteria are provided with an energy source: photosynthate produced by the plant. The practical advantage for farmers is that legumes can be grown without the addition of expensive nitrogen fertilizers, which, if present, actually inhibit the nitrogen-fixing activity of rhizobia. Legumes increase the amount of available soil nitrogen so that nonleguminous crops grown in rotation or intercropped with legumes benefit. Legumes such as alfalfa, vetch, and clover are often grown as "green manure" cover crops to prevent erosion while increasing soil nitrogen.

In the 1970s and early 1980s there was speculation that genes for nitrogen fixation could be transferred to non-nitrogen-fixing microbes that could be used to colonize the roots of cereal crops and provide them with nitrogen (Elkington 1985, 119). In 1971 the United Kingdom's Agricultural Research Council's Unit of Nitrogen Fixation at Sussex University successfully transferred seventeen *nif* genes responsible for nitrogen fixation in *Klebsiella pneumoniae* to

Escherichia coli (Dixon, Cannon, and Kondorosi 1976). The recipient bacteria were then able to fix atmospheric nitrogen. This meant that all of the machinery needed to transcribe and regulate translation of the foreign DNA was contained in *E. coli* (Haslekorn 1986). *Nod* genes, responsible for nodule formation, have been transferred from rhizobia to the non-nitrogen-fixing bacteria, *E. coli* and *Agrobacterium tumefaciens* (Hirsh et al. 1984). The bacteria successfully colonized the roots of alfalfa and formed pseudonodules. But the pseudonodules were nonfunctional and therefore unable to fix atmospheric nitrogen. No team has claimed the ability to increase the amount of nitrogen available to nonleguminous crops by transferring genes from rhizobia to non-nitrogen-fixing microbes. As far are we know, not withstanding a burst of media attention, there is no serious research program to transfer nitrogen-fixing capabilities to non-nitrogen-fixing bacteria for enhanced plant growth.

When it became technically possible to transfer genes into plants in the early 1980s (Bevan 1984), there was both speculation as well as skepticism that cereal crops, including corn, which requires high levels of nitrogen inputs, could be transformed with genes from rhizobia, enabling nitrogen fixation (Barton and Brill 1983). However, the obstacles for transferring nitrogen fixation to plants are formidable. First, one of the bacterial enzymes in the nitrogen reduction process requires an oxygen-free environment. Nodules on legumes are specialized for this function. The primary obstacle to expanding nitrogen fixation to nonleguminous plants is the difficulty of restructuring a plant to bear root nodules similar to those of legumes where nitrogen fixation works. Second, there is a high energy cost to the plant. Nitrogen fixation consumes considerable energy that the plant would expend at the expense of carbohydrate production (crop yield). Third, the physiology of eukaryotes is generally not designed well for nitrogen fixation. Zimmerman (1984, 84–85) notes:

> Not only must the enzymatic machinery be in place within the cell to perform the conversion of molecular nitrogen to the form utilized by the plant (ammonia), but it must be located in a suitable place within the plant for the efficient absorption of the gas. The stomata, the pores on the undersides of the leaves, are the opening through which oxygen and carbon dioxide are exchanged during photosynthesis. But photosynthesis takes place in very specialized structures called chloroplasts, which are well adapted for efficient gas exchange. Although it may be possible to insert nitrogen-fixing genes into plants and

to achieve gene expression, the likelihood of achieving high efficiency of nitrogen incorporation seems remote without additional structural modifications.

The nodule-formation/nitrogen-fixation process requires multiple genes (probably more than twenty) in the bacteria and the plant. The complexity of the nitrogen-fixation process makes it highly unlikely that with current technology nitrogen-fixing abilities can be transferred to cereal crops. However, molecular techniques are being applied successfully to decipher the details of the nitrogen-fixation process, which will increase our understanding of plant physiology and plant-microbial interactions and may lead to breakthroughs in the future (Dixon 1990; Hirsch et al. 1984; Moffat 1990).

During the 1980s several U.S. companies, including Agracetus, Agrigentics, Allied Technologies Division of Allied Signal, and Biotechnica, invested up to $80 million on research and development to improve rhizobia inoculants genetically (Kidd 1994). The research programs employed rDNA techniques as well as other methods of genetic manipulation. After ten years none of the companies had succeeded in successfully marketing a rhizobia product and all had withdrawn from the field. The ill-fated rhizobium improvement story illustrates the high hopes placed on a new molecular technology that remain unrealized due to the difficulties of moving from the laboratory to the field.

Rhizobia are widespread in nature, but because of the specificity of the bacteria-plant association the compatible bacterial species may not be available in sufficient numbers in a particular locale to colonize crop roots effectively. Even when the suitable species is present, crop performance may be poor because many indigenous strains are inefficient nitrogen-fixers (Baldwin and Fred 1929; Helz, Baldwin, and Fred 1927; Leonard 1930). Since the first decade of the twentieth century researchers have been selecting for naturally occurring strains with superior nitrogen-fixing capabilities. Inoculants made up of the choice strains are then applied to seeds before planting or to soils in hope of improving yields of legumes. Thousands of field tests aimed at discovering the best rhizobia strain for particular crop/environment combinations have been performed (Brill 1991). However, the worldwide market for rhizobia inoculants has remained between $20 and $25 million annually for some time (DRI 1992; Kidd 1994). This is largely because farmers remain unconvinced that inoculants give consistent yield benefits. Applications of inoculants, which in the greenhouse provide yield advantages over wild-types, often fail to increase yield because ineffective indigenous strains outcompete the effective inoculant strains for nodulation sites on the host plant's roots (Triplett and Sadowsky 1992).

Because the market for inoculants is relatively small, one might wonder why companies would invest large amounts of capital and research effort in this sector. Considerable acreage in the United States and worldwide is devoted to legume production, but relatively few acres are treated with inoculum. For example, soybeans account for two-thirds of the inoculum used in the United States, but only 15 percent of the soybean crop is now treated (DRI 1992). A company that could demonstrate a nitrogen-fixing product proven to increase yield could charge a premium and have a largely untapped market available. Efforts to improve rhizobia with genetic engineering have focused on boosting the efficiency of nitrogen fixation compared to available selected strains and enhancing the competitiveness of new strains compared to indigenous strains.

A. Technical Development

In 1985 Biotechnica International initiated a research program using genetic engineering to enhance nitrogen fixation in rhizobia. Gene cassettes* containing additional copies of the *nifA* gene along with stronger gene promoters were inserted into the chromosomes of *R. meliloti* (for alfalfa) and *B. japonicum* (for soybeans) (Cannon et al. 1988). The *nifA* gene is regulatory, and its product stimulates transcription of several genes involved in nitrogen fixation (Wilson and Lindow 1993). Greenhouse tests of *nifA*-enhanced strains were very promising, with yield increases over nonengineered strains reaching 17 percent (Cannon et al. 1988). However, the only published field results were much less impressive (Ronson et al. 1990). Differences in greenhouse and field results were attributed to poor nodule colonization rates of engineered nitrogen-fixing stains when in competition with indigenous rhizobia in the field (Hankinson 1992).

Biotechnica came up with a second strategy to increase nitrogen production. Rhizobia rely on the photosynthate provided by the host plant for the energy needed to fix atmospheric nitrogen. The reaction is energy-intensive because the di-nitrogen molecule in the atmosphere is held together by a triple bond that must be broken to form ammonia. Researchers reasoned that if the amount of car-

---

*"Gene cassette" is a metaphor genetic engineers use for having available several different genetic constructs from which to chose for transfer to a recipient organism.

bohydrate available to the bacteria was limiting, then nitrogen fixation and the amount of nitrogen available to the host plant would also be limited.

Dicarboxylic acids (malate, succinate, and fumarate) are actively transported from the plant to the root nodule and are the primary sources for energy for symbiotic rhizobia (Birkenhead, Manian, and O'Gara 1988). Several genes (dct genes) responsible for efficient dicarboxylic acid transport were isolated in R. meliloti and inserted into B. japonicum. Free-living dct-enhanced B. japonicum strains had higher nitrogenase activity compared to free-living wild-type strains (Birkenhead, Manian, and O'Gara 1988). Strains of R. meliloti combining nifA and enhanced dct genes were developed by Biotechnica and have yield advantages over genetically engineered stains with just nifA genes (section B).

Another strategy for rhizobia improvement involves increasing the competitive ability of efficient nitrogen-fixing rhizobia strains relative to indigenous low-efficiency strains. The competition problem is considered by many experts to be key to improving nitrogen fixation in legumes because selection for the most efficient nitrogen-fixers is relatively easy (Triplett and Sadowsky 1992). Several characteristics of rhizobia have been identified as possible determinants of competitive interactions for plant nodulation sites: bactericide production, motility, cell surface properties, and speed of nodulation (Triplett and Sadowsky 1992). Research on competitive interactions is still in a early stage, and it is uncertain that improving competitiveness of selected strains is amenable to genetic engineering. One example of a possible application involves transferring genes for antibiotic production to efficient nitrogen-fixers. A strain of R. leguminosarum bv. trifolii produces trifolitoxin, which inhibits the growth of several other rhizobia. However, the toxin-producing strain does not form active nitrogen-fixing nodules. The trifolitoxin gene was isolated and inserted into an R. leguminosarum bv. trifolii strain that is an efficient nitrogen-fixer (Triplett 1990). The transgenic rhizobia outcompeted toxin-sensitive wild-type strains. These experiments, however, were conducted in sterile soil, and it is unknown how competitive the transgenic strain would be as an inoculant under field conditions (Triplett and Sadowsky 1992).

Dowling and Broughton (1986) pointed out that because competition for nodulation sites involved the plant, the bacteria, and the environment, the system would not be easy to manipulate for agronomic advantage. They optimistically suggested two steps to surmount the competition problem. First, rhizobia could be selected or engineered to make them resistant to environmental variations such as temperature and pH extremes as well as tailored for the agricultural milieu. Second, host and bacteria genes could be manipulated in such a way that only particular plant-rhizobium combinations could successfully form nodulates. In this optimistic scenario rhizobia applied to seed or soil as an inoculant would be robust enough to survive in the environment until they had the opportunity to colonize the crop host. When a host was available, the inoculant bacteria would have the genetically conferred competitive edge over indigenous rhizobia.

B. The Commercial Development and Economics of Nitrogen-Fixing Bacteria

Several *Rhizobium* and *Bradyrhizobium* strains developed by Biotechnica International were tested in the field from 1989 to 1991. The results were equivocal. Yield increases were demonstrated in some tests but not others, and it was not clear whether the advantages were sufficient to convince farmers to pay a premium for bioengineered inoculum (Hankinson 1992). Biotechnica decided that the uncertain commercial prospects of the products did not warrant further developmental efforts and financial investment. The company decided to abandon the program. In February 1991 it sold the entire advanced rhizobia development program, including all patents to the technology and the rights to all the strains developed, to Research Seeds in St. Joseph, Missouri, at a price very favorable to the latter (Wacek 1993). Research Seeds is a wholesale producer of forage seeds, primarily alfalfa, clover, and grasses. Urbana Laboratories, a division of Research Seeds, is one of only two companies selecting and marketing rhizobia inoculants in the United States.

Urbana Laboratories has no plans to develop the *B. japonicum* strains commercially. The firm is cooperating with researchers at the University of Wisconsin interested in the *B. japonicum* strains and has conducted field tests on the genetically engineered *R. meliloti* strains, created by Biotechnica, to ascertain their commercial prospects as an alfalfa inoculant. Urbana Laboratories has no plans to engage in further genetic engineering of either strain.

After three years of experiments (1991–93), one strain of *R. meliloti*, which contains both *nifA* and *dct* genes, has been identified as the best-performing candidate for further development (Wacek 1993). Field trials have shown that alfalfa treated with genetically engineered rhizobia will only outperform commercial inoculants, and, for that matter, uninoculated alfalfa, in fields that do not have high indigenous populations of rhizobia. This underscores the competition problems as limiting the range of situations in which the enhanced rhizobia are advantageous. Yield gains of 7 to 10 percent over parental *R. meliloti* strains can be achieved when alfalfa is grown on sandy soils with low nitrogen levels and low indigenous *R. meliloti* populations. Typically, 90 percent nodule occupancy rates are achieved for the engineered strains, but there is no yield advantage over parental strains in tests on heavier soils, where alfalfa has been grown previously and indigenous populations of *R. meliloti* are relatively high. Nodule occupancy rates of the engineered strains drops to 30 percent on these soils (Research Seeds 1993; Wacek 1993). Because the heavier soils are more typically used as alfalfa pasture in the midwestern United States than sandy soils, one might speculate that the prospects for a viable product seem dim. However, company officials believe that by demonstrating yield advantages of around 10 percent on some soils (10 percent is the level needed for farmers to recognize easily the yield gain) they can charge a sufficient premium for the product to recoup development costs (Wacek 1993).

In 1994 the recombinant nitrogen-fixing bacteria were test marketed in eight states to determine whether farmers will find real value in the product. Research Seeds subsequently requested that the EPA grant commercialization of recombinant *R. meliloti* strains for alfalfa.

Overall, prospects are poor for commercial development of other genetically engineered microorganisms for nitrogen fixation. The biotechnology companies that at one time had research programs to improve rhizobia have all withdrawn from the field. We know of no company developing new genetically engineered nitrogen-fixation products. This lack of commercial interest is due to the small size of the inoculum market and the lack of success of getting products to work in the field. University programs are continuing to uncover the molecular biology and ecology of nitrogen fixation. This is one example where the power of molecular biology was oversold and promoted prematurely in the science and popular press.

C. Environmental Applications

Large proportions of all of the major nonleguminous crops in the United States receive nitrogen fertilizer applications. In 1992 all potato acreage, 97 percent of corn acreage, 85 percent of winter wheat acreage, 81 percent of spring wheat acreage, and 80 percent of cotton acreage received at least one treatment with a nitrogen fertilizer (USDA 1993a). Nitrate-nitrogen is water soluble, resulting in large amounts of nitrogen run-off into surface waters and leaching into groundwater following irrigation or rainfall. Nitrogen contamination of surface and groundwater is a serious environmental problem in the United States and is closely associated with agricultural activity (NRC 1989; figure 14). More than one-quarter of 1,600 counties that the U.S. Geological Survey surveyed in 1987 reported elevated levels of nitrate-nitrogen in at least 25 percent of wells tested (USDA 1987). Many of these counties have large numbers of wells that fail to meet the safe drinking water standards set by the EPA.

Any technology that could reduce the amount of nitrogen fertilizer applied to agricultural lands would have an immediate and significant beneficial environmental effect. This is especially true because it is estimated that world demand for nitrogen fertilizers will triple from 51.4 million tons in 1979 to as much as 180 million tons by 2000 (OTA 1981, 152). Winston Brill (1991, 93), founder of Agracetus in Madison, Wisconsin, has observed that "microorganisms have the potential to be more environmentally compatible than many chemicals used in agriculture. Inoculant practices may play an important role for sustainable agriculture." Improving or extending nitrogen fixation and reducing the demand for nitrogen fertilizer would have the added benefit of decreasing the burning of natural gas (and CO_2 emissions) needed to manufacture inorganic nitrogen (OTA 1981, 153).

Early claims that genetic engineering would lead quickly to the creation of nitrogen-fixing non-leguminous plants or more efficient nitrogen accumulation by legumes were overly optimistic. Improving rhizobia so that leguminous plants would be provided with more nitrogen would increase yields of those plants but in no direct way substantially reduce fertilizer treatments. Most legume crops do not receive any additional fertilizer. Only 15 percent of soybean acreage, the largest acreage legume crop in the United States, receives nitrogen fertilizer applications (USDA 1993a). Manure is often spread on alfalfa pastures as a way of disposing of the wastes, not as nitrogen fertilizer for alfalfa. Improved strains of rhizobia would not reduce this practice.

If inoculation with recombinant rhizobia results in the accumulation of additional nitrogen in the soil, compared to inoculation with nonrecombinant strains or no inoculant treatment, nitrogen

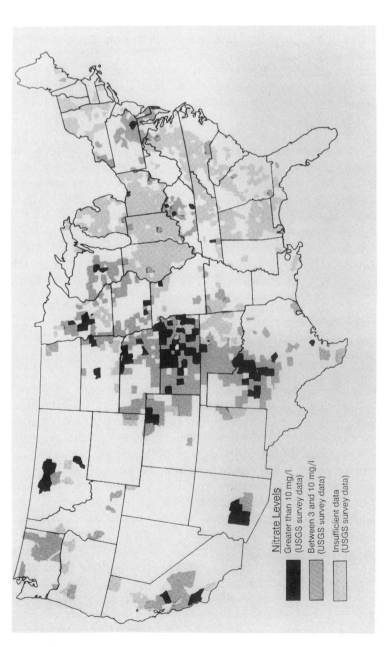

Nitrate Levels

Greater than 10 mg/l
(USGS survey data)

Between 3 and 10 mg/l
(USGS survey data)

Insufficient data
(USGS survey data)

Figure 14. Agricultural Counties with Nitrate Contamination in Groundwater. *Source:* NRC 1989, 100

fertilizer could be spared on corn that is rotated with soybeans. Essentially, all corn planted in the United States receives nitrogen fertilizer, and more than 50 percent of corn is rotated with soybean. Higher soil nitrogen levels at the time of corn planting would allow farmers to reduce exogenous nitrogen amendments.

Were it not so formidable a task to expand nitrogen fixation, the environmental concerns raised by Grobstein (1979, 64) would hold more weight:

> A massive increase of released ammonia into soils due to increased nitrogen fixation for improved agriculture might have unfortunate secondary consequences on the oceans and atmosphere. Ammonia is not only toxic in itself, but also tends to reduce atmospheric carbon dioxide levels, which in turn tends to reduce average world temperatures as well as ozone levels in the upper atmosphere. Reduction of average world temperatures by even one degree can counteract any favorable agricultural effect of improved capacity for nitrogen fixation.

D. Public Response and Oversight

Field tests conducted by Biotechnica from 1989 to 1991 received close scrutiny from EPA regulators. Before the rhizobia tests only two releases of genetically engineered microorganisms had occurred. Biotechnica researchers were required to monitor the air, soil, and water at field sites and track the movement of the genetically engineered rhizobia in great detail. Sites had to be monitored for several seasons following field releases. Volumes of field data were collected, and the cost of the monitoring program was estimated at 50 percent of the research budget for the entire program (Hankinson 1992).

With the accumulation of data, EPA regulators gained confidence that the behavior of the engineered rhizobia was the same as that of the indigenous strains, that there were no negative effects on the crop plants or any other plants, and that ecological disruptions of microbial communities were not observed at the test sites. Site monitoring and data requirements were relaxed progressively as the ecological risk questions were answered to the regulators' satisfaction.

Research Seeds was required to submit a premanufacture notice for all field tests, but the company did not consider these requirements burdensome (Wacek 1993). The request to test market an *R. meliloti* strain in 1994 caused the EPA to evaluate whether additional risks were associated with a large-scale release of the organism. Five major risk questions were addressed: (1) Would there be any negative effects on the treated alfalfa? (2) Would the genetically engineered strains outcompete the indigenous organisms and cause disruption to the microbial community? (3) Would the genetically engineered strains produce an abundance of nitrogen, causing pollution problems? (4) Would the genetically engineered R. meliloti colonize leguminous weeds in the habitat, increasing their fitness and creating a new weed problem? (5) Would antibiotic resistance genes, used as markers in the genetically engineered R. meliloti, spread to other bacteria and cause human health concerns (Clark 1994; EPA 1993)? Data from the small-scale field experiments indicated that there was no significant risk from questions 1 through 3. Alfalfa treated with the recombinant bacteria had never shown yield declines, the recombinant bacteria did not compete well with indigenous rhizobia, and the greatest nitrogen increases observed in test plots ranged up to the 15 percent range, not sufficient to create a pollution problem. For question 4, regulators identified sweet clover as the only weed in the area with which the recombinant strain was compatible. But sweet clover was not considered a weed of alfalfa fields. Experts on antibiotic resistance, consulted by regulators, concluded that the antibiotic resistance genes were stably incorporated on the "megaplasmid" of R. meliloti and unlikely to be transferred to another bacteria and that the antibiotics in question were not clinically important. Based on these results, regulators approved the test marketing of the recombinant R. meliloti.

Public response to the initial releases of the genetically engineered rhizobia was muted compared to the outcry over the release of the ice-minus bacteria in California (chapter 8). In 1990, the state of Iowa banned field tests of the engineered rhizobia for fear that they would disrupt the indigenous microbial community. Since that time there has been no negative publicity regarding field releases of the genetically engineered strains of rhizobia. Research Seeds, however, is concerned that attempts to market genetically engineered strains of R. meliloti may spur criticism and increase public concern. Within the company there has been discussion that commercialization would be halted if any negative publicity, whether well founded or not, occurred that might jeopardize seed sales, the company's main revenue source (Wacek 1993). Company officials indicated that one potential problem area may concern objections that the genetically engineered strains contain antibiotic resistance marker genes, which cannot be removed from the strain before commercialization. A 1995 report of the EPA's Science Advisory Board stated that the inclusion of antibiotic resistant genes do not present an obstacle to commercialization (Gottesman 1995).

E. Economic and Social Implications

The cost of inoculum is minor compared to the cost of seed. For example, alfalfa seed costs $2 to $3 per pound compared to 1 to 2 cents per pound for inoculum. Thus, 95 percent of alfalfa seed comes coated with inoculum even though in most cases the treatment does not provide yield advantages over untreated seed (Wacek 1993). A company is likely to charge a premium for an inoculum that has consistently been proven to improve yields. Still, it is unlikely that the cost of a new inoculum would prevent even the smallest farmer from using the technology. However, the only product nearing commercialization does not appear to provide yield advantages under all growing conditions.

Increasing the nitrogen-fixing efficiency of legumes with improved inoculum would benefit farmers by increasing yields per acre. It would be especially useful for those farmers who use or who would adopt crop rotations. Expenses from purchases of high-nitrogen inorganic fertilizer as well as indirect costs from nitrate pollution would more than offset the cost of the inoculum. Smaller farming operations, which possess greatest flexibility for shifting production to different crops and are already familiar with maintaining a diverse agro-ecosystem, would likely benefit the most.

Were it possible to create corn and other cereal crops that could fix nitrogen, there would be a large economic (and environmental) benefit in reducing the use of high-nitrogen inorganic fertilizers. However, nitrogen-fixing corn would probably lead to increased acreage devoted to continuous corn production. Now, most corn is rotated with soybeans. Continuous corn production leads to increased pest problems from insects and disease, followed by the application of more pesticides. These increased inputs and the danger of widespread crop failure due to reliance on too few crops could offset the benefits of cereal crops with nitrogen-fixing capacity. These crops would need to be integrated into an overall cropping system that would take account of the potential problems with area-wide monocultures.

F. Conclusions

The short but continuing history of using biotechnology to improve nitrogen fixation for crops exemplifies a number of the pitfalls of innovation. Early claims that nonleguminous plants could be made nitrogen-fixers through this technology have proven simplistic and unrealistic. Vigorous industry interest in transferring nitrogen-fixing genes to other bacteria has been dissipated, and all of the biotechnology companies that initiated research in the early 1980s have abandoned the field.

Much innovative technology for improving plant nitrogen fixation has been directed at enhancing the function of existing microorganisms that naturally inhabit the root nodules of plants. This product was developed more because it was technically achievable than because it was the best path of innovation for expanding nitrogen fixation. Transferring nitrogen-fixing capability to nonlegumes would meet an economic and environmental need, to reduce the use of nitrogen fertilizers. In this respect, efforts to improve nitrogen fixation in legumes were a direct outgrowth of the maturity of the science (induced innovation). Receptivity to nitrogen-fixation enhancement for legumes from the governmental and agricultural sectors has been strong. Criticism from environmental groups was based on concerns about releasing GEMs into the environment without environmental benefits. Although criticism from the environmental lobby did not impede the R&D effort, companies did have to address cautious and untested regulatory requirements on a case-by-case basis. As with any of the first-generation biotechnology products, the pathbreakers must be prepared to meet higher regulatory burdens than those who follow, at least until a set of common principles is developed.

It seems that it is more difficult to manipulate microbes genetically to affect the productivity of plants positively than it is to engineer new traits directly into the plants themselves. Molecular biologists have had great success in gene transfer and expression in the laboratory but have failed to appreciate the complexity of organismal interactions in the field. With recombinant rhizobia, early optimism derived from demonstrated increases in nitrogen fixation and plant yield in greenhouse experiments on sterile soils. However, the results were not borne out in field tests when the enhanced bacteria had to compete with indigenous rhizobia better adapted to the environment. The problem of differences between laboratory and field results has been encountered by others attempting to improve microbes for agricultural purposes (chapters 6 and 8). Molecular techniques continue to be applied to decipher the mechanisms rhizobia use to form symbiotic relationships with plants and to elucidate factors in the field that resolve competition for nodulation sites.

8 Frost-Inhibiting Bacteria: The Case of Ice Minus

The first federally sanctioned, genetically engineered microorganism to be field-tested was released in 1987 on a test plot in northern California after five years of regulatory review. The organism was *Pseudomonas syringae*, a bacterium that makes its residence on the surface of plants. The purpose of the experiment was to test the effectiveness of a mutant strain of the bacterium to delay the formation of ice crystals on the plant during sub-zero temperatures. The strain being tested was known as "ice minus" by virtue of its excised gene, which expresses a protein that provides a nucleating point for the formation of ice crystals.

During the mid-1980s the print media carried numerous stories describing the controversy over the release of ice minus in open fields. This genetically modified microorganism (GEM) is in the generic category of "frost-inhibiting bacteria" (FIB).* In this instance, the predominant natural strain of *Pseudomonas syringae*, found on the leafy matter of plants, is called ice plus or an ice-nucleating agent (INA+) for its ability to catalyze the formation of ice crystals from water at sub-zero temperatures.

As a result of extensive international publicity over ice minus and the pathbreaking field tests, it was widely believed that it would be the first GEM to be commercially available under the emerging federal policies addressing the environmental release of genetically altered microorganisms. The analysis in this chapter draws heavily on studies of ice minus by Krimsky and Plough (1988) and Krimsky (1991).

A. Technical Development

By the early 1970s scientists studying soil and plants harboring bacteria *Pseudomonas syringae* and *Pseudomonas fluorescens* learned

---

*Any microbe that protects a plant from frost damage is classified as a frost-inhibiting bacterium (FIB).

that they were catalysts for ice formation at temperatures several degrees below zero centigrade (Maki et al. 1974). When the ice-nucleating (INA⁺) particles are present, ice crystals begin to form at very near zero degrees centigrade. Without INA⁺ particles, water can remain in a supercooled state.

Plants are vulnerable to ice damage by the fact that the ice crystals that form within their tissues disrupt the plant's physiological processes. Scientists have sought ways to protect plants from subfreezing temperatures. The three necessary elements for plant injury from frost are sub-freezing temperatures, moisture, and ice-nucleating agents. In theory, supercooled water can remain in a liquid state at temperatures approaching $-40°C$. and not necessarily damage plants.

Farmers have been known to apply a variety of methods to protect crops from frost damage. Most of those methods are designed to keep the air temperature around the plant above freezing. These practices have included the burning of smudge pots and auto tires, watering the soil, using wind machines to keep warmer air circulating, and applying foamlike insulation around the plants. After it became known that microorganisms can catalyze ice formation, some farmers have applied bactericides to destroy ice-nucleating bacteria (Lindow 1983).

Pseudomonas syringae is a ubiquitous organism found on the leafy surfaces of plants. The term *epiphytic* is the technical term for nonparasitic organisms that take residence on plant surfaces. The role of this bacterium in the agricultural ecosystem has been studied since 1902, when the organism was first isolated (Hirano and Upper 1985).

By the early 1970s scientists had discovered that *P. syringae* was very efficient at seeding ice crystals in sub-freezing water. They also learned that ice formation was catalyzed by a single protein on the surface of the cell. Thus the single-gene, single-protein phenotype of the cell made it a favorable project for genetic engineering. The evolution of ice-nucleating cell-symbiotic bacteria would suggest some survival advantage to the organism. In fact, the frost-damaged cells release nutrients to the parasitic organism (Fincham and Ravetz 1991, 39).

Strains of *P. syringae* that lack the protein fail to exhibit ice-nucleating activity at the higher sub-zero temperatures. Nearly half of the strains of *P. syringae* that have been tested are ice-nucleating agents. Natural mutants of *P. syringae* with the deletion of the ice-nucleating protein are found in nature but at low frequency, indicating that the protein offers a competitive advantage. Otherwise, the ice-minus strain would persist and displace the ice-plus strain.

Most organic and inorganic substances that are ice-nucleating agents are active below temperatures of –10°C. *P. syringae,* however, catalyzes the formation of ice crystals at temperatures between –1.5°C. and –5°C. The special feature of the bacterium brought it to the attention of plant pathologists interested in the biotic and abiotic factors affecting plant development (Lindow 1982).

As plant pathologists became increasingly interested in the properties of *P. syringae,* they found three methods of obtaining a mutant ice-minus strain. First, deletion mutants can be found in cultures of the native species. Second, through chemical mutagenesis, ice-nucleation-active (INA+) *P. syringae* has been transformed into non-INA (INA-) strains. Third, by the use of recombinant DNA techniques and restriction enzymes, INA+ can be transformed into INA- strains. Only the third technique was subject to special regulations and became the cause célèbre of environmental activists and local communities.

The interest in commercializing ice minus was spurred by the development of genetic engineering techniques which, it was initially believed, would produce a stable mutant. The organism would be applied to the seedlings of a plant. If the INA- bacteria could be made to take over the niche of the INA+ strains, frost formation could be delayed, at least until the temperature drops below –10°C. This process requires displacing from nearly .1 to 10 percent of the bacteria on leaf surfaces, because that represents the percentage of ice-nucleating strains (Lindow 1983).

Although the number of INA species is relatively small, the prevalence of the bacteria in the environment is quite high, especially on certain food crops. *P. syringae* is widely distributed in nature and is believed to be one of the largest sources of bacterial ice nuclei that are active at higher temperatures, for example, above –5°C. By reducing the population density of INA bacteria, scientists believed they might have an effective and environmentally safe method of protecting crops from frost damage.

Pathbreaking research on the relationship between INA bacteria and frost formation was carried out by Steven Lindow and Nicholas Panopoulos at the University of California at Berkeley. Their experiments revealed that a reduction in the number of INA+ bacteria correlated with declining frost injury to field-grown plants. The fact sheet issued by the University of California on the ice-minus strain stated that the investigators "were able to remove the single gene (out of some 3,000) that allows ice to form on plant leaves and transform it into a non-ice-forming bacterium such as the one found in nature. These modified bacteria are *new* only in the technique used to make the change. No new traits have been added."

B. The Economics of Ice Minus

It is estimated that about 11 percent of the land mass of the continental United States is allocated to the cultivation of frost-sensitive crops. Projected losses from frost injury have been reputed to be between $1 to 1.6 billion annually (Lindow 1985).

This is a crude and unreliable measure of the economic potential of ice minus were it to be used efficiently across the frost belt. The actual economics of ice minus must be viewed in terms of its micro and macro dimensions. Any individual farmer facing crop frost damage may apply several techniques to mitigate its effects. In this regard, facing both economic and environmental risks, the farmer asks what benefits are gained by using ice minus and how cost-effective the treatment will be. Some of the traditional techniques have adverse environmental effects. Farmers who burn automobile tires or smudge pots create toxic air pollutants; those who spray biocides add potentially dangerous additives to the food supply and introduce occupational risks. Advanced Genetic Sciences promoted ice minus as a safe alternative to polluting technologies. At an estimated cost of $5 per acre it was also considered cost-effective.

On the macro-economic side, investors are interested in the U.S. and world market for ice minus. While ice minus gained a significant share of the media's attention, that visibility created a false market optimism. Risk, therefore, has a double edge. It can excite public concern, and it can also distort the market potential of a product. The level of concern makes the product appear more important in the economy than it actually is. By the 1990s the optimism for the commercial success of ice minus had begun to wane. Glass and Lindemann (DRI 1992, 70), two insiders in the biotechnology business, reported that ice-minus products "will not live up to their earlier *star* billing and may never achieve a significant market share." According to their study, only a single company is pursuing the ice-minus market estimated to be valued at $5 million in the United States. Love and Lesser (1989) evaluated the potential economic benefits of ice minus on reducing frost damage to the New York state fruit industry and found that it would not be economically competitive with existing technologies.

C. Regulatory Review

Ice minus was not the most likely organism to achieve the status of the first field-tested GEM. Before its commercial development, a promising genetically modified organism looked as though it might be the first petitioned for environmental release. In 1980 the U.S. Supreme Court ruled that a strain of *Pseudomonas* capable of degrading crude oil was patentable. Applying techniques involving the transfer of circular elements of DNA called plasmids, a General Electric scientist created a strain of *Pseudomonas* with multiple plasmids, each of which was suited for degrading one of the key constituents of crude oil. The patent was for the process of application and the organism per se. The process involved inoculating the strain of *Pseudomonas* into straw and dispersing it over an oil spill.

Despite the patent victory and the media attention that surrounded the public debate over the first patent of a unique life form exclusive of process, the oil-eating strain of *Pseudomonas* was not commercialized, and therefore no effort was made to test it in the environment. As a result, the first application to a U.S. federal agency for the release of a genetically altered microbe awaited two strains of ice minus originating from UC-Berkeley and a new biotechnology company called Advanced Genetic Sciences (AGS).

Advanced Genetic Sciences, formerly located in Oakland California, was founded in 1979 to commercialize technologies that promoted crop growth and protected crops against disease and frost damage. The company had the exclusive patent right on the use of bacteria that induce snow and ice formation, as well as on naturally occurring and chemically mutated frost-protecting bacteria.

AGS chose to develop a microbial frost inhibitor by removing the ice-nucleating gene from INA *P. syringae.* Initially, AGS accomplished this by exposing the ice-plus strain to chemical mutagens. The ice-minus chemical mutant produced in the laboratory was then field-tested. Special permits were not required for those field tests because genetic engineering techniques were not used in the manufacture of the microbe. AGS reported that the ice-minus bacterium produced by mutagens slowed the effect of frost damage, but the company believed it could enhance the performance of its product.

Using recombinant DNA techniques, AGS deleted the ice-nucleation gene from *P. syringae* (Hirano and Upper 1985). In its submission to a National Institutes of Health (NIH) committee, which at the time was reviewing university as well as industry self-initiated proposals, the company stated that it had moved about a thousand

base pairs of DNA sequences and that the changes were nonrevert-
ible. AGS maintained that the rDNA-derived strain was superior to
its chemically derived counterpart in inhibiting frost damage but
alike in all respects regarding risk. The proposal stated that the
rDNA deletion mutants of *P. syringae* were more stable, better defined genetically, and probably more fit than the ice-minus strain
resulting from chemical mutagenesis.

Around the same period, Lindow and Panopoulos deleted the ice-
nucleating protein from *P. syringae* and *E. herbicola* and discovered
promising frost-inhibiting results in laboratory tests. Through the
University of California, the scientists petitioned the NIH's Recombinant DNA Advisory Committee for approval to field test the organisms.

Initially, NIH proscribed all releases of rDNA-produced organisms
into the environment. On 1982, however, the blanket prohibition
against deliberate releases was removed (DHHS 1982). Between 1982
and 1987 the RAC and the EPA reviewed proposals from UC-Berkeley and AGS for field testing strains of rDNA-constructed ice
minus. Federal regulatory decisions were met by legal challenges and
community opposition in Monterey County and Tulelake, California. Finally, following numerous delays, on April 24, 1987, after a
California superior court denied a petition for an injunction, personnel of AGS, in the presence of EPA inspectors, completed the first
authorized release of a genetically engineered microorganism into
the environment in Brentwood, California. Five days later, on April
29, the UC-Berkeley scientists performed a field-test release of their
strains of ice minus at the Tulelake Agricultural Field Station in
northern California (Krimsky and Plough 1988, 119).

D. Environmental and Social Impact

With the impending release of the first rDNA-GEM, there were speculations about what might go wrong. Could ice minus be toxic to
plants or humans? Would the INA deletion mutants displace the
original INA populations that have played a key role in ice crystal-
lization for plants and other media? In particular, there was concern
that weather patterns might be affected if large quantities of ice
minus wafted up to the atmosphere.

A letter published in *Science* from Eugene Odum, a University
of Georgia ecologist, cited a worst-case scenario for the release of
ice minus. The letter placed the stature of a distinguished environmental scientist behind the precipitation hypothesis. Odum (1985)
wrote, "It seems that the lipoprotein coats of this and other species

of bacteria found on plants and in detritus when shed and wafted up in the clouds form ideal nuclei for ice formation that is absolutely necessary for rain to fall. . . . If *Pseudomonas syringae* does indeed have a beneficial role in enhancing rainfall, then the ecologist's concern about possible secondary or indirect effects of releases of genetically altered organisms is vindicated."

In an affidavit in support of a lawsuit petitioning broader study of ice minus, Odum stipulated two conditions that should be met before the environmental release. First, the organism should be studied over at least one annual cycle involving experimental releases in greenhouses that simulate the external environment as closely as possible. Second, the probability of adverse effects should be examined through computer modeling in which "all conceivable situations are simulated."

Scientists at AGS responded to the letter and criticized Odum for implying that there is any proof that bacterial nuclei initiate precipitation. They argued that it was an untested theory and should not be treated as doctrine. The AGS scientists maintained that there are no published data "on the concentration or activity of bacterial or bacterially derived ice nuclei in clouds" (Lindemann, Warren, and Suslow 1986, 536).

From the AGS perspective, whether or not INA bacteria are connected with precipitation was not the central issue for risk assessment. Rather, it was whether "the release of INA⁻ bacteria could have a significant impact on the number of INA bacteria available for such natural cloud seeding." The company maintained that the experimental releases of INA⁻ would have no competitive advantage over INA⁺ bacteria, therefore the cloud seeding issue was moot.

The Environmental Protection Agency approached the risk assessment for ice minus in a multistaged process based on a framework developed by Martin Alexander (1985). The process involved an examination of (1) the formation of the GEM, including the characteristics of the parent organism, the techniques used, and the sequences added or deleted; (2) the release of the organism into the environment, including the site characteristics and flora and fauna that could be compromised; (3) the potential for ice minus to establish itself in the ecosystem, including survival, multiplication, dissemination, and transfer; and (4) the effect of ice minus on the environment, including the impact on humans and other species.

Within this framework, the EPA posed a series of guiding questions for the applicants. Is ice minus or its parental strain pathogenic to humans, plants, or animals? Will a release of ice minus in a field alter precipitation patterns? Will a release of ice minus affect the range and survival of frost-sensitive or frost-tolerant insects?

After reviewing extensive data from petitioners, the EPA was satisfied that the parental strain of ice minus was not associated with human or animal pathogenicity and that *P. syringae* was not pathogenic to any crops in northern California. However, on the presumption that there is no way to prevent the organism from escaping beyond the test zone, the EPA addressed the issue of whether the ice-minus strain would overrun the existing microbial flora. The agency was persuaded by studies that indicated that wayward ice-minus strains would not out compete indigenous microorganisms. Referring to the UC-Berkeley proposal, the EPA Hazard Evaluation Division wrote, "The applicants' data show that INA⁻ deletion mutants have no competitive advantage over their parental or other INA⁺ strains when applied to potato leaves under a variety of dosage regimens except when INA⁻ deletion mutants are applied in higher concentrations than INA⁺ strains" (Betz 1985).

The EPA required a series of greenhouse studies by the UC-Berkeley scientists. These studies focused on the colonization potential of the ice minus on new vegetation exposed to low-dose inoculation. Colonization studies were conducted with both ice minus and their parental strains on sixty-seven plant species. One deletion mutant was compared to its parental strain for 180 different phenotypic characteristics, another for thirty-two characteristics. The applicant claimed that the strains were identical in all respects except for their ability to nucleate ice (the EPA actually found differences in eleven of the characteristics). The UC-Berkeley scientists tested ice minus and its parental strain for pathogenicity in seventy-five annual and perennial plant species, including agriculturally important crops, native plants in northern California, and all major crops in the Tulelake region.

With the prospect that its decision on ice minus would be challenged in court, the EPA took special precautions in its review of the organism for the first field test. The agency had input from the USDA, the National Institutes of Health, the Food and Drug Administration, and a scientific advisory panel consisting of two microbiologists, a meteorologist, a community ecologist, a microbial ecologist, and a plant pathologist. The various advisory groups agreed with the agency's conclusion that the proposed application of INA deletion mutants on 0.2 acres of land presented, in the agency's terms, "no foreseeable significant risk to human health or the environment."

E. Media Response to Ice Minus

The first phase of the regulatory history of ice minus began in 1982 with the proposals of the UC-Berkeley scientists submitted to the Recombinant DNA Advisory Committee of NIH to field test genetically modified organisms. It culminated in two outdoor tests in 1987 for controlled, supervised releases.

Intermittently during this period, the print media featured extensive coverage of various phases in public response to ice minus. The citizens of Monterey, California, opposed the first test site planned by Advanced Genetic Sciences. The Washington-based Foundation on Economic Trends in collaboration with Californians for Responsible Toxics Management took legal action against the University of California to stop its planned release of the organism in the Tulelake region. Green party members in Europe sent telegrams to local officials in California to warn them of the dangers of releasing a genetically modified organism into the environment. And there was a flurry of media coverage when the EPA fined AGS for an illegal release of ice minus into trees located on the roof of AGS's Oakland facility.

To evaluate the media response to ice minus, we surveyed the number of articles specifically focused on agricultural biotechnology in several leading newspapers and magazines from 1980 through 1991. The newspapers included were the *New York Times*, the *Wall Street Journal*, and the *Washington Post*; the magazines were *Business Week*, *Newsweek*, and *Time Magazine*. In order to avoid product and financial announcements, we limited our analysis to articles longer than one-half of a column. Two search methods were used. First, a search was executed with the Dialogue database, using the key words *agriculture, biotechnology, seeds, pesticides, herbicides, genetic engineering*, and *gene splicing*. Second, a manual search was carried out through the published indexes of the newspapers. News magazine articles were selected based on a search of the Infotrack database.

In total, 130 articles were identified: 45 from the *New York Times*, 39 from the *Wall Street Journal*, 30 from the *Washington Post*, 8 from *Business Week*, 6 from *Newsweek*, and 2 from *Time Magazine*. Thirty-two percent of the articles focussed exclusively or almost exclusively on frost-inhibiting bacteria (figure 15). Insect resistant plants, disease resistant plants, herbicide resistant plants, and nitrogen-fixing microbes were discussed in 42 percent, 28 percent, 25 percent, and 12 percent of the articles, respectively. Between 1983 and 1987 a sizable percentage of the media coverage in these major publications was devoted to a product with an estimated $5 million of market value. In the years 1983, 1984, 1986, and 1987, more than 40 percent of the articles in the survey were centered around ice minus (figure 15).

In general, three types of risk were reported: twenty-five percent of the articles referred to the potential for novel organisms to spread to nontarget organisms and cause ecological disruption; 12 percent referred to the potential for Frostban (AGS's trade name for ice minus) to affect weather patterns; and 7 percent of the articles referred to the risk that engineered herbicide resistant plants would result in an increased use of and reliance on chemical herbicides.

Krimsky and Plough (1989) discuss another media analysis of the ice-minus episode. Three reference periods were chosen for in-depth review of print journalism reports on the social, regulatory, and environmental aspects of the ice-minus field tests. The first period, January through February 1986, centers around the controversy in Monterey County, California, where community and official county opposition eventually caused AGS to find another test site for releasing the organism. A second high concentration of media cov-

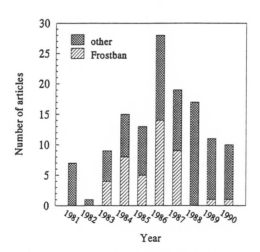

Figure 15. The Number of Articles on Agricultural Biotechnology Published in the *New York Times,* the *Wall Street Journal,* the *Washington Post, Business Week, Newsweek,* and *Time Magazine,* 1981–90.
Note: Articles focusing on Frostban are distinguished from articles on other products of agricultural biotechnology. $N = 130$

erage occurred in May 1986, when field tests were scheduled to take place in the Tulelake region of California. Finally, for the third study period the authors chose the time just preceding and up to the first field test (April 1987) in Brentwood, California.

All the articles were selected from local and national sources for the peak coverage periods and had either been published in a major national newspaper or appeared in a local or regional paper that covered the communities scheduled to host the release of the test organism. The study examined headlines and text devoted to risk, symbols, analogies, benefits, and emotive language. Sixty-seven articles were examined.

With very few exceptions, the primary bearers of risk information in both the local and national media formed dichotomous groups. Those who were not experts carried the warnings about ice minus while scientists recited their views on the safety of the organism. The controversy focussed almost exclusively on ecological risks; comparatively little attention was given to benefits. The press cited estimates of frost damage to crops that varied from hundreds of millions to $20 billion worldwide. Recurrent themes in the discourse fell into two general categories. First, there were references to such broad and unspecific images as unforeseen hazards, catastrophic effects, environmental roulette, interference with natural ecosystems, and blind faith in technology. Second, there were specific risk scenarios, such as the endangerment of wild strawberries, the alteration of rainfall patterns, the overproduction of potatoes, the stigmatization of a region's potatoes or strawberries, and toxicity to humans and animals. Eventually, the EPA's assessment strategy prevailed. The courts rejected any petitions for enjoining the release. Although the first release in Brentwood was met with some early morning sabotage by environmental groups, overturned strawberry plants were mended and sprayed by an employee of AGS. The episode yielded the striking image of an AGS employee dressed like a moon-walker and spraying the test plot as a small child ate freshly picked strawberries from an adjacent field.

F. Conclusions

Between 1987 and 1989, Advanced Genetic Sciences completed approximately one hundred separate field trials of the genetically engineered bacteria. Company officials reported that the results of those tests were encouraging and that the bacteria provided frost protection for plants consistent with laboratory studies. However, during the field tests it was learned that some naturally occurring strains of *P. syringae* lacking ice-nucleating proteins were just as effective in inhibiting frost formation as the genetically engineered constructs.

AGS decided to pursue field testing of the naturally occurring strains and delay further development of the genetically engineered variety. Company officials feared that continued regulatory and community-level difficulties regarding genetically engineered microbes, especially as they came closer to large-scale testing, would make the relative cost of the GEMs much greater than the naturally occurring strains.

In 1989 DNA Plant Technology Corporation (DNAP) merged with AGS. Research on ice minus was halted in 1990. DNAP continued to pursue and was granted EPA registration of the naturally occurring *P. syringae* strains under the name Frostban. In 1992 DNAP entered into an agreement with Ecogen, a biotechnology firm that markets other plant protection microbial products. The expectation was to commercialize Frostban in 1993 (Wrubel 1993).

Ice minus is one of the prime examples of a technology push approach to innovation in the array of new biotechnology products. The organism was conceived, constructed, and largely promoted by academic scientists who consulted with a start-up company that invested in product development, risk assessment, regulatory approval, and field trials. The farm sector stood by somewhat skeptically as the early field trials captured a disproportionate amount of the print media space devoted to biotechnology. Some farmers opposed an innovative frost reduction strategy that could expand the land dedicated to certain crops that were traditionally unsuited to the area.

Ice minus was never destined to be a major advance in agriculture, but it was fated to reach international attention as a milestone in the human use of biotechnology. It is highly likely that in a few years ice minus will recede into the footnotes of the history of biotechnology, perhaps cited as a pathbreaker in the regulatory process or as a symbol of a society struggling to understand and come to grips with innovations in the genetic refashioning of microorganisms.

9 Animal Growth Hormones: The Case of Bovine Somatotropin

Without question, the most publicized, contentious, and complex debate pertaining to the introduction of a bioengineered product has been the commercial development of a veterinary growth promoter that goes by the scientific name "bovine somatotropin" (BST) or the more popular designation "bovine growth hormone" (BGH). BST has been under review by the U.S. Food and Drug Administration (FDA) since the early 1980s. The FDA claims that BST has been studied more than any other veterinary hormone. According to Hecht (1991), BST research has involved more than three hundred studies on more than twenty-two thousand dairy cows. The National Library of Medicine compiled 1,097 citations on BST for the five-year period from January 1985 through October 1990 (Gluckstein, Glock, and Hill 1990). And in its review of health effects of BST, the FDA summarized more than 120 studies on human safety of synthetic BST derived from recombinant DNA methods (rBST) (Gibbons 1990).

BST comes after years of veterinary hormone developments, mostly compounds like estrogens, zeranol, androgens, beta agonists, and hormone releasing factor used to produce leaner animal products. Growth regulators already approved for beef cattle in the United States are endogenous compounds already present in humans and animals (estrogen, testosterone, and progesterone), compounds developed through biotechnology to emulate the functions of endogenous substances. Thus, BST is only the latest veterinary product in a long series of innovations designed to increase dairy productivity: mechanical milking, bulk tanks, embryo transfer, and artificial insemination. In this particular case, the microbially derived bovine hormone is used to induce greater milk production. Some argue that synthetic bovine growth hormone will be a boon to milk production, raising it 15 to 25 percent nationwide. Others claim that it will cause the ruin of tens of thousands of dairy farms, create a higher incidence of bovine disease, and expose consumers to new health risks from contaminants in the milk.

A. Historical Development

Somatotropin is a polypeptide (protein) hormone synthesized by the anterior pituitary gland in mammals. The BST protein molecule contains either 191 or 192 amino acids. The major biochemical and physiological function of BST is that it repartitions nutrients so as to increase milk production or growth of tissue. Somatotropin acts to preserve body protein, increase the oxidation of fatty acids, inhibit glucose transport in cells, enhance cell division, and promote bone growth (Hallberg 1992, 100). In dairy cows, absorbed nutrients are allocated among maintenance of body tissue, milk production, growth of body tissue, and the growth of a fetus. BST directs nutrients toward milk production and away from body tissue storage (MacFarlane 1992, 97).

BST is one of more than twenty proteins found in milk and in smaller quantities than are proteins like casein and lactalbumin. The forms of somatotropin derived from distinct animal groups differ in structure and biological properties. Human somatotropin and bovine somatotropin have only about a 65 percent similarity in amino acid structure. The role of somatotropin in the physiology of animals has been studied for more than seventy years. Until recently, the commercial applications of animal somatotropin were unrealized.

The fact that a substance produced by the pituitary glands of rats when isolated and injected into animals is responsible for the promotion of growth as well as oestrus and ovulation was reported in the scientific literature in 1921 (Evans and Lang 1921). Scientists in France reported in 1928 that milk yield increased when lactating laboratory animals and goats were treated with extracts of the pituitary hormone (Stricker and Grueter 1928). By 1933 scientists had extracted a hormone from bovine pituitaries and treated rats with it. They observed changes in muscle and fat composition (Lee and Schaffer 1933). The extract from the pituitary gland was named somatotropin (ST). The name comes from the Greek *soma* (body tissue) and *tropin* (growth).

The first reported large mammalian experiment was by a group of Russian scientists, who in 1937 treated more than five hundred lactating cows with subcutaneous injections of ST obtained from slaughtered oxen. They reported substantial increases in milk yield

(Azimov and Krouze 1937). Scientists in Britain during World War II, seeking ways to increase milk production, administered pituitary extracts from slaughtered animals to cows. The limited quantity of ST from slaughtered animals was an obstacle to improving milk production, however (Bauman and Vernon 1993, 448).

Knowledge that exogenous BST administered to lactating cows increases milk production was not translated into a commercially useful product until the early 1980s, when an inexpensive method was discovered to produce large quantities of the hormone. Microbial production of BST through recombinant DNA techniques resulted in a race among four major corporations, Monsanto, American Cyanamid, UpJohn, and Eli Lilly, to market a product. The first use of recombinant bovine somatotropin on lactating cows was reported in the literature in 1982 (Bauman et al. 1982). Since then, BST has been administered to cows on an experimental basis in the United States and sold commercially in a dozen other countries. In 1993 the FDA gave final approval for commercial use of one form of BST.

B. The Current State of Development

Before BST could be manufactured on a large scale, some technical difficulties had to be overcome. The eukaryote BST gene is not ordinarily suitable for bacterial expression because of its discontinuous structure. Prokaryotes lack the enzymes for splicing the messenger RNA. Additional promoter sequences from *E. coli* had to be spliced to the BST gene so that the bacterial ribosomes (the protein manufacturing machinery) will recognize the mammalian code. As a result, the hormone had to be purified carefully to remove contamination from bacteria and the culture medium. With the exception of an extra sequence, the resulting purified hormone is virtually identical to that the pituitary gland secretes (MacFarlane 1992, 97). Monsanto added the amino acid methionine, American Cyanamid added a tripeptide, and Elanco added a nine-peptide chain to make their products suitable for bacterial expression. Thus, each commercial product of BST has one or more different amino acids than the mammalian BST sequence. Epstein (1990, 78) cites these structural difference as relevant to the assessment of the human health risks of BST (section D).

Intravenous administration of exogenous somatotropin to cows has long been known to increase milk production. It is generally recognized that the mammary glands of BST-supplemented cows absorbs more nutrients from their bloodstreams and synthesizes more milk. The amount of increased production will vary with the type of herd, its management, and the lactation period. Most research indicates that the increase in milk production per cow annually can be as high as 30 percent from about 6 percent more feed (Hutton 1957; Kroger 1992, 226; McBride, Burton, and Burton 1988; Wyke 1988, 13). Yields of as high as 1.5 grams of BST per liter of bacterial culture could also be obtained.

BST is administered either by repeated subcutaneous injections during a cow's lactation period or by an implant that releases the hormone slowly. During the stormy BST debate, little attention was given to the existing application of growth regulators already approved for use in beef cattle in the United States. Existing growth regulators fall into two categories: endogenous compounds, such as estrogen, testosterone, and progesterone, that are already present in humans and new compounds, such as zeranol and trenbolone acetate, developed through biotechnology to simulate the endogenous substances. According to Byers and Thompson (1991, 270), growth regulators are used in over 95 percent of all cattle on feed in the United States and in 50 to 75 percent of these same cattle during growth as calves and as stockers prior to feeding.

Estrogenic animal drugs are sometimes grouped in the same category despite marked differences in structure and physiological action. The European Community has been extremely cautious about all such veterinary supplements. In December 1985 the Council of Ministers of the European Economic Community (EEC) issued a directive (85/649/EEC) banning the use of anabolic hormones in livestock production as of January 1, 1988, a ban some view as inherently unenforceable (Byers and Thompson 1991, 272). The international publicity directed at the estrogen scandal in Italy in 1980, when DES residues were discovered in samples of baby food, contributed to a general anxiety about exogenous animal hormones. Despite the negative publicity about estrogenic drug use in animals, the World Health Organization (WHO) and the Food and Agricultural Organization (FAO) have declared some veterinary hormones such as estradiol and progesterone safe when used properly (Byers and Thompson 1991, 275).

C. Economics

The economics of BST may be divided among macro markets, the economic decisions of individual farmers, and social economics. The estimates of economic markets are obviously central to investor confidence in veterinary drug biotechnology. Because it is the first major product in this sector, it had great symbolic importance to the biotechnology investment community, which followed the issue with unusual interest. *The Economist* (1988) wrote that BST was expected to generate annual sales of close to $500 million in the United States. In *Lancet*, Sibbison (1990) gave the same figure for expected annual sales worldwide. Molnar, Cumming, and Nowak (1990, 3086) quoted a $500 million figure without distinguishing U.S. or world markets. Schneider (1990) of the *New York Times* placed the annual sales at $1 billion, a figure also cited in a respected market study (DRI 1992) for 2000. The DRI study's conservative estimate is $250 million worldwide. Monsanto, Eli Lilly, American Cyanamid, and UpJohn purportedly each spent between $100 and $500 million to develop BST. Although the *New York Times*'s Schneider (1994b) places Monsanto's investment at more than $300 million, accurate figures have not been published (Hileman 1993; Molner, Cumming, and Nowak 1990, 3086). *The Economist* (Wyke 1988, 13) reported that BST is expected to increase milk production per dairy cow by an average 522 pounds annually. The journal also noted that highly productive cattle already produce twenty thousand pounds of milk a year, giving rBST a 2.6 percent advantage. Under these assumptions the number of dairy cattle needed to meet U.S. consumption would decline from 10.8 million to 7.5 million by the end of the 1990s.

The economics of BST for individual farmers have been studied extensively to determine the market potential of the product. To understand the economics of BST is to understand all the factors of its contribution to milk production: the cost of the drug, the cost of additional feed for BST-administered cows, the cost of increased management and surveillance (labor), the cost of increased care if administration of the drug creates additional veterinary care or the need for drugs, and additional hauling costs associated with additional milk produced.

The daily treatment costs of BST per cow are between 25 and 75 cents. Molnar, Cumming, and Nowak (1990, 3086) report that for dairy farms of nearly all sizes the use of BST increased potential profits at low feed costs in most situations, the exception being herds with low milk production, considered to be 13,200 pounds (6,000 kg) per year per cow. Although the economic benefits to farmers of BST depends on the management of the herd and the overall economic conditions affecting milk and feed costs, Molnar, Cumming, and

Nowak (1990, 3086) believe that "farms that adopt BST will make more money than similar farms that do not."

Based on the experience of farmer adoption practices for new technologies, Butler (1991, 154) argues that farmers will require a two-to-one return on BST before adopting it. Thus, if BST costs farmers 35 cents per day per cow, they would have to make 70 cents per day per cow as a precondition for adopting its use. In a special report on biotechnology in *The Economist* Wyke stated, "To dairymen, the net benefit after subtracting the costs of the drug and additional feed is predicted to be $100–160 for every lactation cycle of the cow" (1988, 13). The economic predictions for BST are based on optimum conditions. Kronfeld (1993, 94) cites as a weakness in the economic forecasts their underestimation of the effects of biological variation and adverse veterinary health outcomes. For example, he points to higher costs resulting from increases in routine veterinary maintenance, variation in drug costs, increases in cows culled, and more expensive drugs for treatment of mastitis.

There is also the social economy. How will BST affect the federal price supports for milk? Because milk consumption is not very elastic, increased production of milk through the use of BST could be followed by an increase in federal price supports designed to keep milk prices stable. Molnar, Cumming, and Nowak (1990, 3090) projected increases in federal price supports to dairy farmers averaging $20 million annually if current support prices are maintained. The media reported 8.4 billion pounds of surplus milk from 1989 to 1990 and 10.4 billion pounds in 1990–91 (Locke 1991). Most of the surplus is bought up by the government and turned into butter for special programs. Fallert et al. (1987, 2) projected that BST will increase government milk purchases by 8 billion pounds within three years after its introduction into the market. In the United States it is evident that milk production is more than sufficient to meet the demand.

Individual and social economies are ultimately linked. Greaser (1992) has observed that calculating the profit from BST of a single farmer is based on the micro inputs of the farm. But if all farmers adopted it and the total supply of milk increased, the macro factor must also be put into the profit equation. It has been projected, in a study of the economic effects of BST use in the United States, that milk production will increase by about 1 percent through FY 1999, and milk prices are expected to drop by 2 percent, resulting in a decline in aggregate farm income by about 1 percent over the same period (Executive Branch 1994).

Monsanto's aggressive marketing of BST may have been the key to a favorable early adoption rate. After the first six months of sales the company reported that more than ten thousand U.S. dairy farmers administered Posilac to more than eight hundred thousand cows.

D. Health and Safety Assessment

BST has been under review by the FDA since about 1980. Officials of the agency maintain that this veterinary drug has been studied more than any other hormone. The agency reviewed 120 studies (Executive Branch 1994, 4). International marketing of BST began before U.S. approval. Monsanto distributed BST in Mexico and Brazil, and Eli Lilly began marketing the hormone in Russia and Czechoslovakia. International development rights organizations cited these cases as examples of industrial countries using the third world as guinea pigs for new products.

FDA's health and safety assessment of BST, which covered both humans and animals, consisted of four parts: (1) safety of milk and meat used for human consumption; (2) efficacy and safety of the product on cows; (3) environmental assessment; and (4) quality of the product.

A variety of government commissions and experts reviewed the risks of administering recombinant-derived BST. These included the Veterinary Medicine Advisory Committee to the Center for Veterinary Medicine (1993); the National Institutes of Health, Technology Assessment Conference on BST, December 5–7 1990 (NIH 1991); the report of the thirty-eighth Joint Expert Committee on Food Additives-Veterinary Drug Residues, "BST 1992"; the Commission of the European Communities' "Final Scientific Report of the Committee for Veterinary Medicinal Products on the Application for Marketing Somatech and Optiflex 640" (January 1993); the National Institute of Child Health and Human Development; National Institute of Diabetes and Digestive and Kidney Diseases; and the Office of Medical Applications of Research at the National Institutes of Health.

In 1985 the FDA reviewed the toxicological data on BST and concluded that the milk and meat from BST-treated cows was as safe and nutritious as that from cows not treated with BST. The FDA initiated a long-term health impact study of BST on dairy cattle from 1985 to 1991. The results of the study played a key role in the FDA's favorable decision toward BST. The key health questions addressed in the risk assessment of BST by federal agencies were: Are there recombinant BST residues in the milk? If there are, can those residues adversely affect consumers? Are there ancillary substances produced when BST is used that might be harmful to people? Will BST affect the health of cows? If it does affect the health of cows, will the treatment of cows for bovine disease add additional risk to the milk supply?

Unusually strong, although not universal, consensus among diverse members of the medical, veterinary, and nutritional community indicates that rBST use on cows does not pose a health risk to humans. There is somewhat less consensus on the direct effects of rBST on animal health and its indirect effects on human health. It is difficult to find coherence and closure from the complex data on rBST safety. Each study opens more questions and new uncertainties. Experts in the field who interpret the complex array of studies place emphasis on different strengths and weaknesses of the research. Critics select the most vulnerable areas of uncertainty and elevate them to places of importance in the risk assessment.

One of the definitive published studies on the safety of BST appeared in the journal *Science* in 1990 (Juskevich and Guyer). In what has been termed a rare event, the journal published some of the data, some of which was proprietary information, of the critical tests. The journal concluded that BST is biologically inactive in children, that BST is broken down in the digestive track when consumed orally, that natural BST in cows and recombinant BST are biologically indistinguishable, and that the use of rBST in dairy cattle presents no increased health risk to humans. These results have been echoed in many other sources (Executive Branch 1994; Fallert 1987; NIH-TAP 1991; OTA 1991).

1. Pituitary and Recombinant BST

There is a significant structural difference in amino acid composition between human pituitary hormone (human somatotropin) and bovine somatotropin. The latter has been shown to be inactive in humans. The concentration of pituitary BST in cow's milk is about 1 part per billion. Because hormones are digested in the gastrointestinal tract and not absorbed into the bloodstream, they are not considered to have biological activity when ingested.

In earlier studies BST was administered by injection to growth-hormone-deficient children and was proven ineffective in enhancing growth (NIH-TAP 1991). Also, when rBST was administered orally in very high doses to species that ordinarily respond to injected rBST, the substance was neither absorbed nor produced a biological effect.

2. Recombinant BST in the Milk

One of the major concerns expressed by BST's critics is that residues of the hormone will end up in the milk. Although this does not seem like it would be an intractable problem to resolve, the scientific literature abounds in ambiguity. When cows are given large doses of rBST, higher levels of BST are detected in the cow's milk. These higher levels could be the result of the cow producing more of its own BST or the result of synthetic BST entering the cow's milk. When the doses of rBST are low, higher BST levels in the milk are not detected.

These results may or may not mean that rBST enters the milk. The methods of detection may not be sensitive enough or there may in fact be no residue. Some studies report that BST levels are raised in milk from industry-recommended doses but that the results are not significant because they fall within natural variations of control groups. Other scientists believe that rBST injected in a cow, even at small quantities, will appear in the milk whether or not we can detect it because there appears to be a direct relationship between the dose of rBST administered and the increase of BST in cow's milk. The fact that rBST may not appear in detectable quantities in the milk, according to some scientists, is not sufficient to ensure its safety.

Daughaday and Barbano (1990) report on a study in which cows, administered up to six times the recommended dose of BST, produced a statistically significant increase in the mean level of BST in the milk, but the levels were still small (less than three nanograms per milliliter). Studies using recommended dose levels (twenty-five to thirty-five milligrams per day) have found that there was no statistically significant rise in the BST levels found in the milk.

Ironically, if there were levels of rBST residue in the milk, its detection under available technologies is practically impossible. The former head of the FDA's Center for Veterinary Medicine testified in May 1993 that "it would be very difficult, and perhaps impossible to develop practical and accurate methods to identify milk or meat from BST-treated cows" (Guest 1993). Radioimmunoassay procedures are used to detect the amount of BST in the milk. Juskevich and Guyer (1990) maintain that these procedures are not sensitive enough to distinguish between the pituitary-derived BST and the synthetic rBST. Therefore, they are treated as virtually identical.

If rBST residues do get into the milk supply, could they be harmful? It is widely held that because BST is a protein hormone, after ingestion it is broken down into small peptides that are not biologically active in the intestinal tract. As NIH's technology assessment panel wrote, "There are no data to suggest that BST present in milk will survive digestion or produce unique peptide fragments that might have biological effects" (NIH-TAP 1991, 231). The biochemical reason given for BST's inactivity in humans, even when injected, is that the growth receptors in humans do not recognize BST. Without the ability of BST to bind to the human somatotropin receptors, the hormone cannot cause a biological effect on humans. Guest (1993, 6) concludes, "Since rBST is orally inactive and since BST, even when injected, has no biological activity in humans, the agency has no human food supply concerns for rBST residues in tissues or milk."

3. Higher Amounts of IGF-1

Insulin-like growth factors (IGFs) are among a number of ingredients present in ordinary milk. These growth factors mediate many of the effects of growth hormone. One variant factor, IGF-1, is found slightly increased in milk of somatotropin-treated cows by two to five parts per billion (NIH-TAP 1991, 230) compared to untreated cows. Critics have focused attention on this point, indicating that IGFs may survive digestion and that they can be a problem to some people, even raising the specter of breast cancer. Some investigators have commented that the significance of increased amounts of IGF-1 from rBST-treated cows is uncertain. The gut of very young infants is an immature organ capable of absorbing intact proteins. Most infants, however, are not given pure milk.

Others have argued that the data on increased IGF-1 must be viewed in the context of the fact that the concentration of IGF-1 in milk varies considerably among cows, herds, and stage of lactation and that IGF-1 content of rBST treated cows is within the normal range of variance from other factors. Furthermore, milk from cows treated with rBST cannot be distinguished from the milk of untreated cows based on IGF-1 values. It is a difference without a significance. The official FDA position is that the consumption of dietary IGF-1 plays no role in either inducing or promoting any human disease, nor does it cause malignant transformations of normal human breast cells (Wilms 1994). As Feenstra (1993, 30) has summarized the state of the controversy over IGFs, "In light of uncertainty about IGF-1 and the contradictory studies about its survival in digestion, critics do not feel confident at this time in concluding IGF-1 is inactivated and will not have any effect on humans."

4. Mastitis

Among the most forceful and frequently cited arguments against the use of rBST is the claim that its use increases the rate at which cows contract mastitis, an infection of the udders that can be treated by antibiotics. According to NIH's technology assessment panel, "An increased incidence of clinical mastitis has been observed in treated cows in some rBST trials, possibly because higher producing dairy cows have a greater incidence of clinical mastitis" (NIH-TAP 1991, 230). Other sources, including a report of the European Commission (CEC 1992; Kronfeld 1993, 86), support the claim that mastitis incidence is increased specifically by rBST. At issue, then, is whether rBST treatment is an independent factor in the rate of mastitis.

The U.S. General Accounting Office (USGAO 1992) reported to the Department of Health and Human Services (HHS) in its own study that the use of BST would increase the incidence of mastitis or udder infections in cows treated with the hormone. The GAO stated that the use of antibiotics for treating mastitis would result in increased drug residues in the consumer's milk. In March 1988 the FDA reported that seventy samples of milk taken in fourteen cities were contaminated with antibiotics that were not permitted in the milk. Among the most prevalent of these was sulfamethazine, which was not approved by the FDA for use in dairy cows. The incident brought to light the fact that farmers sometimes overuse antibiotics or use unapproved brands to treat animals against sickness (Hilts 1990).

Molnar, Cumming, and Nowak (1990) report that "long term studies with BST, conducted in well-managed university herds, have shown few effects on mastitis." Moore and Hutchinson's (1992, 122) review of the studies concludes, "Most studies have reported no difference in clinical mastitis or somatic cell count between BST-treated and control cows." In contrast, the Veterinary Products Committee (VPC) of Britain, recommending against an application for BST approval, expressed concern about levels of mastitis in some injected herds (Watts 1990, 25).

The importance of the mastitis issue was played down by a number of agricultural experts who argued that additional management practices could address that problem. From their perspective, increased mastitis means less milk for the farmer because the milk of diseased cows cannot be marketed; therefore, there is a built-in incentive to reduce mastitis. Patton and Heald (1992, 79) argue that cows with clinical mastitis will be less profitable for BST supplements. In testimony before the Joint Meeting of the Food Advisory Committee and the Veterinary Medicine Advisory Committee (VMAC) of the FDA (May 6, 1993), Michael K. Hansen of Consumers Union noted that the members of the VMAC agreed that there was an increase in mastitis. The debate was over whether or not the risk was "manageable." The "manageable risk" standard, according to Hansen, contradicts established FDA policy under which animal drugs should cause no adverse effects to animal health.

Samuel Epstein, a physician and professor of occupational and environmental medicine, published a paper in the *International Journal of Health Sciences* in which he posited several hypothetical risk scenarios, including the considerations that rBST residues in milk might stimulate premature growth in infants, mobilize carcinogens from body fat, and become absorbed into the blood from the digestive tract, particularly in newborn infants. Epstein contended that "no studies on humans have been conducted with the synthetic hormones, especially the more potent met-BGH, one of the commercially manufactured BST variants" (Epstein 1990, 79).

The Center for Veterinary Medicine (CVM) convened its Veterinary Medicine Advisory Committee on March 31, 1993 to discuss whether increased mastitis and therefore increased antibiotic use represents a risk to human health. At the gathering, the CVM presented its position that the current variation in mastitis incidence in untreated cows due to season, purity, stages of lactation, and herd-to-herd variation is considerably greater than the effects of BST treatment. Also, mastitis cases in BST-treated cows are not more difficult to treat than cases in control cows and are of similar duration (Guest 1993, 5).

The National Institutes of Health Technology Assessment Conference statement (1991, 230) acknowledged data on increases in mastitis but attributed it to productivity and not to rBST. "An increased incidence of clinical mastitis has been observed in treated cows in some rBST trials, possibly because higher producing dairy cows have a greater incidence of clinical mastitis." Monsanto acknowledged that some cows did develop mastitis in their trial, but the company stressed that these cows were given five times the normal dose (Gibbons 1990).

The mastitis issue is unsettling. The official government response is that any increase in clinical mastitis does not represent a public health concern with respect to antibiotic residues in milk, that the new cases would not be more difficult to treat, and that the increases are less than from other sources and much less than what takes place in different stages of normal lactation. When all this is said and done, federal regulatory bodies are confident in the monitoring procedures that would detect milk with antibiotic residues (Executive Branch 1994, 7–8). At the same time, public health professionals are warning that the overuse of antibiotics has been responsible for the development of antibiotic-resistant strains of human pathogens (Levy 1992). The question is, Should innovations in biotechnology be permitted that would likely exacerbate the use of antibiotics in milk production?

David Kronfeld, Distinguished Professor of Agriculture and Veterinary Medicine at the Virginia Polytechnic Institute and State University, reviewed the safety data on rBST and concluded that there is reason to be concerned over animal safety. The most troubling aspect of Kronfeld's analysis is that government and industry reports gloss over or blatantly suppress data on the adverse effects of BST on cows. A possible reason for this is that most safety protocols for veterinary drugs look for a specific endpoint, such as a pathologic lesion or metabolic abnormality. On the existence of such endpoints there have been no unequivocal conclusions, but the suggestive evidence has mounted. Here is the assessment of a scientist-insider in the debate.

> At the technology assessment conference on bovine somatotropin . . . the Panel and other interested participants, including myself . . . were offered five FDA manufacturer documents dealing with safety protocols. . . . These documents revealed the seriousness of infertility and illness in rBGH-treated cows. One massive safety report documented substantial pathology, a high incidence of disease and extensive use of unapproved drugs. . . . At my request, a colleague who is an experienced toxicological pathologist reviewed the safety report. . . . He identified five pathologic lesions affecting the mammary, lung, kidney and joint tissue that increased linearly with dose. (Kronfeld 1993, 76)

Kronfeld concludes that pathologic changes in cows cannot be accounted for by increased milk production but are from rBST treatment. In the package insert of Monsanto's rBST product (Posilac), mastitis, increased body temperature, and localized swelling are listed as possible side effects (table 7).

Table 7. Selected Contraindications of Monsanto's Posilac

1. Cows injected with Posilac are at an increased risk for clinical mastitis.
2. The number of cows affected with clinical mastitis and the number of cases per cow may increase. In addition, the risk of subclinical mastitis (milk not visibly abnormal) is increased.
3. Use of Posilac is associated with increased frequency of use of medication in cows for mastitis and other health problems.
4. Cows injected with Posilac may experience periods of increased body temperature unrelated to illness.
5. Use of Posilac may result in an increase in digestive disorders such as indigestion, bloat, and diarrhea.
6. Studies indicated that cows injected with Posilac had increased numbers of enlarged hocks and lesions of the knee, and second lactation or older cows had more disorders of the foot region.
7. [At the injection site] some cows may experience swellings up to 10 cm in diameter that remain permanent but are not associated with animal health problems.
8. Use of Posilac has been associated with reductions in hemoglobin and hematocrit values during treatment.

Source: Monsanto Co. farmer package insert in Posilac, June 1993

5. Contaminated Milk

According to Hansen (1993), cows receiving rBST require more energy-dense food than ordinary cows. One of the major sources of energy-dense food are the proteins from rendered animals. If, as expected, BST will increase the amount of rendered protein fed to dairy cows, there is a likelihood that more cows will be contaminated with bovine spongiform encephalopathy (a pathogen found in rendered animals), and therefore rBST use will indirectly increase the spread of this organism. This issue was noticeably absent in the published deliberations of the several panels that reviewed the animal and human health risks. As a general matter, the indirect health consequences of new technologies rarely receive the attention given to direct causal effects.

A wide body of opinion within the veterinary, medical, and human nutrition communities seems confident that rBST will either not show up in milk or that, if traces do show up, they will have no direct adverse effects on human health. This opinion neglects the skeptical views of a responsible scientific minority. There is less consensus on the official government conclusion that rBST will not exhibit statistically significant pathological effects on animals and on the importance of these effects on public health. Beyond the debates on animal and human health effects, there remains strong opposition to the use of rBST from those who believe its use would have detrimental social or environmental impacts.

E. Social, Ethical and Environmental Considerations

Will BST accelerate the demise of small dairy farms? Much of the evidence argues affirmatively. But small farms have been disappearing for a host of other reasons. How will BST's influence compare with the other factors? First, cows have become more productive milk producers and therefore fewer cows are needed. In 1985 a cow averaged 13,000 pounds of milk annually, compared with 5,842 pounds in 1955. Some well-managed herds average 20,000 pounds of annual milk production. Second, there has been a continuous trend toward larger dairy farms. In 1955 there were 2.8 million dairy farms, with an average herd size of 8; by 1985 the number dropped to 272,000, and the average herd size rose to 40 (Fallert et al. 1987).

Some agricultural analysts, such as Molner, Cumming, and Nowak (1990, 3085), still remain cautious about linking BST to the reduction in small dairy farms.

> Whether biochemical innovations will significantly accelerate the national trend toward fewer and larger farms depends on how each technology affects the cost structure of the typical farm firm. If the technology requires substantial capital outlays so that fixed costs of production rise appreciably, smaller farms will be placed at a competitive disadvantage relative to larger better capitalized firms because production costs per unit after adoption of the technology are higher for the small firm. Conversely, if the new technology is relatively inexpensive, affecting only variable costs, cost bias in favor of larger firms generally will not exist.

Molnar, Cumming, and Nowak argue that herd management is the key variable, not scale. But management is not the same as animal husbandry. The former involves an assembly-line approach to dairy farming in which there is systematic monitoring of products and quality control operations. The latter focuses on the health and well-being of animals, even as they are exploited for human use. It is generally acknowledged that large herds enable dairy owners to use more advanced technological controls to achieve efficiency of output. Even if rBST were scale neutral in some theoretical sense, once management practices are factored into the scale issue expert opinion leans heavily toward the conclusion that large herds will benefit more from BST. "Successful management of an rBST-treated herd is facilitated by a larger farm's capacity to purchase sophisticated and expensive tools" (Beiswenger 1992, 689). Molnar, Cumming, and Nowak (1990, 3086–87) see management as a proxy measure of the scale impact of BST where the economic return of BST was highest for better-managed herds and where larger herds can afford the capitalization required for better management: "One clear impact of BST is that it increases the complexity of farm operations, narrowing the tolerable margin of error for nutrition and disease management. Such increased risk may present problems for operators with less attentive management styles."

Both proponents and opponents of rBST support the view that the drug will contribute to small farm closings. They disagree over its contribution compared to those of other factors. This message about dairy farm consolidation has appeared in various private market studies and government sources (DRI 1992; Executive Branch 1994; Kalter et al. 1985). The following was stated in a high-priced insiders' market report: "Without government intervention, widespread use of BST will temporarily increase milk supplies, leading to decreased milk prices. For marginal producers, a 15 percent increase in milk production, gained either by using BST or by milking one extra time per day, will not be sufficient to offset the drop of milk prices. Most analysts agree that lower milk prices will drive some farmers out of business and contribute to the well-documented trend of consolidation in the dairy industry" (DRI 1992, 37).

A USDA economic analysis modeled various scenarios of BST impact on the dairy industry. Although the uncertainty of the projections depends on the assumption of government price supports, the study estimated that with BST the number of cows will drop by an additional 315,000 and the number of farms will also drop by 3 percent in seven years over and above non-BST factors. Because the number of dairy farms has declined by 90 percent, or about 3 percent annually, over thirty years, if the trend continues BST would push the decline by .4 percent annually, a 13 percent increase.

BST use is also expected to have an impact on the demographics of dairy farms. As Beiswenger (1992, 690) noted, "Wisconsin produces 17 percent of the nation's milk, has over 36,000 dairy farms. . . . California, second in milk production nationwide, produces 13 percent of the nation's milk, but does so with only 2,400 dairy farms.

The larger farms of the South and the Southwest are likely to benefit from the introduction of rBST, at the expense of smaller farms in the Midwest and Northeast."

A less noticeable concern connected with using BST is its environmental impact, which is not a key issue for the FDA but is nonetheless part of its review process. Johnson, Ward, and Torrent (1992) identified five BST-related ecological concerns: animal manure, production of methane, fossil fuel requirements, water use, and soil loss. The authors evaluated the increase of nitrogen, phosphorous, and methane (which may have adverse effects on the environment) resulting from rBST use against the decrease in the number of dairy cows. Essentially, fewer dairy cows will produce the same volume of milk. As a result, there will be a reduction in waste output and less demand for feed, with its requirements for fossil fuel and water. Johnson, Ward, and Torrent concluded that "all of the environmental impacts of BST adoption that were analyzed were positive. The impact of BST is found to be favorable for all categories except beef production" (161). They estimated that the number of cows will be reduced by 11 percent, which will reduce beef output by 3 percent and require an increase in the national beef herd, yielding additional environmental effects. In balance, the authors argue that rBST has a favorable environmental profile.

The Office of Technology Assessment (1991b) also found that the use of BST could decrease urinary nitrogen excretion, because less feed would be required to produce the same quantity of milk. The OTA reported that the reduction in urinary nitrogen would be expected to reduce nitrate and nitrite contamination of drinking water, eutrophication of aquatic systems, and the denitrification of urea by soil bacteria that produce nitrous oxide and contributes to the greenhouse effect (see also *Food Chemical News* 1993b).

A report of the Executive Branch (1994, iv) summarized the environmental impacts of rBST as marginally favorable on the grounds that it would lead to a slightly smaller U.S. dairy herd, less pollution through decreased use of fertilizers for feed production, and less cow manure and methane production. Most environmental impact assessments fail to consider the positive impact of having a greater number of cows more widely distributed across the national landscape. A large concentrated herd using less aggregate fertilizer may still create a more perilous impact because of the high concentration of the fertilizer in a single region. In addition, the elimination of small farms across rural America would likely decrease biodiversity. Notwithstanding the safety issues of BGH still under contention, it is undeniably true that its use brings dairy farmers one step further down the path of high input, intensive livestock production. For some, this is the path of progress. Byrnes (1993, 334) describes an alternative path as being one of rotational grazing:

> The rotational pasture-management system maximizes efficiency of on-farm resources—soil, water, plants, animals, and human time and effort—that go toward production of milk. By dividing the pasture into smaller paddocks, the farmer fully uses available forage in each paddock before the cows are moved. This allows each area time to maximize its use of water and nutrients, including the manure left by the grazing cattle, and to regenerate before it is regrazed. The low-input approach to feeding also reduces the need to purchase or use other inputs required in confinement dairy production, such as feed production machinery, waste removal equipment, and energy—both human and fossil fuel.

F. Public Policy and Citizen Perceptions

1. FDA Approval

On November 5, 1993, after nine years of review, the FDA announced its approval of Monsanto's formulation of BST (brand name, Posilac) in milk production. FDA head David Kessler called the veterinary drug thoroughly safe; no label would be required. "There is virtually no difference between milk from treated and untreated cows" (Schneider 1993). The FDA stated that it lacks the statutory authority to require special labeling of rBST milk, but that companies may voluntarily label their products as long as information is truthful and not misleading. In the summer of 1993 Congress passed a ninety-day moratorium on BST after the FDA's approval. The FDA has permitted the sale of BST used in cows that were part of experimental evaluations since 1985. When the ninety-day, congressionally imposed moratorium came to a close, the FDA warned dairy producers that BST-free labels on milk might mislead consumers and therefore be illegal under federal law. Companies may voluntarily label milk as BST-free if they add the statement, "No significant difference has been shown between milk derived from cows that were given the drug and cows that were not" (Schneider 1994, A1).

2. The Organization of Opposition

In the summer of 1989, the Foundation on Economic Trends, under the leadership of Jeremy Rifkin, consumer and environmental groups and animal welfare organizations launched a campaign against BST that resulted in a partial boycott of rBST milk produced in experimental herds. On August 1989, Ben and Jerry's Ice Cream, which purchases milk from small Vermont producers, began to note on its ice cream containers that it opposes hormones and supports small farmers. During that same period, five of the nation's largest supermarket chain stores (Safeway, Kroger, Supermarket General, Stop and Shop, and Vons) publicly announced that they would refuse to buy dairy products from farmers who have injected their cows with BST (Sugarman 1989). The country's largest dairy cooperative, Associated Milk Producers Inc., released a statement that its twenty-one thousand members will not give the hormone to the cooperative's cows (Corey 1990). The campaign against BST has witnessed the creation of coalitions among several diverse political forces, including small dairy farmers, milk distributors, animal rights advocates, and international indigenous rights groups. In addition, it has fostered a contentious split within the dairy industry between small and large milk producers.

The strongest media campaign against BST came from the Humane Farming Association (HFA), identified in the press as a San Francisco-based animal rights group. HFA published advertisements against BST in the *U.S. News and World Report* and *Time Magazine* during December 1991. These news magazines have a circulation of more than six million readers. The advertisements compared BST to diethylstilbestrol (DES), a drug that resulted in uterine cancer in the daughters of women who had taken it. People writing to HFA received a glossy brochure that stated: "Researchers suspect that its [IGF-1] effects could also include premature growth stimulation in infants, breast growth in young children, and increased risk of breast cancer among women. No one knows what effect this secondary hormone will have upon consumers of BGH treated milk."

In response to the negative publicity over BST Monsanto supported a national advertising campaign that featured a large glass of milk and the statement, "You've had BST and cookies all your life." Monsanto also directed its lobbyist to inform the USDA that the company would withdraw from agricultural biotechnology if the administration would let socioeconomic factors dictate the approval of a new product (*Food Chemical News* 1993a). The FDA warned the company about making any safety or efficacy claims before the product was approved. Among the objectionable statements cited by the agency was, "If a cow is given extra BST, the milk doesn't change, but the cow is able to make more milk more efficiently" (Guest 1991).

3. Public Attitudes

Smith and Warland (Hallberg, ed. 1992, 262) reviewed eleven studies of consumer attitudes on BST covering a period from 1987 to 1990. The studies involved more than seven thousand individuals. In summarizing their findings the authors state that most consumers are concerned about BST, most want milk from BST-supplemented cows to be labeled, a significant number indicated that they would decrease their consumption of milk if it came from BST-supplemented cows, and a majority indicated that their image of milk as a pure food would change. The overall consumer reaction would be negative.

Show, Mather, and Noel (1992) examined the attitudes of dairy farmers, veterinarians, and dairy processors. One-quarter of the dairy farmers indicated that they would not use BST under any circumstances, whereas another quarter said that they would accept its use if it became an economic necessity. While dairy farmers against the use of BST were more concerned about the price of milk, veterinarians against the use of BST were concerned about milk supply and consumer reaction. A study released in October 1993 indicated that only 11 percent of the Wisconsin dairy farmers surveyed would use BST if labeling were not required (*Biotech Bulletin* 1993). Consumer surveys also showed consistently that milk consumption will decrease if BST is used. In a New York state survey, Kaiser, Scherer, and Barbano (1992) found that milk consumption in the state could decline by 5.5 percent to 15.6 percent. A Wisconsin survey found that 77 percent of respondents would prefer to drink milk from untreated herds and 67 percent would be willing to pay an extra 22 cents a gallon for it (Beiswenger 1992, 686). A National Dairy Board survey taken in 1990 indicated that more than half of the respondents were very or extremely concerned about the use of rBST (Feenstra 1993, 12).

New England dairy processors declared that they would pay premium prices to farmers who do not supplement their herd with BST. When the processors considered using a BST-free label, Monsanto was alleged to have threatened them (Dillon 1993). As Feenstra (1993, 3) summed up public reaction, "Uneasiness about BGH [BST] runs deeper than concerns about consumers' own short-term health. BGH represents for many consumers the widespread use of a new technology about which they know little and over which they have no control."

4. International Adoptions and Prohibitions of BST

While the United States was reviewing the safety and efficacy data on BST, at least twelve nations had already given approval and in some cases started using Monsanto's version of BST in milk production (table 8). After a moratorium on BST use, during the summer of 1993 the European Community banned BST for seven years. The EC indicated that the usual criteria of safety, quality, efficacy, and ethics could only be met by radical dairy management changes that are unenforceable. By early 1995 the European Union Agricultural Council permitted its member states to authorize limited use of Monsanto's BST over a five-year period in order to study the effects of the product. This decision did not affect the European Union's general moratorium, which lasts throught the end of 1999, on the use of supplemental BST hormone.

In Australia, the Agricultural and Veterinary Chemicals Council (AVCC) decided "solely because of trade implications" to prohibit BST use in Australia (*Gene Report* 1993). BST has been banned in Australia since 1993. Britain's Veterinary Products Committee recommended that bovine somatotropin should not be approved because of concern about harm to animals and questions about its manufacture (*The Economist* 1990). The four Scandinavian countries

Table 8. Nations That Have Approved Monsanto's BST Product for Milk Production

Nation	Date of Approval
South Africa	November 1988
Czech/Slovak Republics	July 1989
Zimbabwe	February 1990
Nambia	February 1990
Brazil	March 1990
Mexico	May 1990
Bulgaria	July 1990
CIS (Russia, Ukraine, etc.)	February 1991
Jamaica	April 1992
Costa Rica	October 1993
European Union	January 1993
U.S.A.	November 1993
Puerto Rico	March 1994
Malaysia	October 1994

Source: Monsanto

also banned BST, and all Canadian provinces except Quebec termi-
nated BST trials. Meanwhile, in the United States, Wisconsin and
Minnesota issued a moratorium on the sale of BST that lasted until
June 1991. The Monsanto Company provided its brand of rBST for
experimental trials in Zimbabwe, where, as reported in the *African
Farmer* (Spoor 1990), milk yields began increasing within days of the
BST injection. Monsanto's synthetic bovine growth hormone has
been approved for marketing in Mexico, Russia, Czechoslovakia,
South Africa, Bulgaria, and Nambia (DRI 1992, 38).

In 1995 Monsanto reported that the human safety of dairy and
meat products from dairy cows receiving rBST supplements has been
confirmed by more than thirty countries around the world, including the United Kingdom, Germany, France, Australia, Canada, Italy, the Netherlands, and Spain. The company made an effort in its
public relations literature to highlight the nations that declared BST
a medically safe product even though they decided not to use it on
social or ethical grounds.

5. The Public's Concept of Milk as a Pure Food

The public harbors the fiction that milk is a natural product drawn
from the udder of a cow. In actuality it undergoes considerable processing; milk is pasteurized, homogenized, vitamin D fortified, and
reduced of fat content. Yet the combined symbolism of hormones,
genetic engineering, and injecting the cow creates an unsettling
image. Despite assurances from manufacturers, federal agencies, and
health scientists, these powerful negative images are not easily negated or neutralized. The industry is counting on time and acclama-
tion, as was the case before people began to respond favorably to
margarine as a substitute for the "high priced" spread. Statements
in the scientific literature that question the nutritional quality of
rBST milk will undoubtedly fuel public skepticism (Kronfeld 1993,
97; Mepham 1991). The concept of a pure or natural food is culturally determined, mediated by historical tradition and corporate per-
suasion. There has been publicity against the use of milk as a core
component of the U.S. diet; animal rights groups, for example, argue that human infants did not evolve to drink bovine milk. This
may be a small movement, but it does indicate how changing fashions can take hold of the consumer preference for pure food.

G. Conclusions

After the voluminous studies on the health effects and efficacy of
BST are presented and the massive amount of data processed, we are

left with two principal conclusions. First, government agencies have sought to present a consensus position on the safety of BST that is questionable in the face of continued scientific skepticism. Second, the public policy debate over this veterinary hormone is fundamentally about agricultural values. Emblazoned in the political discourse that frames this controversy is the question of what the structure of our agricultural system will look like in several decades.

Reputable scientific opinion, albeit a minority, remains skeptical over the official government conclusion on such key issues as safety of rBST to cows, the appearance of rBST in milk, the nutritional quality of milk, and the relationship between the synthetic growth hormone and residues of antibiotics and other secondary products in the milk, including the production of IGF-1 and its public health implications. This body of opinion, which cannot be summarily dismissed, challenges the all-clear signal that the FDA and other federal bodies have issued for BST since the mid-1980s.

Amory Lovins (1977) wrote about the hard and soft paths of energy. The hard energy path is symbolized by the development of nuclear power, which presupposes a hierarchical, centralized, high-risk, and technologically remote system of energy production and distribution. The soft energy path is characterized by smaller units of decentralized producers, sustainable energy systems such as solar and conservation. Agricultural policy can be seen as having hard and soft paths to the future. The BST controversy has highlighted the alternative social visions of food-processing systems. The hard path of agriculture is characterized by high-energy inputs, intensive chemical use in farming, and efficiency optimization of land, genetic resources and animals. It is quintessentially anthropocentric in that human value is the measure of all things. The soft path views agriculture as more than a food-producing mechanistic system; it is the wellspring of our agrarian culture and the central human contribution to our rural ecology. The soft path of agriculture seeks to preserve the diversification of agrarian culture in the United States, to provide people with meaningful and healthy work, and to create sustainable ecosystems where the interests of diverse species and human food cultivators can be met simultaneously.

The BST controversy tells us that our legal and institutional structures are situated squarely in the hard path, while a strong segment of the popular culture and a part of the agricultural industry are seeking softer approaches to food production. The FDA is constrained to evaluate BST under the hard-path criteria; no provision is in the Food and Drug Acts for evaluating the social, ethical, or economic impacts of the veterinary hormone. Agri-industry has acclimated to certain rules in product development. After it is shown that a product is safe to humans and does not endanger the environment, the product may be marketed. The BST debate indicates that the public's concerns are reaching beyond the concepts of safety and security. Questions such as whether society will limit the use of animals as surrogate machines are not meaningful in and of themselves when viewed through current policy frameworks. The public's interest in preserving farmland extends beyond the price of food. Beiswenger (1992, 693) states that "the choice for policy makers is whether rural life and rural families are worthy of protection at the expense of some level of inefficiency in dairy farming."

Regulators involved in assessing BST are also caught in a policy and legal matrix that reinforces the hard agricultural path. If a soft path is sought, policymakers must replace the current framework through which technologies are adopted with a new set of principles. For example, one study argues for rotational grazing—a flexible system that promotes sustainable pasture management as an alternative to veterinary drugs (Liebhardt 1993, 131–88).

The BST case has brought the significance of technology assessment to the surface. It is a test case not for the FDA, because the agency more or less fulfilled its narrowly framed statutory mandate, but for Congress. Will the health and safety laws for new products and technologies be rewritten or amended to include social, ethical, and economic distributive effects? Biotechnology in general and BST in particular has stimulated proposals that call for widening the lens of technology assessment (Beiswenger 1992, 708; Krimsky 1991, 205–29).

The use of veterinary drugs has played an increasingly important role in animal agriculture. Since the early 1970s farmers have administered DES, antibiotics, beef tenderizers, and other medicinal and enhancement products. In this context, the introduction of BST into animal agriculture represents an incremental innovation, while its method of production—cell culture and rDNA techniques—is revolutionary. The introduction of BST was met with significant backlash from diverse consumer, small farmer, and animal welfare groups as well as diverse segments of the general public.

In terms of the theories of innovation, BST is a textbook case of science-technology-induced change. The development of recombinant bovine growth hormone came at a time when many farmers were dubious about increasing milk yields. Certainly from a macro-industry perspective it was destabilizing. Agriculturalists were also aware of the public concerns over biotechnology and the possibility of food products associated with genetic engineering becoming stigmatized. Recombinant BST was largely motivated by a few multinationals that invested heavily in the idea of a veterinary growth hormone for raising milk productivity, a concept known for fifty years but only economically viable during the 1980s. Although we found no evidence that the dairy sector was investing in, advocating, or anticipating this area of development, the large mechanized farms were receptive to innovations that could easily be integrated into their technological milking processes and would offer a profit without compromising the quality of the milk. The market for BST was the milk producers not the consumers, who see no added value.

The successful development and marketing of BST came about as a result of the commitment, heavy investment, and aggressive program of direct farmer contact by a multinational, along with strong endorsements from nutritionists, farm organizations, food technologists, physicians, health scientists, and toxicologists. The product might have been too risky to seek market approval for a traditional venture capital-funded biotechnology firm with insufficient capital and infrastructure for addressing regulation, the support of scientific and professional associations, public relations, farmer education, liability, and legal challenges.

10   Transgenic Animals

The application of reproductive technologies to farm animals began in the 1930s with the development of artificial insemination (AI) techniques. By the 1960s the use of frozen embryos in conjunction with AI became widespread. Another major innovation in the control of animal reproduction was introduced with oestrus induction through the use of steroid hormones and prostaglandins. Scientists could artificially synchronize ovulation with fertilization while advances were being made in AI, in vitro fertilization, and embryo transplantation.

The next major breakthrough in animal reproduction came with the development of techniques for implanting foreign DNA into a fertilized egg. The resulting organism is referred to as a genetically modified or genetically engineered animal. The most commonly used and efficient method for making genetically engineered animals is by injecting DNA into a fertilized egg or zygote and then allowing the egg to develop in a pseudo-pregnant mother. The transgenic animal that is born is termed a founder. The new DNA randomly integrates into the genome, sometimes in many multiples of copies in several sites (Sedivy and Joyner 1992, 124).

Genetically modified animals developed from fertilized eggs in which foreign DNA has been inserted are classified into two types. When foreign DNA has been introduced into a fertilized egg before the egg has divided, there is strong likelihood that the DNA will be inherited by all the offspring cells, including germ-line cells (cells involved in reproduction). Under these conditions, the offspring of the adult animal are also expected to carry the foreign DNA in their genome. Animals that have had foreign DNA introduced in this manner are called transgenic. Alternatively, when foreign DNA is introduced into the embryo and cell differentiation has begun, the resulting animal will contain tissue made of cells, some with and some without the foreign DNA (a mosaic). Because the resulting organism possesses cells with different components of DNA, it is called a chimera (MacFarlane 1992, 68).

A. The Current State of Development

The first successful experiments creating transgenic vertebrates were reported in the early 1980s. Palmiter et al. (1982) created a transgenic mouse by transferring a growth hormone gene into the embryo of the mouse. Following that, in 1988 a patent was awarded for a mouse with human genes that can be used as a model system to deliver malignant tumors. Because the mouse was developed to be tumorgenic, it is referred to commonly in scientific parlance as the oncomouse (oncology is the study of tumors). It was the first patent issued for an animal (OTA 1989, 12). The genetically engineered mouse was developed by Harvard scientists Philip Leder and Timothy Stewart. They were working on a genetic sequence called *c-myc*, which was associated with childhood cancers. They spliced the gene fragment into genetic material from a mouse mammary virus. The virus carries the oncogene (a gene associated with the formation of tumors) into the fertilized egg of the mouse, and under controlled conditions mice with the oncogene experience a higher incidence of breast cancer.

Transgenesis—the transfer of genes across species lines—opened the way for animals to be used as an alternative to tissue-culture production of human protein. The term *transgenic pharming* was coined to characterize the role of genetically engineered animals as bioreactors (usually a mechanical system like a fermenter, where cells are grown to harvest protein products) for the manufacture of human pharmaceuticals. In 1987 a transgenic mouse was created that demonstrated the viability of tissue-specific expression of foreign proteins in milk (Gordon et al. 1987). The mouse was genetically engineered to make clot-dissolving tissue plasminogen activator (TPA), which is viewed as a highly promising drug for the treatment of coronary disease and a strong competitor of the widely acclaimed streptokinase. The procedure involved the surgical removal of zygotes, followed by microinjection of the desired DNA and promoter sequences. The transformed embryos were implanted in the oviducts of recipient mice through a second surgical procedure.

Because mice do not produce sufficient milk to harvest foreign proteins commercially, it was natural for pharmaceutical companies to seek other animals with higher-volume milk productivity—sheep, goats, pigs, and cows, for example. Some dairy cows are capable of producing ten thousand liters of milk a year. Following the successful development of a transgenic mouse, prototypes of other transgenic animals were reported with foreign protein expressed in the milk, including sheep producing anti-hemophilic Factor IX (Clark et al. 1989); mice with CD4 protein (Yu at al. 1989), urikinase (Meade et al. 1990), and alpha-antitrypsin (Archibald et al. 1990); rabbits with interleukin-2 (Buhler et al. 1990); goats with TPA (Ebert et al. 1991); and cows with human lactoferrin (HLF) (Krimpenfort et al. 1991) (table 9).

The application of transgenesis is more complex for large animals than for mice because of multiple surgical procedures. In the case of transgenic dairy cattle, investigators have succeeded with a single surgical procedure that reduces the risk of egg loss. First, bovine oocytes were collected from the follicles present in the ovaries of slaughtered animals. Second, the oocytes were fertilized by frozen semen from several different bulls. Third, foreign DNA was microinjected into the fertilized eggs. Finally, the genetically modified fertilized eggs were implanted into the womb of a cow.

While fertilized eggs may be prepared in several different ways for different species, the procedure of choice for transplanting foreign DNA is microinjection. In the case of the transgenic sheep, artificially inseminated eggs were collected from superovulated ewes. A gene construct was microinjected into the eggs, which were then reimplanted into surrogate mothers.

Table 9. Milestones in the Production of Human Proteins in the Milk of Transgenic Animals

1987	Human plasminogen activator in milk of transgenic mice (Gordon et al. 1987)
1989	Human anti-hemophilic Factor IX in milk of transgenic sheep (Clark et al. 1989)
1989	Human CD4 protein in milk of transgenic mice (Yu et al. 1989)
1990	Human interleukin-2 in milk of transgenic rabbits (Buhler et al. 1990)
1990	Human urikinase produced in mouse milk (Meade et al. 1990)
1990	Human alpha-antitrypsin in the milk of transgenic mice (Archibald et al. 1990)
1991	Human TPA in the milk of transgenic goats (Ebert et al. 1991)
1991	Human lactoferrin (HLF) in the milk of a transgenic cow (Krimpenfort et al. 1991)
1992	Human hemoglobin in transgenic swine (Swanson et al. 1992)

Source: Compiled by the authors

Transgenic animals under development include swine with the human growth hormone gene, genetically engineered livestock designed to tolerate extreme climatic conditions, transgenic sheep that grow faster than normal sheep, engineered sheep that secrete insect repellent to protect them from pernicious insects and produce moth-proof wool, chickens with the growth genes of cows for accelerated growth, and genetically modified sheep and cows that produce milk that can be consumed by individuals who are lactose-intolerant.

Several universities in the United States have begun research programs to engineer edible fish genetically. Among the goals of the research are to increase the size of the fish or make a species that will grow faster or survive better in new environments. For example, by transplanting antifreeze genes taken from an arctic flounder into salmon, it is hoped that the transgenic salmon will be able to live in subfreezing seawater. Scientists are also experimenting by transplanting growth genes from rats, cows, and humans into a variety of fish species (Crapo 1993).

The scientific world heralded the news that a gene responsible for cystic fibrosis had been identified and characterized. Although a number of mutations in the gene have been correlated with cases of CF, defects in a very small region of the gene are responsible for 70 percent of the cases. Once it could be shown that mice contain a gene similar to the cystic fibrosis locus, the rationale for creating a CF mouse was compelling. Since the discovery it has been learned that mice that are homozygous for a number of the alleles on the CF locus exhibit many of the same phenotypic effects of humans stricken by cystic fibrosis.

The Genzyme Corporation of Boston, Massachusetts, and researchers at Tufts University's Veterinary School are working on a transgenic mouse that can produce human membrane proteins (cystic fibrosis transmembrane regulator, or CFTR) that may be used to treat cystic fibrosis. Finnish researchers have developed a genetically modified cow that purportedly can produce milk containing large amounts of red cell growth factor (erythropoietin) used to treat anemia. If successful, this method will replace costlier cell culture techniques. Other more remote applications of transgenic animals include human blood and organ production.

B. Benefits and Applications

Four major areas of anticipated benefit of TGAs are in pharmaceutical manufacture (transgenic "pharming"), the development of research animals, human tissue and organ harvesting, and food production. It is widely recognized that producing human therapeutic proteins in the milk of transgenic livestock is a viable alternative to cell culture systems and in vitro chemical synthesis.

Among the advantages cited for agricultural pharming are the ease of access to the expressed therapeutic protein in the milk, the higher production capabilities of the mammary gland, especially of cows and goats, and the facts that animal bioreactors are relatively easy and inexpensive to reproduce for expanding production and the operating costs of these systems (animal bioreactors) can be significantly lower than fermentation facilities. The purity of the product and the competitive efficiency of manufacture are two hurdles to commercialization. Ebert et al. (1991) have summarized the benefits of a goat as a living bioreactor: high milk production (four liters per day), a modestly long gestation period of five to eight months, and the fact that goat milk is well characterized biochemically. Milk from farm animals produces tens of grams of pharmaceutical protein per liter, whereas commercial bioreactors make milligrams per liter of such protein. No therapeutic agent derived from a transgenic animal has thus far been approved for commercial use.

A second promising area opened by transgenics is the production of specialty animals for research. Donnelley, McCarthy, and Singleton (1994, S5) note that transgenic animals may vastly improve the modeling of human disease: "The technological innovations used to develop transgenic organisms allow researchers to design laboratory organisms that mimic or duplicate many human diseases such as cystic fibrosis, diabetes, AIDS, cancer, or sickle-cell anemia. Such animals become valuable models to follow the sequelae and treatment possibilities for these diseases. Thus transgenic organisms provide exciting models to understand and perhaps to intervene in human disease processes."

In 1987 scientists at the National Institutes of Health began raising litters of mice that carry a copy of the AIDS virus in their chromosomes. The experiments were restricted to a maximum security laboratory, where investigators used the transgenic AIDS mouse to study how viral genes are activated and to test drugs that might obstruct the production and spread of the virus (Okie 1987). As Comstock (1992, 75) has summarized the advantages to cancer research of creating transgenic animals, "By introducing an activated oncogene sequence taken from humans, scientists can produce transgenic mice with an increased propensity for developing neoplasms. The physiology of the resultant mouse makes an improved animal 'model' of human diseases such as cancer. From the transgenic mouse research program, scientists have learned the location and function of mouse genes and hope to use that information in identifying the location and function of human genes."

Not everyone, however, is convinced that studies on animals are useful or successful models for humans. Many animal models have proven ineffective to human disease. Even the revered animal bioassay, which for more than a quarter of a century has been the bedrock of toxicological testing for chemical agents, has been called into question as providing misleading information about carcinogenic substances (Marx 1990).

Contemporary affluent societies have become alerted to the adverse effects of high-fat, high-cholesterol diets. Beef consumption per capita in the United States has declined precipitously as medical news about excessive animal fat in the human diet has begun to make an impression on consumers. Several venture capital companies, sensing that lower-fat beef or pork is what consumers desire, are pursuing the application of transgenesis to create animals with lower fat content.

There are methods other than genetic engineering that can lower the fat in animals, for example, the administration of veterinary hormones such as bovine or porcine somatotropin. However, the use of exogenous drugs for altering an animal's muscle to fat ratio or for increasing lactation has been met with consumer resistance (chapter 9). An alternative being considered, to engineer an animal genetically to produce the same hormone at the requisite quantities, although technically more complex than administering veterinary drugs, is viewed by some as more consumer friendly. Some observers believe this will receive a more favorable consumer response because the public distinguishes between exogenous drugs and endogenous genes.

Another target for transgenic animals in food production is fish. Commercial fish stocks are being depleted rapidly in most coastal regions, a result of improved technology for locating and catching fish and increased consumer demand. Aquaculture is viewed as a way to increase fish supply while reestablishing sustainable yield in the open waters. However, not all fish are adaptable to fish farming. Some people believe that fish, through genetic engineering, could be given new traits and made more suitable for aquaculture.

Transgenic fish are also being engineered with growth genes, projects that drew protests from the environmental community. Once released, these enlarged species of fish could destabilize the marine ecology. Kapuscinski and Hallerman (1990, 2) cite fourteen species of transgenic fishes produced as of 1989; the foreign genes introduced included growth hormone, antifreeze proteins, and marker proteins. "Besides the expected direct effects of inserted DNA," Kapuscinski and Hallerman note, "Indirect phenotypic effects might occur as a consequence of uncontrolled genomic integration or expression of the introduced DNA. . . . Because aquatic ecosystems function through complex interactions involving transfers of energy, organisms, nutrients, and information, it is reasonable to expect difficulty in predicting the community-level impacts of releasing transgenic fishes that exhibit one or more type of phenotypic change."

Since the onset of the AIDS epidemic, considerable attention has been directed at protecting the quality and supply of human blood banked for transfusions. Among the innovations being considered for in vitro transgenesis is the creation of animals that would produce blood functionally identical to human blood. The firm DNX of Princeton, New Jersey, has initiated research on developing human hemoglobin in pigs. According to a report by Hodgson (1992, 866), which cites company estimates, one hundred thousand pigs killed and desanguinated would provide $300 million worth of human hemoglobin.

These cases represent the four main areas where transgenic animals are being sought for commercial applications. The investments are high and so, therefore, are the economic stakes. Generally, these investments are made with the expectation that substantial markets exist for transgenic products.

C. Economics of TGAs

The science and technology of animal transgenesis have been developing rapidly since the early 1980s, and with striking accomplishments. However, the commercial success of harvesting therapeutic proteins, human organs or blood products, and nutritionally higher-quality food is not yet proven. The success of transgenic animals for drug production depends on its competition from alternative forms of manufacture. For pharmaceuticals, the competition is between transgenic animal products and cell culture production, cadaverous sources, and human subject contributions.

Human alpha antitrypsin is an amino acid (a serum glycoprotein) normally present at two grams per liter in plasma. The primary locus for antitrypsin production is the liver. Alpha-1–antitrypsin has been approved in the United States as a replacement therapy for individuals with a genetic deficiency that is responsible for a life-threatening form of emphysema. The disease alpha-1–antitrypsin deficiency (AAT deficiency) afflicts more than twenty thousand individuals in the United States and seven hundred thousand people worldwide. The therapeutic needs for a treatment are estimated to be two hundred grams per patient per year of antitrypsin. Supplies of the drug are obtained from purified plasma. Scientists created transgenic sheep that produced up to thirty-five grams per liter, and "a moderate sized herd would provide several thousand kilograms during one lactation period" (Bialy 1991, 786). The annual worldwide market for the drug is estimated at $100 million (Spalding 1992, 498).

Clark et al. (1987, 23) estimate that the world's requirement for Factor IX (a chemical that plays a key role in the blood clotting cascade) is about one kilogram of purified protein per year. With a value of $25,000 per gram, the potential world market for Factor IX is $25 million. The size of the transgenic herd needed to meet this production is modest: "If the expression of recombinant Factor IX is of the order of endogenous milk protein genes and the efficiency of downstream processing were 10 percent, then a flock of ten lactating ewes would be sufficient to supply the world's needs" (Clark et al. 1987, 23).

Lactoferrin is a protein that facilitates iron absorption and fights bacteria. A biotechnology company named Gen Pharm International of Mountain View, California, has been seeking to develop human lactoferrin in transgenic cow milk that could be used as an alternative to infant formula, a $4 billion market.

The drug tissue plasminogen activator (TPA) produced by transgenic goats at Tufts University's Veterinary School is being used for research purposes. A single treatment with TPA costs $2,200, making each goat that produces TPA worth more than $1 million. Supplies of TPA for treatment therapy are derived from microbial sources.

Establishing human hemoglobin in the blood of transgenic pigs may solve some problems but will surely raise others. The purity of the product is clearly of the utmost importance. Human hemoglobin must be separated from that of the transgenic pig, which contains about 9 percent human serum. Also, the response of people to animal-derived human hemoglobin is as yet untested. Some analysts see little distinction between the public's acceptance of bovine and porcine insulin and human blood products derived from animal milk. Seventy million units of human blood are transfused worldwide, a $10 billion market. Public fear that blood for transfusions may be contaminated with the AIDS virus makes the commercial prospects of transgenic blood more realistic. Among the uses of transgenic animals, pharmaceutical applications appear to be the leading investment strategy, particularly in cases where drugs are not available from other production techniques.

D. Social and Ethical Considerations

Sorting out the social and ethical issues associated with the treatment of animals is destined to produce some thorny problems, particularly where social consensus is sought. In large part, this is due to the fact that subgroups in society do not share a common metaphysical, religious, or ethical framework on the status of animals. Donnelley, McCarthy, and Singleton, (1994, S14) have observed that "we confront an eradicable moral plurality: a bewildering variety of values and ethical obligations, each claiming attention and not readily coordinated with the others." Moreover, the differences among groups are manifold. For example, Michael W. Fox, who is vice president of the Humane Society of the United States, believes that transgenic animals present unique ethical problems because, unlike plants and bacteria, animals are sentient beings. Fox (1992, 90) adds rhetorically, after noting that a genetically modified animal might induce a unique form of suffering, "Is it morally and ethically acceptable to turn animals such as mice, pigs, and sheep, which are sentient, into biomachines for the manufacture of proteins and other biological materials?"

Within environmental ethics there are theories that offer a wide spectrum of viewpoints on the moral status of animals. Among the leading perspectives are the hard-core biocentrism represented in Paul Taylor's *Respect for Nature* (1986) (humans do not have any more inherent worth than other living things and therefore are deserving of no greater consideration on the part of moral agents) and the moral pluralism of Christopher Stone in *Earth and Other Ethics* (1987) (the moral response to nonhuman entities are petitioned into several distinct frameworks governed by their own principles and logical texture). We are, with respect to animal policies, at any time in history, at an unstable equilibrium that could be shifted to a new balance point in response to swings in public opinion and organized citizen actions. Membership in animal advocacy organizations has increased substantially since the 1970s. At one time these organizations were composed mainly of pet owners, but that is no longer the case. Animal welfare advocates, wildlife conservationists, and vegetarians have found a common cause (Rowan 1989).

What makes the issue of transgenic animals particularly complex is that it not only is being considered by competing metaphysical, religious, and ethical frameworks but also that within these frameworks it does not quite fit the traditional mold for rendering decisions on the treatment of animals. Donnelley, McCarthy, and Singleton (1994) note, "With varying emphasis we can be both for and against animal biotechnology, for different moral reasons and according to different world visions." It is, therefore, incumbent on the proponents of one of the distinctive perspectives to address a somewhat novel situation. In this sense it is analogous to the situation where prelates of the Catholic or Jewish orthodoxy must assess the compatibility of a new technology with traditional norms. And for those groups for whom it is abhorrent to manipulate, control, experiment with, or consume animals of any type there is still the question of where the issue of transgenic animals is situated in the hierarchy of concerns.

In the political discourse on transgenic animals, adversaries often follow a pattern of analysis that is characteristic of one of several distinctive belief structures. Among these structures there may be areas of common concern or even nodes of consensus. But the controversies over transgenic animals can be traced to norms that fall into distinctive patterns. An ethical norm may fit comfortably in one belief structure and seem incoherent in another. A useful way to reveal the basic logic, metaphysics, and values of the distinctive schemata—or what Stone calls the "planes of moral pluralism"—is through an analysis of the belief structures that frame the ethical discourse. The study of the conditions under which ethical reasoning takes place is sometimes referred to as meta-ethics.

E. Applications of Transgenic Animals

The ethical choices we shall describe and the conflicting rights and responsibilities associated with these choices are relevant to established traditions in the care and treatment of animals as well as any unique situations that arise from the techniques of animal transgenesis. Six applications of transgenic animals are commonly discussed in the literature: wild species released into natural systems, physically controlled or domesticated species, food-producing animals, animals used to manufacture drugs, animals used to harvest human organs, blood, or tissue, and research animals or animals developed for intellectual curiosity.

1. Transgenic Species Designed for Release into Natural Systems

Several benefits have been suggested for producing genetically engineered animals that are released into the environment. These include commercial interests in modifying the size, shape, or nutritional quality of game animals. Improvements in the food supply are usually cited as a rationale. The human growth hormone gene has been inserted into fish embryo, resulting in an oversized fish. This increases the total poundage of marine species suitable for consumption and also provides new incentives for sports fishing. Tests of the oversized fish, however, brought criticism that such introductions could create ecological imbalances and that any such releases should be studied for their effects on the entire ecosystem (Kapuscinski and Hallerman 1990, 2–5).

A genetically modified animal might be introduced as part of a wildlife maintenance strategy to control the overpopulation of another species. In past years, species that are not indigenous have been introduced to certain regions as predators of overpopulated prey. Even if the introduced species is successful in maintaining the growth of another species, the introduction might have other, unintended impacts on the ecosystem (such as on the community of flora and fauna) that warrant consideration.

Another form of instability is represented by species that are dying out. Human intervention into the environment has created unfavorable survival conditions for many species. Some have suggested that modifying the species could make wildlife more robust and capable of procreating in otherwise unfavorable conditions. For example, genetically engineered wildlife might be created to resist the feminization of males that results from exposure to xenobiotic estrogenic chemicals (Colborn, vom Saal, and Soto 1993).

2. Domesticated or Physically Contained Animals

In this category, we might consider new species of animals used in controlled sports such as greyhound or horse racing. Alternatively, there is certainly a market for exotic pets that combine characteristics of domestication with the exotica of wild animals. This class of transgenic animals is generally well contained and not subject to spontaneous breeding in the wild. Once we mix the traits of domesticated and nondomesticated animals, however, the obstacles to breeding in the wild for domesticated pets may be moot.

3. Food Production

The system of factory farming in conjunction with consumer food fashions creates a demand for larger, leaner, physiologically restructured or hormonally modified animals. This might include transgenic animals modified to digest fiber more efficiently, or to use cheaper feed stock, or to improve resistance to disease so costs of raising the animal or of antibiotics are lower. Examples cited in the popular press are of chickens with larger breasts, of pigs with less fat, or of cows that produce more milk without the use of an exogenous hormone.

When human genes or other foreign genes are transplanted into fertilized eggs of animals, the success rate is about 1 percent. Animals for whom the genetic modification fails are often judged to be normal. They are often sold to slaughterhouses and eventually end up on consumers' dinner tables.

The United Kingdom's Advisory Committee on Novel Foods and Processes (ACNFP) has noted that animals resulting from transgenic experiments might turn out to be mosaics, some cells having the foreign genes and some not having them. This raises ethical questions for consumers who, because of religious or cultural norms, are forbidden to eat certain types of transgenic animals (Aldridge 1994, 11–12).

4. Pharmaceutical Production

The use of farm animals as bioreactors for the manufacture of valuable human proteins, enzymes, and hormones is a relatively new idea and made possible through the use of transgenesis. Pilot studies have been successful in implanting human genes in the fertilized eggs of goats, and the protein products are subsequently harvested from the goat's milk. Although the use of animals as sources of human protein is new, animal proteins have traditionally helped save human lives, as indicated by the use of bovine and porcine insulin for the treatment of diabetes. What makes animal-derived pharmaceuticals (those made through pharming) of special significance? It is perhaps in the public perception associated with tinkering with the animal genome. Some view species as a protected gene pool that should not be subject to refashioning by human whim. Others who reject the essentialist and protectionist view of species are opposed to transgenic animals because no stopping point exists that would prevent creating animals that have ever-greater quantities of the human genome that would eventually breach a moral threshold.

5. *Harvesting Human Organs*

The scarcity of human organs for transplants has turned the attention of the medical community to genetically engineered animals with organs (hearts, kidneys, and livers) that are functional and not rejected in humans. There is already precedent for transplanting animal organs into humans when the human organ loss presents a life-threatening condition. In the famous Baby Fae case, the heart of a baboon was transplanted into the body of an infant. The experiment failed, and public opinion was mixed. It is too early to predict whether physiologically successful animal organ transplants in humans will result in some form of stigmatization or psychological distress. But the ethical concerns about animals created with functional human organs may be less about the human recipient than about the animal harboring human anatomical parts. It would seem that public anxiety increases along with the percentage of the animal genome devoted to human genomic elements.

6. *Intellectual Curiosity, Basic Research*

Animal models for human disease have been a cornerstone of biomedical research. Transgenesis offers scientists precisely defined animal models for controlled studies. Examples include the creation of a mouse that has a defective cystic fibrosis regulator (CFTR) gene for the purpose of studying the gene in humans. According to Donnelley, McCarthy, and Singleton (1994), this is an excellent model to mimic cystic fibrosis in humans, because the CF mouse shows many of the same symptoms found in humans. Another application of transgenic animals is the creation of new recreational or learning habitats. A popular fictional account of creating a community of cloned extinct species from fragments of DNA is found in Michael Crichton's *Jurassic Park* (chapter 11, section C).

F. Value Perspectives on Transgenic Animals

Each of the following four approaches to the issue of transgenic animals frames problems differently, operates under a unique set of value assumptions, and poses a different set of moral considerations. The four positions fall under two main categories designated by the terms *androcentric* and *biocentric*, which refer to the moral status of human beings in relationship to other living things. Androcentrism holds that humans have a unique moral status relative to other species, whereas biocentrism posits a moral universe that includes humans along with other species interests and rejects the view that humans are a morally superior species.

Organized social responses to transgenic animals follow the pattern of behavior and attitudes people exhibit when faced with other animal welfare issues. Individual responses are best understood within archetypal value structures associated with various political and ideological constituencies. Four value structures built around androcentrism and biocentrism have been selected for analysis and provide an organizing framework for situating alternative value responses to the creation of transgenic species: androcentric scientism, androcentric culturalism, biocentric individualism, and biocentric holism (table 10).

1. Androcentric Scientism

Scientism is characterized by the search for consistency in applying moral principles, the use of analytical reductionism under which all problems are divisible into component parts, and the compatibility of moral claims with scientific tenets. Ethical considerations are most easily addressed when the rights, obligations, and consequences apply to persons now or in the future. The issues of concern are primarily secular in orientation. Scientism is best able to address ethical issues that are subject to empirically testable hypotheses. Androcentrism means that only humans have intrinsic value and are therefore deserving of absolute moral consideration. The treatment or development of animals is viewed exclusively in terms of their moral relevance to individual human values. From this perspective, the questions that shape the political discourse reveal an underlying value structure and proper points of consideration that focus, ultimately, on human welfare.

1. If we release a transgenic animal into the environment, will it upset the balance of nature and result in losses to humans?

2. How are transgenic animals used in food or pharmaceutical production in ways that are morally different than the ways that other animals are used for these purposes? How is the use of the traditional milk-producing cow any different from the use of transgenic cows for pharmaceutical production, assuming that similar humane treatment provisions are followed?

3. In what morally relevant ways are the use of transgenic animals for harvesting human organs different from breeding animals for food?

4. Is there a relevant moral distinction between transgenic animals and those breeds of animals developed through other forms of

Table 10. Belief Structures and the Ethics of Developing Transgenic Animals

Uses of Transgenic Animals	Androcentric Scientism Individual/Human	Androcentric Culturalism Group/Human	Biocentric Individualism Individual/Life Form	Biocentric Holism Group/Life Form
1. Released into nature	animal welfare; human benefits	religious values; tampering with nature; "brave new world" considerations	animal rights; animal cruelty	respect for species
2. Domesticated or physically contained animals	consumer safety; animal welfare	religious prohibitions; socioeconomic impacts	animal cruelty; violation of species nature	species integrity
3. Food production	consumer safety; animal welfare	religious prohibition; socioeconomic impacts	cruelty to animal; violation of species nature	species integrity
4. Animal pharming (drug production)	consumer safety; animal welfare	hubris	animal cruelty; animals as bioreactors	species integrity
5. Harvesting human organs	human safety; animal welfare	hubris; species mixing; human animal chimera; slippery slope of human eugenics	animal cruelty; pleiotropic effects	restricted evolutionary impact
6. Research/intellectual curiosity	danger of escape; animal welfare; human/animal cost benefit	hubris; slippery slope of human eugenics	animal cruelty; pleiotropic effects	no evolutionary impact; respect for species boundaries

Source: Compiled by the authors

human intervention (for example, artificial insemination, cross-breeding, drugs, or modifying developmental environments)? Because animals are slaughtered for food, what can be wrong with slaughtering animals for organs that would benefit humans?

5. What secular norms proscribe creating transgenic animals for research purposes? Are those norms based on consequential circumstances, such as the escape of a dangerous species, for example, an "AIDS mouse"? If they are not based on consequential circumstances, what other basis could there be for proscribing the creation of new animal types?

Much of American law and regulation is based on this value structure. In recent years emphasis has shifted, as illustrated by laws that protect animals from inhumane treatment in experimental research, wildlife preserves, and agriculture. There is nothing in law that informs society about the rights and responsibilities of creating transgenic species.

2. Androcentric Culturalism

In contrast to scientism, the term *culturalism* signifies that societal norms evolve historically and that consistency is not an ultimate goal; for example, norms may or may not be based on a logically consistent set of moral criteria (some animals are selected out for special consideration based on historical and cultural traditions and outdated or indefensible science). This approach to policy reflects cultural and species diversity.

Androcentric culturism describes a system of values that is human-centered and that places moral primacy in the individual. Greater latitude is given to moral pluralism and the diverse cultural constructions of rationality. Although the issues raised do not demand a "rational" consistency among the moral criteria, they do demand respect for cultural history, identity, and cohesion. As an example, within this moral perspective Eskimos can hunt wildlife that would be restricted to other groups. In this category it is perfectly reasonable to raise questions about the impact of transgenic animals on human culture, religion, and overdependency of society on science for controlling nature (e.g., re-breeding the earth with wild animals that cannot spread rabies). The following questions express the significance of culturally developed norms.

1. Will the creation of new species of animals reinforce to society a dysfunctional value of hubris that gives humans a false sense of empowerment over the biosphere? Humans may feel that they can alter the earth's distribution of species, seed new species, or that

transgenic species can be used as a substitute for replacing endangered species.

2. Is the release of transgenic animals into nature inconsistent with a preservationist ethic? Will it create an overly dependent relationship between society and its scientific institutions? For example, in wildlife management, transgenic species might be used to repopulate an area that is no longer able to support indigenous species.

3. Are there religious prohibitions against certain genetically engineered food products or against the mixing of species genomes?

4. Can the development of transgenic species serve a positive functional role to the general social framework that distinguishes animals from humans, or will transgenic animals create social-psychological dissonance in people and destabilize patterns of relationships between humans and nature? Is there a positive cultural function in having (more or less) distinct animal species? In *Purity and Danger* (1966) Mary Douglas argues that each culture must have its own notions of dirt and defilement which, contrasted with its notions of positive structure, must not be negated. Douglas maintains that there were important functional reasons why some animal species were treated as unclean in ancient cultures. Holiness was exemplified by completeness. This meant keeping the categories of creation in distinct classes. What effect will a research program for mixing species lines have on how humans view their own species? In whose social interest will transgenic species serve?

5. Will popular opinion find it objectionable to mix species traits (chimeric animals) for food production? What about, for example, crosses between fowl and pig?

3. Biocentric Individualism

The emphasis of this value structure is on individual entities. Its biocentric designation indicates that some classes of nonhuman entities have some intrinsic moral worth. It extends the notion of rights and moral obligations associated with the theory of persons to other forms of life. All life forms with some set of designated characteristics have moral status under biocentric individualism. The characteristics vary among biocentric positions (e.g., sentience, interests, cognitive capacities, teleological centers of activity, and response to environmental stimuli). The primary concern is with the abuse of individual animals (cruelty, pain, taking of an animal's life when it is not part of a struggle for survival) and a violation of the animal's well-being or species nature. In considering transgenic animals, biocentric individualism applies the concepts of ethical analysis commonly employed by animal rights advocates and animal welfare societies.

1. Would releasing into nature a transgenic animal that has no means to protect itself from predators or has lost its capacity to compete for food be considered a morally suspect position?

2. Will the creation of transgenic animals expand the human use of animal suffering? Fox (1992, 101) argues that animal suffering is underestimated in the assessment of transgenesis: "Following gene insertion into the embryos, the embryos often fail to develop normally. Some may die in utero and be aborted or resorbed, or some may be born with a variety of defects, sometimes due to what are termed *insertional mutations*. Because these defects may not be manifested until later life, there can be no accurate prediction of whether engineered animals will suffer."

3. Is it possible to create transgenic species without inflicting pain on the novel animal type? Those concerned about the well-being of individual animals were appalled at the creation of the "Beltsville pig," which had numerous afflictions.

4. Is it morally legitimate to intentionally create transgenic animals such as a CFTR (cystic fibrosis regulator) strain of mice that will endure great suffering. We have rules for the treatment of some laboratory animals but none that address the genetic modification of species. Can we talk about a species nature for animals that have been transformed genetically? Can we speak of the animal realizing its species nature?

4. Biocentric Holism

This perspective takes a long-term and systemic look at the biosphere in considering the possible introduction of transgenic species into nature. Moral value derives from the class concept (e.g., species), and those values are egalitarian across species. Primacy is given to classes of entities over the individuals in those classes. Concepts like species nature, species diversity, or species integrity play a central role in this perspective and take precedence over welfare considerations of individual organisms.

Environmental ethicists distinguish between transgenic manipulation of wild animals (the true species prototype) and domesticated animals (which have not evolved into species lines and a social community under natural conditions). Under these circumstances humans do not have moral responsibility for the species integrity of domesticated or laboratory animals, because these species have been artificially manipulated. The value system of biocentric holism may be more permissive of transgenic manipulations of controlled laboratory animals than would normally be proscribed for animals in the wild. Species evolution and animal social groupings have moral relevance, including the relationship between animals and ecosystems. Considerations are given to natural versus human-induced evolution (Colwell 1989). This value structure focuses on classes of living entities, species, and their ecosystems. Critics of this view contend that concepts like 'species' and 'species nature' are artificial constructions and are not consistent with modern evolutionary thought. Nature is a web of life. Boundary lines among organisms are blurred. Humans have always altered the world around them in ways that affect individual organisms and species. Some have argued that human interventions have not always been damaging to species— "We are under no intrinsic moral obligation to respect species barriers" (Donnelly, McCarthy, and Singleton, Jr. 1994, S11).

The following queries are seminal to the political discourse in which species integrity, extinction, biodiversity, and balanced habitat are central categories of analysis.

1. By releasing transgenic animals into nature might one displace an evolved species? Should any consideration be given to the primacy of evolved species over the creation and introduction of transgenic species? Should science and species managers be entrusted with the task of respeciating the planet?

2. Is the jump-starting of evolutionary process through creating new forms of life released into the wild consistent with a concept of biodiversity and respect for nature?

3. Are there some discernable restraints on the transformation of animals, a boundary beyond which it would be deemed unacceptable on evolutionary grounds? One might imagine introducing new species into nature that would disrupt the natural balance of other species or that could not propagate without continuous human intervention.

4. Are there any limits to creating new breeds or chimeras of animals for the sake of expanding human knowledge? Because manipulating small numbers of animals without intention to release them into the environment does not have evolutionary consequences (this cannot be said to hold for transgenic microorganisms, which could easily escape the laboratory and establish themselves in the environment) this framework may be agnostic on the issue of creating chimeric animals for research purposes.

G. Conclusions

The creation of transgenic animals for drug development and food represents the greatest leap beyond conventional agriculture that we have discussed in this work. It is not only a technological innovation but also an innovation in our concept of the farm. The transgenic farm will produce not only food but also pharmaceuticals and human organs. Government policies in patenting and regulation have been highly supportive of transgenic farm animals. The early science looks technically promising, but there appears less public resistance to a transgenic goat that emits a therapeutic protein in its milk than to an animal administered a protein that has been produced in cell culture. A major factor shaping the innovation of transgenic animal drug development is its economic competitive advantage over other methods of drug manufacture. Obstacles to innovation in animal pharming include the low rate of transgenic egg development, the difficulty in putting the foreign gene with its regulatory sequences in the correct place in an animal's germ cell, low expression of foreign protein, and concerns about viral contamination.

Relatively little attention has been given to the alternative paths of transgenic food animals. Whether the Flavr Savr tomato proves to be a useful analogy stands to be seen. The transgenic tomato opposition, after all, does not have the animal rights lobby behind it. That lobby has thus far not stopped the marketing of bovine growth hormone, and it is not clear yet whether it will be a noticeable force in obstructing the development of its transgenic counterpart, a super-lactating cow.

Animal welfare policies, once the sole moral lens for the protection of domesticated pets, have increasingly been applied to farm animals reared for food. How do transgenic animals enter into this debate? Do they add a unique moral dimension? If transgenesis is exclusively seen in welfare terms, then the principal obligation is to ensure that a genetically engineered species does not incur suffering or pain as a result of the gene modification. No special proscriptions regarding the type of animal created seem germane. However, some ethicists have introduced the animal's telos (species nature) as a morally relevant category (Rollin, 1986). Such notions as the telos of an animal are undeveloped, but they suggest a prima-facie obligation not to interfere with or obstruct the telos or obstruct the fulfillment of the animal's special place in nature. This leaves open the question of creating a new telos based on utilitarian criteria. For example, the creation of a transmogrified animal optimally suited to human consumption and mass-produced factory farm feed-lots is, for some animal ethicists, acceptable if the treatment of the animal does not violate its new species nature and if there is no evidence of protracted suffering.

Animal biotechnology has challenged environmental ethicists to establish rational grounds for treating transgenic animals as a mor-ally unique problem. The challenge has led some ethicists to advance a philosophically deeper analysis. But this analysis taps into a lan-guage of metaphysics, religion, or esthetics not likely to create a consensus across varied moral planes. The secular scientism and economic utilitarianism of modern industrial societies resist ab-stract ethical or religious perspectives as a grounding for public policy. Therefore, philosophical or religious critiques of transgenic animals often seek interpretive links to the secular scientific do-main. Protection of natural ecosystems of wildlife has thus gained some currency without the need for ontological justification or the introduction of metaphysical constructs.

The introduction of transgenic animals has not yet found a sta-ble value base in secular society. Instead, there is a translation pro-cess that carries religious or spiritual messages into secular policies. The emotive value of the messages, untranslatable in the syntax of a positivist science, is functional in the political process. The En-dangered Species Act does not speak of sacred species or species nature but rather of near-extinct ones, which translates into an empirically decipherable language in science.

11 The Cultural and Symbolic Dimensions of Agricultural Biotechnology

The nature of land-based farming has remained fundamentally intact through most of agricultural history, as societies have cultivated crops and domesticated animals for consumption and commerce. Crop production has been closely tied to a region's genetic resources and such environmental offerings as climate, soil, and rainfall, as well as the introduction of labor-saving and land management techniques. Agricultural historians point to the mid-nineteenth century and the first quarter of the twentieth century as critical nodes in the development of scientific agriculture (Grigg 1974, 55).

Changes in the mode of agricultural production, whether deep or modest, reflect concurrent changes taking place at many different locuses in society, often involving legal, political, economic, sociological, and technological changes. The interdependencies of agrarian and industrial life are never more evident than when agriculture experiences a revolution (e.g., the change from cultivating the soil with a hoe to a plow), although they also reveal themselves when there are incremental changes (e.g., the change from a spade plow to a crook plow [Curwen and Hatt 1961]). Changes in agriculture rarely if ever are isolated from other cultural happenings such as labor laws, wars, migrations, communications, and enclosure practices. The more clarity that is brought to bear on these relationships, the richer the historical analysis.

Among the most salient impacts of industrialization is that the population engaged in land-based agriculture and the amount of acreage per capita that is devoted to farming has declined steadily. Fewer and fewer people are involved in producing the bulk of a nation's food requirements. In the United States, according to Loew (1993, 106),

"Fewer than 2 percent of Americans now live on farms and engage in production agriculture." That is, with a population of 250 million, barely 2 to 3 million people are involved in the primary production of food. Between 1969 and 1982, for example, the number of U.S. small farms were reduced by 39 percent, while the number of very large farms increased by 100 percent (OTA 1986, 9). According to a report by the U.S. Office of Technology Assessment (1986, 9), "If present trends continue to the end of this century, the total number of farms will continue to decline from 2.2 million in 1982 to 1.2 million in 2000. The number of small and part-time farms will continue to decline but will still make up about 80 percent of total farms. . . . The large and very large farms will increase substantially in number. Approximately 50,000 of the largest farms will account for 75 percent of the agricultural production by year 2000."

Agriculture, once a mode of life, has become a mode of production. Once the cornerstone of local and regional economies, agriculture has become vertically integrated into a global economy. The traditional symbols and metaphors of agrarian life seem dissonant with the industrialization of farming.

Children reared in urban, industrial contexts are introduced at a very early age to the image of the farm through folk tales, rhymes, and story books. Farms are presented as warm and friendly places where extended families form a relationship with the land and where docile and domesticated animals are cared for, protected, befriended and personified. The iconography of farm life embodies the symbols of virtue: hard work, respect for animals, moral responsibility for stewardship of the land, independent entrepreneurship, and respect for family and cultural heritage (Burns 1989). The farm has also been a symbol of an ecologically protected area. No one would think otherwise of the place where food is produced. Images of the farm in proximity to a nuclear power plant or a chemical processing facility have been skillfully used in media campaigns designed to shape public attitudes and gain public acceptability for these technological systems.

In the United States, these powerful images of agriculture and the virtues of agrarian life are embodied in the principles of Jeffersonian democracy. As noted by Buttel and Flinn (1975, 135), "Agriculture was not viewed merely as the source of wealth, but as the foundation of those human virtues and traits most congenial to self-government—a sociological rather than economic value." Even as the modern farm has lost much of its folk character, the mythology of agrarian values persists.

Agriculture [is] one of the main supports of American democracy because it is an occupation embracing millions of freemen who own property and cultivate land on a somewhat equal basis. (Schafer 1936, 289)

As opposed to the great city's mad pursuit of wealth and the things an excess of wealth has made fashionable, the small city, town, village and the countryside, dominated up to now by a rural psychology, still retain the old primal American virtues: a sense of human values, neighborliness, morality, and religion. The farmers from this point of view, are the hope of the nation's future as they have been the chief dynamic force of our country's past. (Schafer 1936, 293)

Against these romanticized images of working and living units where humans and animals form a harmonious balance with nature is the modern high-input farm, which is closer to being a chemical processing facility for plant germ plasm. "The farm's originally organic, coherent, independent production system was expanded into a complex dependence on remote sources and manufactured supplies" (Berry 1981, 130).

Enter biotechnology, a set of genetic and cellular techniques that may further revolutionize certain aspects of agricultural production. The applications of biotechnology to agriculture are beginning to manifest themselves on the deep symbolism associated with contemporary agrarian culture. The notions of what the farm is and what it ought to be, of what food is, and what livestock are, play themselves out in the political discourse emanating from the public wars over biotechnology. Combatants include small farm advocacy organizations, start-up companies, international Green organizations, traditional environmental groups, multinational corporations, natural food associations, and animal rights supporters. The issues are also diverse: a tomato with an inverted gene to slow the ripening process, a microorganism that inhibits frost formation on crops, herbicide resistant crops, microbially produced animal growth hormones, animals that excrete pharmaceuticals in milk, and transgenic animals that yield leaner or breastier meat. The common thread linking these product controversies is a set of genetic technologies that offer highly characterized genetic modifications of bacteria, plants, and animals.

The controversies represent the surficial phenomena of a deeper set of issues that reach beyond the biotechnology industry. The issues tap into a cultural immune system that triggers a response to new product technologies. At a superficial level the global debates over products of biotechnology are about controlling the system of regulation, the conditions of technology transfer, and the criteria according to which technology is approved for commercial application. At another level, the focus of this chapter, the struggle occurs among forces that seek control over the symbolism of agricultural biotechnology and seek to promote a techno-mythology based almost exclusively on the power of genes. Those who eventually gain control over bio-mythology will affect the pathways of innovation for future generations.

The following discussion is about the struggle for control over the symbolic meaning of biotechnology and about the process of myth-making in science. The term *myth* is used judiciously and is not meant to denigrate one side or another in the battles that have erupted over biotechnology. Rather, the term signifies a cultural story that embodies hope, expectations, moral attitudes, and fears or positive visions of modernity. Myths are constructions out of reality and transcend the real into a virtual world of expectations. The following myths and anti-myths will be discussed in their socio-scientific context.

- Biotechnology gives us natural (unnatural) products.
- Biotechnology offers us greater (less) control over nature.
- Biotechnology will contribute to greater (less) biodiversity.
- Biotechnology will be friendly (unfriendly) to the environment.

The propositions are not necessarily independent; for example, being friendly to the environment should be consistent with increased biodiversity. They have been selected as organizing schemas for the analysis of current debates. The first three propositions will be examined in a series, and the fourth will be discussed in the context of the first three. The discussion is organized around the thesis that political debates in biotechnology are essentially about control over techno-mythmaking, defined as the shaping of social expectations through the association with technology of symbolic powers and simple moral virtues.

We are less concerned about the truth or falsity of these claims as we are about how they are used to construct an image of biotechnology.

A. Biotechnology and the State of Nature

Ronald Reagan once commented that trees emit pollutants. As an anti-regulator, his remark was not meant to imply that trees must be controlled. It was, perhaps, designed to rupture the distinction that is widely held within the popular culture between the natural and the unnatural and the association between the natural and the good. Despite Reagan's ploy, the majority of people feel comfortable with the natural/unnatural dichotomy and hold a deeper skepticism toward the unnatural. It is not surprising, therefore, that representatives of the biotechnology industry have described the techniques associated with genetic modification and the resulting pesticidal products as offering a natural alternative to agrichemical products. By advancing the thesis that biotechnology uses nature's own methods of pest control, plant fertilization, or toxic waste degradation, its advocates are hoping to give biotechnology a more favorable image as they drive a wedge between chemical and biological agents used in agriculture.

Not all representatives of the industrial community (e.g., large chemical companies) find it in their self-interest to pit biological agents against synthetic chemical agents. But it is a theme the small venture capital companies advance, in part to win public confidence in genetic technologies and also to create receptive market alternatives to the chemical inputs produced by a few leading corporations.

Efforts to gain control over the term *natural* can be observed in other policy debates. Public anxiety over synthetic additives to the food supply has been met with studies indicating that "natural carcinogens" in the food are more hazardous to consumers than the traces of food additives and pesticides (Ames and Gold 1990). Taken to its logical conclusion, food products would not be regulated any differently if ingredients were indigenous to the plant, taken up in the roots, sprayed on, or added in processing. All products, whether naturally found or synthetically produced, would be on an equal footing. Only demonstrated risks would be subject to regulation, not methods or generic materials of production.

The U.S. Food and Drug Administration (USFDA 1993, 25839) has issued guidelines for regulating transgenic food. The guidelines state that a crop is not made unnatural, nor, as a class, does it exhibit attributes different from foods derived by other methods of plant breeding, by the insertion of a foreign gene. The agency decided not to regulate genetically engineered food as it would food into which synthetic chemicals had been added. Under FDA's proposal, transgenic plants are considered to be no less natural than plants that have been bred selectively. The difference, according to the agency, is that the latter has many undefined genes making up its phenotype whereas the former has a well-characterized genetic locus added.

Within the critical discourse on biotechnology are examples that illustrate efforts to stigmatize genetic engineering as unnatural. There are also efforts to present it as a natural process. Critics who maintain that transgenic plants are not simple extensions of selective breeding emphasize that genetic engineering makes it possible to exchange foreign genes (a gene from a peanut transferred to a tomato) that would otherwise not be introduced by selective breeding or hybridization. But what makes hybridization natural? Could the hybrid seed arise from processes in nature that were not under human direction? The U.S.-based Foundation on Economic Trends has organized a Pure Food Campaign that opposes any genetic manipulations of plants. At least one of the arguments of the campaign is based on the unnaturalness of transgenic food.

Another struggle for control over the symbol *natural* can be found in the controversy over agricultural pesticides. *Natural* in agriculture is synonymous with *organic*, which has been identified by the term *chemically free*. Despite efforts by certain sectors in society to break the link between "natural" and "safe" there remains a powerful association between these concepts. Even though food produced on chemically free farms may contain fungi, insect viruses, and natural carcinogens, organically grown food has a strikingly powerful grip in the public's consciousness over the terms *natural* and *safe*.

Among the boldest promises of biotechnology, and one repeatedly emphasized in the popular scientific press, is that its products will replace synthetic chemical pesticides and fertilizers with biological controls (Gasser and Fraley 1992). For the antichemical pesticide lobby, this would place biotechnology on the side of the angels. The evidence for these claims comes directly from laboratory experiments on pest resistance, nitrogen fixation, and viral resistance in plants. The mythmaking behind this view is that biotechnology has the power to displace a system of chemically intensive agriculture that has evolved for more than a hundred years. The idea that biotechnology will wean agriculture from its chemical fix is widely accepted and cautiously promoted (Harlander 1991b, 156; Miller 1991, 13) despite four significant constraints on the realization of its goals: technological, economic, educational, and political. The products replacing chemical pest controls will have to match or exceed existing efficacy criteria. In addition, economic benefits must equal or outweigh the costs of using chemical controls; farmers need to know how to use alternative products and practices effectively. Finally, a powerful chemical lobby will have to be overcome as biological methods are introduced in conjunction with a softer path to pest control.

While the FDA has sought to treat genetically modified food as it would conventionally bred crops, the U.S. Environmental Protection Agency has a policy that distinguishes transgenic organisms from natural substances. Transgenic organisms other than pesticides are regulated under the Toxic Substances Control Act, a major piece of gap-filling legislation passed in 1976 that requires premanufacture notices of all new chemicals, which has been interpreted to include genetically modified microorganisms. The EPA's commitment to regulating transgenic organisms as chemical substances further blurs the distinction that some proponents of biotechnology have made between nature's "biological friends" and its "chemical enemies."

The importance of the biological friends symbol is exemplified by the bioremediation industry, dedicated to developing microbial techniques for degrading chemical and biological waste. Conventional microorganisms have been used successfully in sewage treatment plants and somewhat less but with some success in degrading toxic chemicals in situ. The industry is comprised mainly of companies that use natural strains of microorganisms that have been screened for their efficiency to degrade a selected substrate. Very few companies in the bioremediation industry in the United States have shown interest in developing genetically engineered strains. Many are concerned that the methods of biotechnology may tarnish the image of an industry that exploits the earth's natural recyclers, those microorganisms that break down chemicals into simpler elemental forms. Unless the biotechnology industry can remove the stigma of genetically engineered microorganisms as a product of a new and untested technology, the field of bioremediation will move with extreme caution into genetically engineered strains.

In another example, industrialists are seeking to exploit the so-called natural qualities of microorganisms in food additives, although the public is strongly apprehensive of artificial chemical additives. Harlander (1989, 200) notes that "consumer concern regarding chemical additives in foods and consumer demand for 'natural' products have resulted in demand for microbial metabolites which can be used as natural ingredients in foods." Microbially produced additives, such as Xanthum gum and monosodium glutamate, come from natural isolates. Seeking to expand microbially produced additives, the food industry will have to persuade the public that genetically engineered "food-grade" microorganisms will also yield natural ingredients if these products are to be received more favorably than synthetic chemical additives. In a somewhat analogous situation, the pharmaceutical industry has advertised microbially produced human insulin as a natural alternative to porcine or bovine insulins.

The perception of biotechnology as natural or unnatural will no more be resolved by empirical study than will our perception of hybrid corn. The reason that the symbol is important, however, has more to do with risk than with the essential meaning of natural. Once the issue of risk is managed, the question of "naturalness" will slowly disappear. Considerable effort has gone into communicating to the public the idea that bioengineered products have inherently no greater risk than products that are not bioengineered.

A National Academy of Sciences report addressed the question of unique hazards of recombinant DNA research (NAS 1987). Finessing the question of whether scientists could create something totally unique to nature, the NAS stated that rDNA presented no unique *hazards*. There is certainly an inferred connection between unique risks and those that are unnatural. If we had a technology that was safe by universal criteria (e.g., passive solar energy), the issue of whether it is natural or unnatural is not likely to be of concern.

In the struggle over symbols, the report represented a major victory for the biotechnology sector. Although somewhat tentative, it contained enough language to serve the interests of a war-torn industry often forced into a defensive posture to justify its existence. For example, it argued that "there is no evidence that unique hazards exist either in the use of R-DNA techniques or in the movement of genes between unrelated organisms" (NAS 1987, 21). It has been argued elsewhere that the NAS conclusion about unique hazards has less to do with good science than it does about political correctness within the scientific fraternity (Krimsky 1991, 142). Regal (1994) has disputed the notion that the safety of transgenic organisms can be established by a generic argument.

B. Greater Control over Nature

One traditional measure of human progress is the degree to which we can control, accommodate to, or survive the forces of nature. Humans have overcome the gravitational force field of the earth, exercised some control over swelling rivers, redefined the landscape by making artificial lakes, rerouted natural water flows, drained wetlands, and irrigated deserts. Yet a growing movement argues that progress is not found in subduing or dominating nature. This group rejects the premise that the goal of humanity is to make nature more rational—that is, more predictable and controllable.

A widely held view is that the new science of molecular genetics offers qualitatively greater degrees of human control over natural processes while releasing a new bounty of benefits to civilization. How much can we extract from nature without paying a price? Does genetic engineering provide more control, or is that an illusion? And if biotechnology does offer more control, is it desirable to exercise that control?

In agriculture, the targets for increased control are weeds, insects, temperature fluctuations, and instability of water supply. For biotechnology to offer greater control over agricultural production it must help to reduce the erratic effects of these external impediments while sustaining high productivity. A case in point involves herbicide resistant crops (HRCs). In theory at least, HRCs can improve weed control by enabling farmers to exercise postemergent herbicide treatment that does not harm the crop. HRCs also give farmers the option of rotating crops that possess different herbicide tolerances. Proponents of HRC development maintain that it offers a more predictable and dependable regime of weed control that is friendlier to the environment because it allows industry to shift from higher-toxicity herbicides (e.g., triazines) to lower-toxicity herbicides (e.g., glyphosate and sulfonylureas).

Battle lines over HRCs were taken up at an early stage in their development while companies were seeking permits to field test transgenic plants. Leading the cause against HRCs in the United States was the Biotechnology Working Group, a coalition of influential environmental public interest organizations. The publication of a widely circulated report titled *Biotechnology's Bitter Harvest* (Goldburg et al. 1990) set the parameters of the environmental offensive. The report excoriated the biotechnology-chemical industry for initiating a vigorous R&D effort for creating new plant species with herbicide resistance. In effect, the report argued that herbicide-tolerant crops will result in farmers' increased dependence on all types of herbicides, the spread of herbicide resistant weeds, an increase in ground and surface water contamination, greater human exposure of applicators and farm workers to toxic chemicals, increased herbicide residues in food, and the contamination of ecosystems. Overall, the report inveighed that this industry initiative represents a cynical disdain for the goals of a sustainable agriculture.

It is inescapable that the widespread use of herbicide-tolerant crops and trees will prolong the use of chemical herbicides for weed control . . . From a social and economic standpoint, the introduction of herbicide-tolerant crops could exacerbate trends toward economic concentration in agriculture, the decrease in farm numbers, and the deterioration of rural communities. Applied to the Third World, such plants could have unwelcome impacts on human and environmental health and genetic diversity, as well as increasing petrochemical dependence. (Goldburg et al. 1990, 55)

Predictably, the reaction from industry was combative. Significant efforts were being made to craft an image of biotechnology as nature's alternative to chemical pesticides. Corporate CEOs spoke optimistically of the new synthesis between environmentalism and agriculture (Harbison, Jr. 1990; Miller 1990). The critics of HRCs, exploiting the difficulty of fitting these products into the newly constructed image, undermined industry efforts to control the symbols of biotechnology as environmentally and economically friendly. In response, supporters of HRCs dismissed the arguments of environmentalists as unscientific and ideological. The high-profile environmental magazines carried a message that the biotechnology industry hoped to avoid—that companies are engineering herbicide resistance into all major crops and the upshot is more chemical dependence (Russell 1993; Weintraub 1992).

The subtle details of the controversy over the environmental impacts of HRCs are linked to the broader struggle over the importance of herbicide resistance in the future of agriculture. Two distinct images of the farm view herbicide resistant crops as having either a rich or a dim future in food production. Rooted in the texts of Judeo-Christianity and later reinforced in the post-Baconian scientific Enlightenment, the largely dominant view of nature is that humans must place under their control the wild and irrational forces of their environment. Such control is obligatory if we are to exploit nature's largess at highest efficiency, and there are esthetic, moral, and religious justifications for exacting such control. In brief, when nature is rationalized it looks more pleasing, it better serves people's interests, and, according to Western religious doctrine, it rewards the Creator, who has implored humans to harness nature's secrets and subdue its irrational impulses.

An alternative vision of the farm is that of an organic and dynamic ecosystem that cannot function under the type of mechanistic control found in industrial manufacture. In the agricultural system humans must still understand their role as one among other species living in balance. Pests are an inevitable part of a farm's landscape;

farmers must learn to cohabit the land while reaping a generous but not overly selfish yield. Efforts to eradicate unwanted intruders totally in the growing area have generally failed. Once the mindset is changed from eradication to management, however, a more ecocentric approach to agriculture is possible. Perkins (1980) distinguishes between the total population management and the integrated pest management paradigms that were both developed during the 1950s. The former held to the assumption that annihilation of certain pests was within technological capability; the latter school of pest management was content in maintaining pests below certain economic thresholds. These alternative visions of the farm result in vastly different roles for HRCs.

Among the current justifications for greater weed control are fears over food security. Because the world population increases by ninety to a hundred million annually, Malthusian logic tells us that greater political instability due to scarcity of basic food will result if agricultural yields are not increased (Rogoff and Rawlins 1987). Levidow (in press) argues that industry has embraced food security as the raison d'être for a total systemic control which chemical-intensive methods failed to achieve. The failure of chemical control methods has been documented by Pimentel et al. (1992, 750): "Despite the widespread use of pesticides in the United States, pests (principally insects, plant pathogens, and weeds) destroy 37 percent of all potential food and fiber crops. . . . Although pesticides are generally profitable, their use does not always decrease crop losses. For example, even with the tenfold increase in insecticide use in the United States from 1945 to 1989, total crop losses from insect damage have nearly doubled from 7 percent to 13 percent."

And why should biotechnology offer the prospect of eradicating pests or improving the efficiency of pest control that has eluded the chemical enterprise? The new hubris of controlling nature arises from the distinction between internal and external controls. To control nature externally is to apply physical force, chemical modifications, or energy supplements on the existing agricultural system. In contrast, internal controls involve modifying the genetics of plants to establish a more efficient system of food production with greater accommodation to external variations. An example of internal controls is the production of virus or insect resistant plants through the introduction of genes that immunize the plant or emit a protein toxic to the insect. The use of HRCs represents a combination of internal and external controls where transgenic plants are used in conjunction with chemical controls (Schell, Gronenborn, and Fraley 1989).

The prospect of controlling agricultural yield through the genome of plants evokes a greater degree of power over nature than that of manipulating external factors. Part of the reason for this is the success of scientific reductionism. Explaining a phenomenon by reducing it to its smallest components remains the ultimate objective of contemporary science. Elementary particle physics, which for all practical purposes has no commercial utility, remains among the most revered of the scientific enterprises. It garners social expenditures of billions of dollars to explore the smallest particles of nature. It is perhaps part of the general scientific ethos inherited from the philosophy of physics that prediction and control are linked and that the power of prediction is heightened as one moves to smaller and smaller units of analysis.

Does biotechnology offer the possibility of greater control over insect resistance than is achievable with chemical pesticides? It is well recognized that insect populations are highly adaptable to chemical pesticides. Georghiou (1988) notes that at least 504 insect species have developed resistance to one or more chemicals. On the basis of what is known about insect ecology, Gould (1988, 146) concludes, "There is no reason to expect that insects will not be able to adapt to these biopesticides."

Ironically, as Harlander (1989, 196) notes, the solution to the pesticide dilemma may be sought in a radically alternative system of agriculture, such as massive tissue culture factories, which have no ecological pests and therefore no need for chemical pesticides: "Plant cell culture used for the production of natural food ingredients offers several distinct advantages over extraction of these components from plants. Seasonal variations, unfavorable weather conditions, and epidemic diseases are not problems when plant tissue is grown under well-defined and controlling laboratory conditions."

The concept of control is deceptive, as critics of the hypothesis that biotechnology will offer greater control over nature point out. To control a single variable might mean losing control over others. The idea that we will gain greater dominance over complex interactions among plants, insects, and environmental factors by manipulating a few choice genes is, nevertheless, an appealing if not fanciful notion (section E).

C. Biotechnology and the Diversity of Nature

The United Nations Conference on Environment and Development, held in Brazil in 1992, brought considerable attention to the question of biological diversity. The Convention on Biological Diversity was adopted by ninety-eight countries. Noticeably absent as a signatory nation was the United States. The Bush administration opposed the convention on the grounds that it would undermine U.S. patent protection for the biotechnology industry. A specifically targeted concern of the treaty was that "the original possessor of naturally occurring materials can assert an interest in derivative materials after allowing them to leave their possession" (Burk, Barovsky, and Monroy 1993, 1901). Although the controversy was over intellectual property rights and the ownership of genetic resources, its outcome was that biotechnology and biodiversity are in opposition.

The connection between patent rights and the loss of biodiversity was first raised in the mid-1980s when it was noted that small seed companies were being bought out by multinationals like Monsanto and Ciba-Geigy, where the synchronous development of seeds and agrichemicals was being pursued (Doyle 1985). According to the logic of this argument, patenting of genetic resources results in fewer plant varieties and the control over those varieties by a group of oligopolistic enterprises. Fox (1992, 133) is among those skeptical that biodiversity is compatible with large-scale industrial interests in biotechnology: "There is an accelerating loss of biodiversity caused by agribusiness's overreliance on a few utility strains and varieties of seed stock and livestock." In the view of Hobbelink (1987, 8), the outcome of patent rights for germ plasm would mean "the total loss of genetic diversity that is maintained in the field by farmers through the selection and use of their own seed."

Ironically, representatives of the biotechnology industry have been actively promoting the new industry as inherently compatible with biological diversity, particularly since the symbolism of biodiversity has gained a prominent place in public consciousness. Environmentalists have invoked biodiversity as a standard to which agricultural biotechnology must measure up. The battle over control of the symbolism has been particularly complex because so many different aspects of biodiversity are involved. The message emanating from the community of international development nongovernment organizations is that biodiversity is a political and not a technical problem, therefore it could never be solved by biotechnology (Shand 1994).

The practice of diversity can be ensured only through decentralization. Centralized systems of research, production, or conservation force the spread of genetic uniformity and genetic erosion (Shiva 1990, 47; Shiva 1993).

Another concern linking threats to biodiversity with the release of genetically engineered plants is that the latter could run amok in the environment and overtake other plant species, particularly those already on the endangered list. Faced with hypothetical prospects of species displacement, worldwide attention has focused on the risks of releasing transgenic plants into the environment (Stevens 1993; Wrubel, Krimsky, and Wetzler 1992).

Industrial interests have vigorously promoted biotechnology as compatible with and nurturing of biodiversity. Some of their arguments have persuaded mainstream environmentalists (Speth 1989). One argument is based on improving agricultural productivity through biotechnology. This will enable more food to be grown on less land, resulting in more land used for other purposes (Macer 1990, 32). This is an all-purpose argument that could apply to any technology, even chemical technology or innovations in high-yield seeds, that improved productivity. Increases in the world population could wipe out any biodiversity benefits derived from higher productivity. The argument also assumes that by improving productivity and narrowing diversity in agricultural land we increase or maintain biological diversity in the fields left fallow (Dixon 1990). The argument would be more credible if there were evidence that improvements in production per hectare resulted from technological innovations, for example, high-yield strains, mechanization, and increased biodiversity in land that was protected from cultivation.

Finally, there is another link between biotechnology and biodiversity that is uniquely associated with the creation of novel species. With new techniques that enable scientists to create intergeneric crosses of plants, animals, and microorganisms there is the prospect of an artificially created biodiversity. This initiative may take several forms. One path is the substitution of hardier strains of plants and animals that can survive new environments that have been affected by human development. Plant and animal germ plasm can also be banked for withdrawal if a crisis of extinction arises. Finally, the fictional dinosaur park in the novel and then film *Jurassic Park* offers an extreme view of an artificially constructed ecological system reinstituting extinct species. The symbol of a Jurassic Park is precisely what the biotechnology industry seeks to avoid, that is, the introduction of uncontrollable and possibly irreversible risks in an effort to create greater diversity.

D. Agricultural-Industrial Inversion

The rapid industrialization and corporatization of farming that has taken place since the end of World War II has little to offer the image of the farm as the embodiment of pastoral life. Despite the transformation of agriculture and the decline of agrarian culture in many industrial nations, the farm is still the place where germ plasm, sun, water, and earth are transformed to basic foodstuff. With the exception of certain fruits and vegetables, most food undergoes some amount of processing before reaching the marketplace (Harlander 1989, 197). The trend is toward fewer unprocessed crops; even apples are sprayed routinely with pesticides and chemical ripening agents, and cucumbers are waxed in preparation of their route to market.

The distinction of farm and city has always been a central theme in American cultural history. Although we understand that modern large-scale farms are not pristine habitats and well-balanced sustainable ecosystems, there is still enough in the practice of farming, particularly its dependence on sunlight, soil, plants, and animals to distinguish it from industrial manufacture, characterized by a closed system of production and nonrenewable sources of energy. Moreover, the romantic view of the traditional farm as a place where food is grown without synthetic chemicals remains a powerful anchor for the advocacy work of numerous groups that refuse to accept the premise that the trade-off for modernization is the abandonment of a chemically free agriculture.

Biotechnology, however, raises the possibility of an industrial agricultural inversion. The characteristics of this inversion are twofold. First, increasingly, the farm will be used to manufacture products that have traditionally been produced in industrial settings. Second, food production will take place to a greater degree outside of the farm in enclosed continuous process bioreactors. In an essay titled "Food without Farms" Anderson (1990) describes a process of food production involving plant tissues, enzymes, and a basic nutrient feedstock. The author describes research in which citrus juice vesicles can be produced from cells in culture without need for the orange, grapefruit, or lemon.

The change of food production from a land-based system to a tissue-culture system would enable food producers to have much greater control over their output. First, food production would not be seasonally dependent, because tissue cultures can be grown in controlled industrial settings in a continuous process. This would be the ultimate rationalization of food production that could overcome biotic and abiotic factors affecting food security—droughts, floods, crop diseases, and the cut-off of fossil-fuel supplies. The feedstock

in the tissue-culture production system would still be agriculturally derived, which still requires some land-based farming. But crops
grown only as feedstock would be much less vulnerable to environmental threats. "If the basic crops were trees or brush, they would
require less fertilizer and water, and they would probably need less
expended effort to help them fight off their enemies. . . . So, instead
of farms as we know them, with their seasonal crops, we would have
plantations of trees or brush that would be harvested periodically
as needed. The wood would then be broken down by a biochemical
process into simple sugar syrups, eventually transported to food factories" (Anderson 1990, 20).

The trend in agricultural biotechnology is to allocate land-based
agriculture for the raw materials of production. Differentiation of
food products, once under the control of farmers, may begin to shift
to industrial tissue culture farms, just as food processing, which
began after World War I in the form of canned products, became so
prevalent after World War II with the introduction of frozen foods.
Technological advances in refrigeration, spoilage retardants, and
transport in large part were responsible for the shift to processed and
packaged foods.

Proteins harvested from bacteria (called single-cell protein, or
SCP) are already being used as a source of animal feed (Smith 1980).
The basic concept is to convert an inexpensive waste feedstock into
protein through the use of microorganisms. Jeffcoat (1991, 478) cites
as possible feedstocks carbon dioxide, methane, methanol, sugars,
and hydrocarbons. Even if the feedstock for microbial fermentation
derives from land-based agriculture, the metaphor of the farm may
more closely approximate a mining industry whereupon raw materials (carbohydrates and sugars) once "mined" are processed into
consumer products (proteins).

Traditional boundaries between agriculture and industry, particularly in drug and chemical manufacture, are becoming blurred.
Transgenic animals have been modified with foreign genes that express scarce human proteins. Through this process called "gene
pharming," useful pharmaceutical products have been produced in
sheep, goats', and cows' milk. Gene pharming is an example of the
type of role reversal we have been discussing; industrial production
is transferred to the farm. A Dutch company called Gene Pharming
Europe BV has developed the world's first genetically engineered bull
with a gene that allows his daughters to produce human milk protein (*Journal of Commerce* 1992). The benefits of this process lie in

the fact that producing drugs in animal milk costs a fraction of producing them in a traditional bioreactor.

Genetically modified tobacco plants show promise for producing enzymes for the food industry. Polyhydroxybutyrate is a biodegradable thermoplastic derived from many species of bacteria. The genes from a bacterium that encodes the enzymes required for synthesizing PHB were placed in a plant virus, which is then able to infect a plant by inserting the desired genes. If this promising technique works, it may be the initial step in the production of novel biopolymers in plants through genetic engineering (Poirier et al. 1992).

The distinction between products of industrial and agricultural origin is one of the boundaries that biotechnology calls into question. There is plenty of precedent, however, for the breakdown of farm-industry polarities. The modern, high-efficiency farm uses Tayloristic assembly-line practices. Much of the machinery must be supplied from the sources outside of the farm's operation. And the Industrial Revolution created a new demand for selected agricultural crops such as cotton, wool, jute, rubber, and vegetable oils (Grigg 1974, 284). The products themselves may undergo processing or treatment before distribution into consumer markets. Thus, innovations in biotechnology are giving new emphasis to an agricultural-industrial nexus that has been evolving for more than a century.

The distinction between rural and urban contributions to an industrialized economy can no longer be grounded on an essentialist view of production-sector modalities. Food, fibers, and commercial chemicals may come either from an industrial processing plant or from land-based agriculture. If biotechnology is successful, Busch et al. (1991, 190) predict that the "elimination of major portions of the farming enterprise" will "displace farmers and farmworkers on a scale never before possible. . . . we can expect the not-so-gradual reduction of spatial, temporal, and climatic barriers to food and fiber production. This change alone will bring with it substantial social upheavals as the location of production changes. In addition, we can expect the elimination of major portions of the farming enterprise if field crops are grown *in vitro.*"

These changes notwithstanding, the concept of the traditional small family farm rooted in a popular mythology persists, possibly because of its historical significance in the nation's development (there are still more than one million small farms in the United States) and the fact that a farm is an archetypal symbol of family values and independent entrepreneurship that people refuse to give up easily.

E. Genetic Power and Techno-Mythmaking

Every ancient culture has created myths. These are the stories in which fantasy, reality, moral education, sacred values, cosmogony, life's lessons, and the transmission of valued traditions are all mixed together. In the many studies of myths in history scant attention has been given to mythmaking in contemporary society. Perhaps it is because of arrogance that scientific secularism refuses to see itself as creating myths, which it views as an activity relegated to prescientific societies and a study of folklorists. Mythmaking, after all, is a revelatory approach to truth and a substitute for scientific rationality. But if we view mythmaking as a process of inventing powerful new symbols that introduce a set of values or expectations that explain our origins or essential being and help define a path to the future, then it is possible to see the role that myths have had in contemporary societies.

Cultural anthropologists have learned that myths are more than the expressions of primitive wisdom. Some have observed that myths are the precursors to a system of law and moral truths, in that myths provide a unifying cognitive structure for social cohesion: "Myth fulfills in primitive culture an indispensable function; it expresses, enhances, and codifies belief; it safeguards and enforces morality; it vouches for the efficiency of ritual and contains practical rules for the guidance of man" (Eliade 1963, 20).

Mythmaking in contemporary science has less to do with practical rules for the guidance of individual human behavior than it does with the choice of future pathways for societal development. Techno-myths, as we call them, provide hopeful symbols and comforting beliefs during periods of uncertainty, anxiety, and change. These beliefs may be speculations, exaggerations, or even false notions of hope, but they are designed to achieve social commitment to unanimity of purpose. Scientific myths are anchors of belief in a selected conception of modernity. "Myth is above all a cultural force . . . an indispensable ingredient of all culture" (Malinowski 1926, 91–92). For example, each technological revolution has its power myth. Nuclear energy was going to produce so much inexpensive electricity that it would not have to be metered. The myth of nuclear energy was replaced with the myth of fusion power, according to which energy would not only be plentiful but also compatible with a safe environment. We also witnessed the myth of DDT, a safe and universal solution for the eradication of insect pests followed by a grander myth about a chemical utopia built on synthetic organic molecules.

After decades of studying myths in native cultures, anthropologists began to recognize the parallels in functional roles between ancient and modern myths. Mythmaking, ultimately, is about securing beliefs: "Every culture will create and value its own myths, not because it may not be able to distinguish between truth and falsity, but because their function is to maintain and preserve a culture against disruption and destruction. They serve to keep men going against defeat, frustration, disappointment; and they preserve institutions and institutional processes" (Gotesky 1952, 530).

It is now generally, although perhaps not universally, accepted that genetic technology is capable of transforming biological entities significantly beyond what could be achieved with traditional technology. Modern biotechnology has brought biology from a predominantly analytical phase to a new synthetic phase in its historical development. The possibilities for rearranging species are, for all practical purposes, unlimited. Various interests are involved in a struggle over the power images of modern biology. Power is central to the mythmaking that is taking place. For staunch supporters of biotechnology, genetic power translates into investor confidence. Venture capitalists ride the wave of biotechnological power while the established corporate sectors reinforce the notion that genes hold the key to a new economic order.

In the postchemical period of industrialization, a new folklore of a healing technology has emerged. According to this new wisdom, biotechnology will reestablish our balance with nature; it will offer a cornucopia of curative and safe products. The same promoters of biotechnology are not blind to the critics who also embrace the metaphor of genetic power. In this case, however, power is read as the potential for a technological disaster and must be played down, especially in communications with the media. The great abundance of discourse on biotechnology cites its power to cross species barriers and introduce completely new traits into indigenous organisms (Olson 1986). Periodically, scientists dispute this message, as illustrated in a *Boston Globe* headline, "Splice Genes? Nature Did It Long Before the Geneticists" (Fellman 1992, 45). There is no dearth of inconsistency in how the science media reports on the power of genetic technology.

Promoters of biotechnology must walk a fine line in this game of symbols. They accept the power metaphor but interpret it as inherently safe power, like the power of solar energy. The grand techno-myth is that with genetic engineering we can fine-tune nature, preserve its diversity while reaping its bounty. Organisms can be genetically modified "in less time and with greater precision, predictability and control than possible with traditional methods" (Harlander 1991, 84).

In the cultural sphere of environmental activism, power signals apprehension. Political activists exploit the power metaphor by emphasizing risk and uncertainty. There is no safe power. The means by which one controls a powerful technology is not with more technology. Therefore, unless the social values are worked out in advance, genetic power is greeted with suspicion. While critics emphasize genetic power as a threat, they also dismiss it as a false power that will not solve societal problems (Tokar 1992).

In the social arena, stakeholders who may disagree about the value of biotechnology continue to advance the myth of genetic power. Not only has the mythology developed around the power of techniques, but the gene has also, uniquely, been afforded a special metaphysical status. "The myth of the all-powerful gene is based on flawed science that discounts the environmental context in which we and our genes exist" (Hubbard and Wald 1993, 6). Ultimately, as the myth of genetic power gains in significance, less emphasis is placed on alternative technologies and on social determination rather than corporate determination of technological futures. Myths are social constructions designed to protect beliefs and invoke order. If this interpretation is correct, then the strongest effort at mythmaking for biotechnology is expected in those periods where the greatest threat to the success of commercialization of biotechnology takes root, for example, periods of social mobilization against specific products or technologies.

Once embedded in public consciousness, techno-myths are difficult to displace. For this reason, different constituent groups view the struggle to control, at the outset, the images of biotechnology as so essential. Successful techno-myths will blunt society's critical perspective. New information inconsistent with the orthodox view is easily discredited or ignored. It is the responsibility of independent scientists and policy analysts to compare the constructed images of biotechnology with empirical reality. Increased collaboration between university scientists and industry is eroding the value of the critical independent perspective of academic scientists on the assessment of new technologies. If that role is relinquished, biotechnology will become self-reifying. The media, the general public, and much of science will not be in a position to distinguish appearance from reality.

Conclusion: Agricultural Biotechnology in the Public Arena

Our review of agricultural biotechnology is based on the research and developments that have occurred since the early 1980s. Biotechnology, at this early stage, is changing so rapidly that it would be presumptuous for us or anyone else to extrapolate our results into the future. Whether the first generation of agricultural bioengineering serves as a template for the next generation remains to be seen. On the basis of our analysis it is fair to say that the level of pre-market public scrutiny of some of the first products of agricultural biotechnology has been unprecedented. Citizens are demanding earlier entry points and broader participation in technological decisions.

A. Elements of Social Critique

The policy issues in agricultural biotechnology have been exceptionally well articulated in diverse media sources. In part, this may be due to the fact that at no time in modern history has a society had so many "watchdog" groups made up primarily of nonprofit advocacy organizations dedicated to promoting an idea, a way of life, or simply democratic participation in technological decisions.

The record for the largest public mobilization in opposition to a technology probably goes to nuclear processes divided between weapons production and electric power generation. Those popular movements brought many middle-of-the road Americans into electoral politics, citizen coalitions, and, in some cases, nonviolent militant actions. While there has not been a comparable citizen mobilization for other technologies, the antinuclear movements fertilized the soils of citizen participation, enabling many other grass-roots organizations to get started. The citizen mobilizations over nuclear power created a culture of expectation that spilled over to public actions in the areas of toxics, treatment of animals, and local environmental movements.

Social movements in biotechnology began in the mid-1970s. A few individuals from national environmental groups like Friends of the Earth, the Environmental Defense Fund, the Sierra Club, and the Natural Resources Defense Council set their sights on the recombinant DNA controversy, which took its most visible form at the community level in Cambridge, Massachusetts. One of the most influential individuals during the early stages of public examination of biotechnology was a New York–based Friends of the Earth organizer by the name of Francine Simring, who helped create a group called the Coalition for Responsible Genetics (CRG). Drawing from environmental organizations, public health fields, labor, and universities, CRG brought public attention to the issue of laboratory safety in biological research. Beyond that, it also addressed the ethics of science and the responsibility of business in launching a new technological frontier. Much of the campaign of the coalition was directed at lobbying for regulations at the local, state, and federal levels. The coalition later became the committee and then, after further maturation, the Council for Responsible Genetics.

Another leading advocacy initiative was spearheaded by Jeremy Rifkin, director of the nonprofit Foundation on Economic Trends, a Washington, D.C.–based media and litigation-focused public interest organization. Rifkin, unlike his counterparts in the mainstream environmental organizations, questioned whether genetic engineering should ever be used. His organization launched public campaigns and litigations against many segments of the biotechnology field (Krimsky 1991, 119–24).

In the area of agriculture and food, developments in biotechnology brought new voices of protest from some unsuspecting sectors. The debate over ice minus in several communities in California prompted protests from members of the German Green Party. Local officials and community representatives in Monterey County, California, opposed the secrecy of site selection for field tests and demanded the community have informed consent before the release of a genetically engineered organism. When Advanced Genetic Sciences, the company that developed ice minus, worked with community leaders in advance of the test, local opposition faded. Subsequent to the first federally sanctioned release in Brentwood, California, of ice minus, there were hundreds of field tests for transgenic plants and a few GEMs without community opposition or national controversy. The ice minus debates in the mid-1980s were a precursor to the later social controversies over food products in biotechnology. At the time of the proposed field tests, some farmers opposed ice minus on the grounds that the antifrost organism would destabilize the potato economy by opening marginal land in the frost belt to potato farming. The equity issue never went beyond the farm community.

Calgene's Flavr Savr tomato prompted public concerns about the safety and purity of the food supply. Like ice minus, no new proteins were added to the tomato genome, although existing genes were rearranged (such as the antisense gene). The Flavr Savr raised the prospect that genes from different food sources, exchanged and re-arranged, might alter the quality, toxicity, or nutritional value of food sources. The media delighted in the term *frankenfood*. Opposition to genetically modified food came from the nation's leading chefs. At issue was the dignity of the food supply even more than its safety. Arctic fish may have an antifreeze protein in their blood, but the chefs questioned whether the genes for foreign proteins ought to be transposed willy-nilly to other food products.

The National Wildlife Federation was host to a project on biotechnology under the helm of two able public interest advocates, Margaret Mellon and Jane Rissler. Their work focused on environmental release of transgenic organisms and herbicide resistant crops. Funded by the Joyce Foundation, Mellon and Rissler publish the *Gene Exchange*, which provides detailed information about industry initiatives and agency decisionmaking. Rissler and Mellon transported the biotechnology project to the Union of Concerned Scientists, which distributed their 1993 report *Perils amidst the Promise* (Rissler and Mellon 1993), evaluating the ecological risks from transgenic plants and citing inadequate government oversight.

Many environmental and sustainable agriculture groups viewed transgenic food as a symbol of the assault on traditional sources of food. A small number of groups opposed any form of genetically modified food, but the general focus of public policy turned toward the question of labeling. Other issues raised in policy debates, such as allergenicity and dietary concerns of religious groups, were subsumed under the labeling issue.

The impact of biotechnology on animals became visible to citizens in three ways. First, the decision of the Patent and Trademark Office to grant patents for animals brought concerns from animal breeders who wished to protect breeders' rights. Second, the creation of transgenic animals signaled a new era that some likened to *Jurassic Park*, where animal species boundaries represented a new conquerable frontier. The "Beltsville pig," a transmogrified chimeric animal, was used to exemplify the claim that biotechnology applied to animals means cruelty. Animal rights groups and humane associations asked for bans or strict controls on manufacturing life forms. Transgenic animals raise a striking irony. If a new species is created with genetic engineering, is that organism protected from extinction by the Endangered Species Act? What are society's obligations to protect a chimeric species and its habitat?

The treatment of farm animals became one of the principal causes célèbres directed at bovine growth hormone (BGH). Some evidence suggests that animals on a BGH diet experience more stress and possibly a greater incidence of disease. Humane societies, food cooperatives, sustainable agriculture groups, vegetarians, and consumer advocates brought their concerns to FDA, the lead agency over veterinary drugs. In addition to the concern about the treatment of animals and the lingering fear of contaminated milk, small farmer organizations formed coalitions with soft technology advocates opposing BGH for its adverse impact on small family dairy farms.

B. Environmental Impacts of Biotechnology

The promotional writings about biotechnology's place within the new ethic of a sustainable planet are manifold. Speaking of the expectations of biotechnology, the Office of Technology Assessment wrote about its role in developing "environmentally benign methods of managing weeds and insect pests (OTA 1991, 99). In previous chapters we have reviewed a series of agricultural innovations arising from biotechnology. Some are seeing the light of commercial profitability; others have not succeeded beyond the concept stage. Many of the most promising products of biotechnology, from an environmental perspective, such as nitrogen-fixing and drought-tolerant plants have proven to be unattainable with the current level of scientific expertise. Microbial products that could improve the biological control of insects, weeds, and pathogens have been slow to develop (chapter 6). Enhanced nitrogen-fixing bacteria that are to be applied to crops that already fix nitrogen might increase alfalfa and soybean yields but would have little impact on the amounts of nitrogen fertilizer applied to crops (chapter 7).

The greatest progress has been made in creating transgenic crops resistant to pests and herbicides. The eventual environmental impact of herbicide resistant crops remains controversial, and critics argue vociferously that they do nothing but reinforce the pesticide treadmill (chapter 2). We have argued that herbicide resistant crops might have an environmental benefit if the use of older, more hazardous herbicides is curtailed and integrated weed management is encouraged. These potential benefits would be compromised if the adoption of HRCs leads to a proliferation of herbicide resistant weeds. Virus resistant crops are beginning to reach the marketplace (chapter 4). Their potential environmental benefits include some reduction in insecticide use and possibly reduced crop acreage arising from increased yield. Insect resistant crops have the most obvious and favorable environmental impact by reducing the use of insecticides. However, the possibility that insects will develop resistance to the *Bt* δ-endotoxins looms large over the success of this strategy.

There are other indicators of environmental friendliness. If we can produce the same product with less cultivated land, more land could be left as a natural habitat in support of biodiversity. This was the line of argument that resulted in claims for a positive environmental result from the use of bovine growth hormone. If milk can be produced with fewer cows, that would reduce the manure in the waste stream and remove cultivated land from dairy farming. However, the loss of dairy farms may not result in opening more natural habitats. Without local and regional land use statutes protecting farmland, more than likely the farms will be sold off as developments. Therefore, the outcome of BGH is that there would be fewer farmland habitats distributed over sectors of exurbia.

Another measure of environmental impact for BGH is whether fewer cows producing the same quantity of milk would require less resources from the earth (e.g., grain per liter of milk produced). It is possible that there could be a gain here, but it would be at the expense of stressing the organs and metabolic processes of an animal. Public debates over BGH have forced the value issues to the foreground, particularly human responsibility to other living forms. Even though animals are exploited for human use, are there limits beyond which it would be immoral to stress their bodies?

A popular guidepost of environmental quality in food production is the degree to which biotechnology contributes to a sustainable agriculture. Among the salient conditions of a sustainable agriculture are reduction of high-intensity inputs, maintenance of soil fertility, protection of biodiversity, attention to renewable resources and pollution prevention, and a focus on indigenous crops. There is nothing intrinsically sustainable or nonsustainable about biotechnology. It represents a set of tools that must be viewed within the political economy of agriculture. In itself, biotechnology cannot be a sustainable process unless it is embedded into a system of sustainable agriculture.

We can see two paths for biotechnology. The first is analogous to the path of the Green Revolution, where high-yield varieties were developed as generic seeds to be used in widely divergent locales under prescribed conditions involving the application of chemical adjuvants. The second path uses biotechnology to improve the efficiency of indigenous or locally adapted introduced crop varieties (e.g. corn in the United States or cassava in Africa) to meet abiotic and biotic impediments without intense chemical inputs. For example, biotechnology might be used to improve the salt and drought tolerance of plants already being used in a certain region.

The first plant products of biotechnology that will have environmental impacts are transgenic crops for pest control. Generally, these transgenic crops follow closely the pesticide paradigm of using a single control mechanism, usually a toxin, to protect crops. As such they do not fit neatly into the ideal sustainable agriculture model. However, we can envision ways in which each of the product types can be used within the existing agricultural system to reduce reliance on environmentally harmful pesticides and encourage a more sustainable approach to pest management.

Strategies that exploit transgenic plants or microbes as the sole solution to pest problems will likely suffer the same fate as reliance on pesticides. Pests, like all populations of organisms, are dynamic systems that respond to changes in their environments through natural selection. There is no reason to believe that resistance to biotechnology-based pest controls will not evolve among insects, weeds, and pathogens as has happened for pesticides. To have an important and long-lasting positive environmental and agricultural impact, the products of biotechnology should be considered as tools to be incorporated into larger pest management systems rather than as *the* solution to pest problems. The judicious use of insect resistant crops would allow farmers to conserve the natural enemies of pests and design systems that promote reduced pesticide use. In contrast, the planting of thousands of acres of insect resistant crops as insurance against having a pest problem would likely result in the rapid evolution of new pest resistance. Will companies refrain from selling transgenic seed as quickly as possible to conserve a valuable tool? Our concern is that the pressure to gain markets and show profits will result in companies releasing transgenic pest control products without proper consideration of the long-term impacts on pest management.

BGH use also reinforces intensive livestock production and views food production as an isolated system rather than being integrated with other agricultural practices. In contrast, rotational grazing represents an alternative path to high-input, high-polluting dairy farming (Byrnes 1993).

Transgenic fish with a growth gene represents another example of a product that drew protests from the environmental community. Ecological concerns over transgenic fish were heightened when it was learned that scientists at Auburn University had created a genetically engineered carp that contained a growth hormone gene from a rainbow trout. The Auburn scientists planned to introduce the carp in outdoor ponds at a university aquaculture research facility. The facility was built on a flood plain, rendering it vulnerable to storm runoff, which would introduce fish into the creek breaching the aquaculture containment. No federal guidelines were in place to regulate this type of release of a transgenic fish, an outcome that illustrates the incremental nature of standard-setting and the fact that the technology was outpacing regulatory oversight.

C. Biodiversity and Biotechnology

One of the key questions linking biotechnology and the environment relates to biodiversity. Is biotechnology neutral to biodiversity? Critics of biotechnology, like Shiva (1993), Doyle (1985), and Fowler et al. (1988), see a clear path from biotechnology to a reduction in biodiversity and eventually to a diminution in environmental quality. A form of this argument can be reconstructed as follows. Biotechnology has the capacity to create a greater variety of commercial plants, but this is unlikely to happen. The strategy of the multinational corporation is to create broad international markets for any single product. Shiva (1993, 114) distinguishes between the diversification of commodities and the diversification of nature. "Although breeders draw genetic materials from many places as raw material input, the seed commodity that is sold back to farmers is characterized by uniformity."

The second link between biotechnology and biodiversity is found in the contributions biotechnology makes to the ownership of genetic resources. The U.S. Patent and Trademark Office has favored increasing patent protection for plants, microorganisms, and animal species. Full patent rights to plants were granted in 1985 and to animals in 1987. If patent protection is extended through international agreements like the General Agreement on Tariffs and Trade (GATT) to cover seeds of farmers in developing countries, they may lose power over their vital agricultural inputs because they cannot sequence and modify the genes of germ plasm used in their region. Thus, a patent claim over a seed variety with a specific phenotype, for example, high oil content or insect resistance, can cover all variations of the genotype with these characteristics.

Because patent protection is deemed vital to the commercial success of transnational companies and the protection of intellectual property raises the prospect that a few varieties will dominate the seed market, a connection is established between the unique tools of biotechnology (gene sequencing) and the legal support for the privatization of genetic resources. This makes a strong case that uniform international seed markets, and thus agro-monoculture, are a likely outcome.

If this argument is sound, then the first plant variety that receives international patent protection should be the one aggressively marketed in place of indigenous strains. If the techniques of genetic engineering for seed production were available to local breeders in every nation and if plant germ plasm were a common resource, there would be less reason to believe that biotechnology and the narrowing of biodiversity were linked (Hobbelink 1991).

D. Consequences of Innovation on Agriculture

The techniques of biotechnology applied to agriculture have given rise to changes in the instruments of research, the processes of manufacture, as well as product varieties unique to this technology. Without gene engineering and microbial fermentation, commercial bovine growth hormone would not be possible. Without embryo DNA transplantation, deriving pharmaceuticals from goats' milk would also not be possible.

Many of the innovations in agricultural biotechnology that we have discussed in the preceding chapters are science-driven rather than need-driven. Industry has developed powerful tools to manipulate organisms genetically and is seeking ways to develop products using those techniques that will generate economic value. That is not to say that there are not agricultural problems that biotechnology could not be helpful in resolving, but the thrust of the biotechnology industry is not to solve agricultural problems as much as it is to create profitability. Sometimes the two coincide, but not necessarily. Perhaps herbicide resistant crops could be used effectively in Africa to prevent large losses to parasitic weeds (chapter 2). To our knowledge no company is directing research to solve that problem. Instead, herbicide resistant corn and cotton are being developed for North American markets although there are already myriad herbicides available to control weeds in those crops.

Will biotechnology have a deep and enduring effect on agriculture, or will it simply contribute incrementally and on the margins to our system of food production? This is one of those elusive questions that occupies the minds and journals of rural sociologists and futurists. We can divide the question into two parts. Will biotechnology's impact be revolutionary, and will biotechnology have a structural impact on agriculture? By dividing the question we are distinguishing between revolutionary change and structural change. Following the criteria of Buttel (1989) for a revolutionary technology, we shall mean that it would lead to miracle products or result in major agricultural productivity and output increases.

For structural change, we adapt criteria developed by the Office of Technology Assessment (OTA 1986) in which the change affects the nature of the agricultural system: modes of production, ownership of farms, size and number of farms, and the overall concept of agricultural production.

Our analysis has thus far not identified any miracle products for the agricultural sector. What would such a miracle product look like? Perhaps it would be a product that could provide inexpensive and plentiful nutrients at low cost to developing countries. Or it might be a product that is completely safe to all forms of life yet protects plants from injurious pests.

Buttel has argued that the high-visibility "revolutionary type" products such as plants that can fix their own nitrogen and crops with increased photosynthetic efficiency have not been developed. He notes that the annual growth rate of world agricultural output is 2.4 percent. Even if biotechnology can match this output, it would lack the luster of being revolutionary next to the impressive improvements that took place in the 1960s and 1970s. Referring to the post-World War II baseline, Buttel argues (1989, 173) that "it seems implausible that, even if reasonably optimistic scenarios for biotechnology innovation over the next two or three decades are realized, the result will be a qualitative disjuncture from this baseline." Based on the commercial products analyzed in earlier chapters, thus far we have no reason to dispute this claim.

Structural change refers not to the products of agriculture but rather to its institutional framework. Even without creating miracle products, biotechnology could easily be responsible for structural change in the industry. We will begin by looking at whether biotechnology is associated with transforming the way food is produced and the types of products originating on the farm.

1. Modes of Production

Will biotechnology contribute to fundamental changes in the modes of production of food? What would count as a fundamental change? If certain food products that traditionally are derived directly from crops, such as sugar cane, can be manufactured through fermentation processes using the genes for a desired protein, this would qualify as a fundamental change in the mode of production. Fowler et al. (1988) cite a protein called thaumatin from a West African plant *Thaumatococcus daniellii* that is several thousand times sweeter than sugar. According to the authors, "The development of a thaumatin product via biotechnology is just the beginning of a transition to alternative sweeteners which will displace Third World sugar markets in the coming years" (Fowler et al. 1988, 103). In fact, the transition has already begun with the replacement of sugar cane by high-fructose corn syrup and aspartame.

Other modal changes in production would include the use of plant tissue culture as an alternative to seed-based agriculture. Shand (1994) describes the work of a California-based biotechnology company, Escagenetics, which is producing natural vanilla from culturing the cells of the vanilla plant. If such a product were commercially successful, consumers might benefit from a less expensive food flavoring, but the hundred thousand small farmers of Madagascar and East Africa who now cultivate vanilla plants might be put out of business. The possibility that a variety of spices, flavorings, and other food additives could be produced more cheaply in bacterial or plant tissue culture would seemingly have significant negative impacts on the farming sector, especially in tropical countries.

Increasingly, plants traditionally used for food production are being thought of as chemical factories for the manufacture of a variety of consumer and industrial products. By the beginning of the next century as much as 25 percent of corn production will probably be devoted to nonfood products such as oils, sweeteners, starches, proteins, and fuels (Abelson 1994). New plant-based outputs might displace traditional plant-based products (e.g., new oils produced in North American oilseed rape supplanting tropical oils [chapter 5]). Other new plant-derived products will compete with petroleum-based products (e.g., as biodegradable lubricants and packaging materials).

Biotechnology provides some of the tools for a new mode of food, food additive, and material production. In some instances tissue and cell culture techniques will either replace current whole-plant agriculture or shift the geographical locus of production, with negative impacts on current producers. Alternatively, farmers can benefit if advances in biotechnology create novel plant products that add new markets.

2. Political Economy of Farms

Will biotechnology significantly affect patterns of farm ownership or the control of food production? Although our research did not address this issue directly, advances in biotechnology appear to be fostering continuing trends toward vertical integration of agricultural production in the United States and globally (Busch et al. 1991, 24–27; Hobbelink 1991; Kloppenburg 1988). Since the mid-1980s many seed companies have been acquired by transnational chemical corporations (TCC) with interests in pesticides and pharmaceuticals. Many of the TCCs have in-house agricultural biotechnology programs and have alliances with other biotechnology firms (Busch et al. 1991). Pioneer Hi-Bred, which has remained an independent seed company, has invested heavy in biotechnology firms and is marketing its own improved seeds.

Biotechnology has made the patenting of seeds viable, which provides an economic incentive for corporations to invest in both biotechnology start-up companies directed at new seed genotypes and traditional seed companies that supply farmers with plant germ plasm. Chemical companies are not in the business of farming, but they see their market as providing the inputs to agriculture. According to Buttel (1990, 241), "Large corporations will probably continue to be disinterested in most agricultural commodities. Put most bluntly, the way to make money in agriculture will continue to be selling inputs to and merchandising the outputs of farmers, rather than in farming itself."

Our research confirms Buttel's notion that biotechnology companies are unlikely to take on the risks of farming directly. However, we have found that these companies will increasingly dictate to farmers what to produce. The case of Calgene's strategy in promoting its delayed ripening tomato is illustrative. Calgene has developed a vertically integrated approach to produce its genetically modified tomato seed and market its tomato products while avoiding the actual on-farm crop growing. The company provides the improved seed to farmers who are contracted to do the crop production. The

tomatoes are then shipped to a Calgene-owned facility for processing, packaging, labeling, and marketing to retailers. Calgene intends
to follow the same production and marketing strategy for its specialty oil seed products.

The outcome of the large investments companies have made in
plant biotechnology is embodied in the seed. It seems reasonable that
those companies will try to control the germplasm from seed to sale
in order to extract the most profit from their investment. Hiring
farmers to grow genetically improved seeds into marketable products fits into that objective. So while farmers will continue to grow
the crops, the choice of which crop to grow will increasingly be influenced by large corporations.

Shand (1994, 81) laments that "the American farmer becomes a
'renter of germplasm,' rather than an independent, owner/operator."
It is predicted that 40 percent of U.S. farmers will be contract producers of "value-added" crops by 2000 (M. Boehlje 1992, cited in
Shand 1994).

3. Size and Number of Farms

The continued evidence of farm concentration in the United States
is indisputable. Figure 16 shows the change in the average number
and size of farms from 1960 to 1993. The question is whether biotechnology will accelerate, in any appreciable manner, the reduction

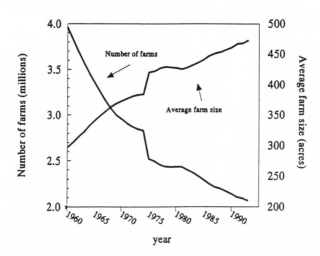

Figure 16. Changes in the Number of Farms and Average Farm Size in the
United States, 1960–93. *Source:* USDA 1976, 1986, 1993c

in the number or size of farms. Alternatively, is biotechnology scale-neutral with regard to farming? The example of bovine growth hormone supports the hypothesis that biotechnology will accelerate the foreclosure of small dairy farms, although the numbers associated with the wide use of the growth hormone differ. If animal pharming or the use of crops for chemical synthesis becomes lucrative, there may be niches for new farms or reinvigorated declining farms to emerge and meet the new biotechnology markets.

4. The Transformational Vision of Agriculture

Much discussion around agricultural policy has centered on conventional versus alternative agriculture. In the same way that Amory Lovins distinguished between the hard and soft energy paths, advocates of an alternative agriculture speak about high-energy and low-energy inputs into farming. The terms *alternative* or *sustainable agriculture* apply to a class of techniques that depart from intensive chemical use, animal feedlots, high energy, and high capitalization at the expense of soil sustainability and the overall health of the agro-ecosystem. Our results have thus far shown that the biotechnology innovations have been designed to meet the requirements or remediate the problems of conventional agricultural systems such as the intensive management of dairy farming, the increased use of antibiotics, or chemical-intensive farming.

Biotechnology does not favor a shift to an alternative vision of agriculture as might be expected from some of its publicists. However, this alternative vision is only one of several ways that biotechnology can contribute to structural change. We have argued that structural change is possible within a conventional agricultural framework as in the development of more intense vertical integration between farms and other industrial sectors. Our results are consistent with the findings of Buttel (1990, 240), which state that biotechnology will continue to deepen the pattern of structural change in American agriculture because they are capital and management-intensive, and will increase output that will exert downward pressure on commodity prices. In no sense will they offer a new vision of a sustainable agriculture. Nevertheless, some of the innovations in agricultural biotechnology are designed to soften the effects of intensive agriculture. Examples of this include transgenic crops adapted to tolerate herbicides with a more favorable environmental profile and insect resistant crops that conform to the requirements of monoculture.

Agricultural biotechnology is more than a biological endeavor. We have shown that the biological aspects of plant and animal development are optimized against social objectives. Certain crop varieties are better adapted to specific forms of production (machine tools or herbicides) and distribution. We have seen how genetic engineering is used to create crops with a greater shelf life (the antifreeze gene in frozen foods or delayed-ripening tomatoes). Other products are being engineered so that they will conform better to the machinery of harvesting.

Modern agriculture symbolizes more than human cultivation of the wilderness. There is nothing particularly modern about extracting use value from land. What is especially notable about the past two hundred years are the goals and methods of evening out nature, destroying its diversity, and eliminating uncertainty and spontaneity in growth patterns. These objectives are sought by whatever instruments are available: irrigation, machines, selected seeds, chemicals, and now genetic engineering. The "smoothing out" of nature is not an end in itself; it is a means to production efficiency and maximization of profit. The model of controlled production became the cornerstone of American entrepreneurship following the tradition of the assembly line and the social organization of labor. It is this context in which biotechnology has been embedded.

E. The Question of Risk

Most observers agree that there is some degree of risk to the environment from transgenic organisms. We have described various risk issues raised for each of the broad product classes. This is not surprising. Genetic engineering is a new technology whose creations are being released into the environment, where the interactions among organisms and between the biotic and the abiotic world are not fully understood. Other new technologies that have been quickly embraced because they appeared benign and miraculous have turned out to have overlooked limitations and flaws. Society's experience with pesticides and nuclear energy demonstrates that the proponents of new technologies tend to embellish the potential benefits while discounting detrimental effects.

Controversy over the environmental risks from the applications of biotechnology to agriculture rests on differences of opinion regarding the level of uncertainty in assessing the probability and consequences of an adverse impact. Environmental critics of biotechnology generally argue that the degree of uncertainty is great and the negative outcomes are potentially very damaging. In the case of the ice-minus bacteria, possible alteration of global weather patterns was one of the main questions critics of this early field test raised (chapter 8). The degree of risk of large-scale bacterial releases was unclear because little was known about the importance of airborne bacteria on precipitation. More intensive study of the question reduced concerns about weather pattern effects of small field experiments while leaving unresolved the effects of large-scale releases of airborne microorganisms.

Food safety concerns from unexpected allergenic or toxic effects resulting from the insertion of a foreign gene into crops or food animals have also been cited. At issue is whether a foreign gene can activate the expression of a latent toxin gene. There is ample evidence that a gene may have multiple functions. The term *pleiotropy* is used to describe the conditions where a gene product can affect more than one trait. For example, the southern corn leaf blight was caused by a gene that both conferred male sterility and caused increased susceptibility to a fungal pathogen. The term *epistasis* describes the condition where one gene modifies the expression of another gene that is not an allele of the first. Rissler and Mellon (1993, 23) maintain that it is reasonable to expect the effects of pleiotropy and epistasis in certain transgenic crops. A new generation of questions are beginning to be asked about genetically modified organisms. Without direct empirical knowledge, some scientists are resorting to historical, theoretical, or analogical reasoning to address this new generation of questions. For example, in response to the latent activation hypothesis, Berkowitz and Kryspin-Sorensen (1994, 249) comment:

> If unexpressed toxin genes were present in normally safe fish, it is likely that toxic varieties of the fish would have been found. The insertion of an exogenous gene is only one of many routes to "turning on" an unexpressed gene. Naturally occurring genetic changes such as deletions, inversions, translocations, and transposon insertions all lead to the formation of new sequences, some of which may activate genes. So if quiescent toxin genes did indeed exist, they would be turned on by naturally occurring genetic events. And yet, hereditary toxin production by normally safe fish has not been observed.

According to the authors, none of the several hundred cases of seafood poisoning reported has been attributed to a hereditary (endogenous) fish toxin. The authors conclude that the transgenic fish is likely to be as safe as the parental line if the transgene is not infectious, the fish are healthy, and the transgene product is safe. Others are less sanguine about using natural background data to draw conclusions about the risks of genetically modified food products.

In *Perils amidst the Promise*, Rissler and Mellon (1993, 2) envision a series of "cascading effects that can ripple through an ecosystem" were transgenic plants to be commercialized. These authors contend that "the long-term cumulative risks to ecosystems of introducing large numbers of transgenes and transgenic plants are not well enough understood to allow their prediction except in the grossest sense" (3). Their analysis points to large degrees of uncertainty that prevent the proper assessment of risk. They emphasize the potential for great environmental harm. Rissler and Mellon conclude that much more research is needed to understand the nature of the risk and that "no company should be permitted to commercialize a transgenic crop . . . until a strong government program is in place that assures risk assessment and control of all transgenic crops" (4).

Critics of Rissler and Mellon contend that genetic engineering and the other "new biotechnologies" are merely extensions of classical plant breeding. Genetic engineering, it is reasoned, is actually safer than traditional methods because of the greater control allowing the transfer of specific traits to crops (NAS 1987, 11). Henry Miller, the former director of the Office of Biotechnology at the Food and Drug Administration and one of the most outspoken critics of federal policies toward biotechnology, advocates a risk-based approach to regulation (Miller 1994). The familiarity with crop plants and the transgenic traits of interest, according to Miller et al. (1993, 1324) provides the basis for making sound decisions regarding risk so that "there is no necessity to conduct risk assessment experiments to ensure confidence about field testing of new plant varieties in general or those crafted with the newest genetic manipulation techniques in particular." Miller goes on to attack the biotechnology regulatory structure established in the United States and Europe: "The United States Department of Agriculture, the Environmental Protection Agency, and the European Community have built huge, expensive, and gratuitous biotechnology regulatory empires preoccupied with negligible-risk activities, and have succeeded in protecting consumers only from enjoying the benefits of the new technology" (1076).

Should development of transgenic organisms be halted until all the risk questions are definitively answered? Our analysis shows that there are many unanswered ecological questions regarding the impact of transgenic plants and microbes released into the environment. It would be foolish to ignore or minimize these issues. But there is also reason to argue that the safe history of release of classically bred crops as well as numerous releases of nonindigenous microorganisms without mishap provides some degree of assurance that the release of genetically engineered plants and microorganisms for agriculture will not result in global catastrophe. At the same time, the novelty of the phenotypic combinations possible through genetic engineering argues for caution, review, and vigilance of environmental releases. The possibility of localized ecological disruptions arising from transgenic organisms introduced into the environment underscores the necessity for establishing a base of empirical information upon which to make reasoned judgments. In fact, experiments directed at the environmental risk issues are now being conducted as commercial development of products proceeds (Kareiva and Stark 1994). However, there are many gaps, and they are growing as new product releases accelerate. Risk assessments of small-scale field tests conducted by regulatory agencies often have not required submission of experimental evidence necessary to evaluate properly the ecological risk issues for large-scale tests or commercialization (Wrubel, Krimsky, and Wetzler 1992). This is a mistake, and government oversight should require the development of ecological risk data early in the product development process. Although we believe the regulatory policy is short-sighted, it conforms well to the current policy trends postulating a regulatory minimalism based on a clear and present danger standard.

F. Biotechnology Policy

After several years of debate between 1976 and 1980 over whether the techniques and the products of biotechnology should be regulated, no new laws were enacted. Instead, Congress expected the relevant agencies to adapt their existing statutory frameworks to bioengineered products. The Executive Office of Science and Technology Policy facilitated an interagency task force that resulted in a Coordinated Framework for Regulation of Biotechnology (OSTP 1986). Under the Coordinated Framework, the regulatory agencies divided the responsibility of oversight based on their traditional roles: The USDA focuses on plants and the problems of weeds, the FDA addresses new food products, and the EPA regulates microbial pesticides and other applications of genetically engineered microorganisms. Each agency was given the mandate to promulgate rules regulating the use of bioengineered products under its jurisdiction.

However, for half a dozen years rulemaking was thwarted by the failure of a consensus within the government over how to define boundaries of the regulated products. One of the key issues in debate was over the distinction between process and product regulation. One group believed that bioengineered organisms are more likely to introduce new hazards than traditional methods of modifying living things (e.g., hybridization of plants). Another group was emphatic about the need to regulate hazardous products exclusively by their characteristics and ignore how they are made. According to the risk-based approach, the evaluation of the health or ecological effects of a microbial pesticide should not be determined by whether the organism is found in nature, produced by cell fusion, mutagenesis, recombinant DNA, or through a process of selection. "Just as with traditional breeding techniques, the production of organisms using new molecular techniques of genetic manipulation may or may not pose a risk, depending on the characteristics of the organism, the target environment, and the type of application" (OSTP 1992, 6755).

In February 1992, after eight years of discussion and debate, the Office of Science and Technology Policy published a scoping document that defined a regulated entity for biotechnology (OSTP 1992). The publication of the scoping principles signaled to the individual agencies that rulemaking, consistent with the risk-based approach, should proceed.

Agency policies developed and evolved concurrently with new product innovations. As soon as consensus was reached over the risk management of one type of product, another product innovation challenged the rules. The USDA began receiving scores of applications for field tests of transgenic plants. Initially, these were reviewed on a case-by-case approach. However, in 1993, the USDA began relaxing its requirements for field-testing transgenic crops. New rules allow companies to field-test six common crops that are genetically modified (corn, cotton, tomatoes, potatoes, tobacco, and soybeans) without obtaining prior approval from the agency. The companies are required to notify the agency thirty days before transgenic crops are planted and to certify that the tests comply with agency performance standards.

The EPA received fewer but no less controversial bioengineered product applications for field-testing, such as ice minus. And the FDA approved, without expressions of public concern, the use of genetically modified yeast containing an animal chymosin gene for making cheese, but its review of the Flavr Savr tomato and BGH provoked major public debates.

Environmental interest groups called for mandatory experimental risk assessment programs for the purpose of screening out potentially hazardous products intended for release into the environment. In contrast, the thrust taken by regulatory agencies has been, first, toward regulatory exemptions for selected classes of products and, second, self-directed guidelines for use by firms that seek to test a new product in the environment. This means that a firm can decide from a decision tree whether to submit transgenic food to the FDA for rigorous review and whether or not to treat the addition of foreign genes to a food product as an additive. The agency has also issued a policy that transgenic food will not require mandatory labeling.

The overall thrust of the regulatory response to biotechnology may be termed a minimalist, cost-effective, priority-driven approach requiring a burden of proof that regulation is warranted. Regulatory practice grows out of the February 1991 report of the President's Council on Competitiveness and the 1992 scope document issued by the Office of Science and Technology Policy. The former policy states that "regulations should be issued only on evidence that their potential benefits exceed their potential costs" and should not discourage or penalize innovation in biotechnology. Regulations that seek to reduce health or safety risks should be based on scientific risk assessment and should address risks that are "real and significant rather than hypothetical or remote." The burden of proof, then, is on those who advance a risk scenario to show that it is "real and significant" and poses a clear and present danger. Finally, the Council on Competitiveness posited the use of voluntary private standards and disclosure in lieu of what it termed "inflexible regulations" (OSTP 1992, 6761–62). The OSTP policy of 1992 builds directly on the policy of the now defunct Council on Competitiveness. Much of its language is derivative of the council's philosophical underpinnings. Regulations will be issued only when there is evidence that the risk is unreasonable. Translated, this means that the value of the reduction of risk must be greater than the cost of regulation. Also, agencies are implored to set priorities on high-risk events because, the policy states, "Agency resources are scarce, and cannot be applied to every possible problem; responsible officials must choose carefully the risks of highest concern and find the best way to combat them" (OSTP 1992, 6756).

Federal biotechnology policy was designed to stimulate the innovative potential of American science and industry, to foster technology transfer, and to enable the U.S. biotechnology industry to achieve hegemony in global markets. At the outset of the rDNA controversy, the United States led in establishing standards for laboratory experimentation. The rDNA guidelines issued by the National Institutes of Health served as a model for most nations of the world. Now, with the rapid growth of industrial genetics, the United States is no longer a leader in setting policy. There is significant divergence between American and European regulations on environmental release, genetically engineered food, and veterinary drugs. Moreover, on questions about patenting, biodiversity, and the ownership of genetic resources, the United States has been at odds with nations of the developing world.

Our research indicates that there is little basis for the claim that biotechnology has been burdened with overregulation and that such regulation has thwarted innovation. Some evidence suggests that regulatory inaction or confusion has kept firms from investing in transgenic microorganisms. Furthermore, there is little doubt that biotechnology is having a significant impact on agricultural research, that it is responsible for inducing structural change in sectors involved with plant germ plasm, but that there are no signs of significant change in the refashioning of agriculture toward environmental goals.

References

Abelson, P. H. 1994. Continuing evolution of U.S. agriculture. *Science, 264,* 1383.

Ag Biotechnology News. 1993. Company news. January, 10.

Agrichemical Age. 1990. Another look at viral inputs. *Agrichemical Age,* October, 26–27.

Akçakaya, H. R., and L. R. Ginzburg. 1991. Ecological considerations in EPA's review for field tests of genetically engineered organisms. In *Assessing ecological risks of biotechnology,* ed. L. R. Ginzburg, 267–87. Boston: Butterworth-Heineman.

Aldridge, Susan. 1994. Ethically sensitive genes and the consumer. *Trends in Biotechnology, 12,* 11–12.

Alexander, D., R. M. Goodman, M. Gut-Rella, C. Glascock, K. Weymann, L. Friedrich, D. Maddox, P. Ahl-Goy, T. Luntz, E. Ward, and J. Ryals. 1993. Increased tolerance to two oomycete pathogens in transgenic tobacco expressing pathogenesis-related protein 1a. *Proceedings of the National Academy of Sciences of the United States of America, 90,* 7327–31.

Alexander, Martin. 1985. Ecological consequences: Reducing the uncertainties. *Issues in Science and Technology, 1,* 57–68.

Alper, J. 1987. Will biotechnology save U.S. farms? *Chemical Week,* January 21, 60.

Alstad, D. N., and D. A. Andow. 1995. Managing the evolution of insect resistance to transgenic plants. *Science, 268,* 1894–96.

Altmann, M. 1992. 'Biopesticides' turning into new pests? *Trends in Ecology and Evolution, 7,* 65.

Ames, Bruce N., and Lois S. Gold. 1990. Too many rodent carcinogens: Mitogenesis increases mutagenesis. *Science, 249,* 970–71.

Anderson, J. M., P. Palukaitis, and M. Zaitlin. 1992. A defective replicase gene induces resistance to cucumber mosaic virus in transgenic tobacco plants. *Proceedings of the National Academy of Sciences of the United States of America, 89,* 8759–63.

Anderson, P. A., and M. Georgeson. 1989. Herbicide-tolerant mutants of corn. *Genome, 31,* 994–99.

Anderson, Walter Truett. 1990. Food without farms: The biotech revolution in agriculture. *The Futurist, 24,* 16–22.

Andrews, R. E., R. M. Faust, H. Wabiko, K. C. Raymond, and L. A. Bulla. 1987. The biotechnology of *Bacillus thuringiensis*. *CRC Critical Reviews in Biotechnology, 6,* 163–232.

Angus, T. A. 1956. Association of toxicity with protein-crystalline inclusions of *Bacillus soto* Ishiwata. *Canadian Journal of Microbiology, 2,* 122.

Archibald, A. L., et al. 1990. High level expression of biologically active human alpha 1–antitrypsin in the milk of transgenic mice. *Proceedings of the National Academy of Sciences of the United States of America, 87,* 5178–82.

Asakawa, Y., F. Fukumoto, E. Hamaya, A. Hasebe, H. Ichikawa, I. Matsuda, T. Matsumura, F. Motoyoshi, K. Noguchi, Y. Ohashi, M. Okada, M. Sato, M. Shiyomi, M. Ugaki, Y. Ukai, and K. Yokoyama. 1993. Evaluation of the impact of the release of transgenic tomato plants with TMV resistance on the environment. *JARQ, 27,* 126–36.

Asimov, G. J., and N. K. Krouze. 1937. The lactogenic preparations from the anterior pituitary and the increase in milk yield from cows. *Journal of Dairy Science, 20,* 289–306.

Aspelin, Arnold L. 1994. *Pesticide industry sales and usage: 1992 and 1993 market estimates.* Environmental Protection Agency, Office of Pesticide Programs, Biological and Economic Analysis Division, Economic Analysis Branch.

Aspelin, Arnold, L., A. H. Grube, and R. Torla. 1992. *Pesticide industry sales and usage: 1990 and 1991 market estimates.* Environmental Protection Agency, Office of Pesticide Programs, Biological and Economic Analysis Division, Economic Analysis Branch.

Baldwin, I. L., and E. B. Fred. 1929. Strain variation in the root-nodule bacteria of clover, *Rhizobium trifolii. Journal of Bacteriology, 17,* 17–18.

Bandeen, J. D., G. R. Stephenson, and E. R. Cowett. 1982. Discovery and distribution of herbicide-resistant weeds in North America. In *Herbicide Resistance in Plants,* ed. H. M. LeBaron and J. Gressel, 9–30. New York: John Wiley & Sons.

Barton, Kenneth A., and Winston J. Brill. 1983. Prospects in plant genetic engineering. *Science, 219,* 671–76.

Bauman, D. E., M. J. DeGieter, C. J. Peel, G. M. Lanza, R. C. Goreit, et al. 1982. Effect of recombinant derived bovine growth hormone (bGH) on lactational performance of high yielding dairy cows. *Journal of Dairy Science, 65* (Supplement 1), 121.

Bauman, Dale E., and Richard G. Vernon. 1993. Effects of exogenous somatotropin on lactation. *Annual Review of Nutrition, 13,* 437–61.

Bayley, C., N. Tolinder, C. Ray, M. Morgan, J. E. Quisenberry, and D. W. Ow. 1992. Engineering 2,4–D resistance into cotton. *Theoretical and Applied Genetics, 83,* 645–49.

Beiswenger, John. 1992. Moving beyond risk in assessing technological artifacts: The case of recombinant bovine somatotropin. *Vermont Law Review, 16,* 667–710.

Benbrook, C. M., and P. B. Moses. 1986. Engineering crops to resist herbicides. *Technology Review, 89,* November–December: 55–61, 79.

Berkowitz, David B., and Ilona Krypsin-Sorensen. 1994. Transgenic fish: Safe to eat. *Bio/Technology, 12,* 247–51.

Berry, Wendell. 1981. *The gift of good land.* San Francisco: North Point Press.

Betz, Frederick S. 1985. U.S. EPA Hazard Evaluation Division, Science Integration Staff. Memorandum to Tom Ellwanger, Technical Support Section, Registration Division. Hazard Evaluation Division position on Lindow EUP application. March 27.

———. 1992. EPA, Office of Pesticide Programs. Interview, March 13.

Bevan, Michael. 1984. Binary *Agrobacterium* vectors for plant transformation. *Nucleic Acids Research, 12,* 8711–21.

Beversdorf, W. D., D. J. Hume, and M. J. Donnelly-Vanderloo. 1988. Agronomic performance of triazine-resistant and susceptible reciprocal spring canola hybrids. *Crop Science, 28,* 932–34.

Bialy, Harvey. 1991. Transgenic pharming comes of age. *Bio/Technology, 9,* 786–87.

Binswinger, H. P., and V. W. Ruttan. 1978. *Induced innovations.* Baltimore: Johns Hopkins University Press.

Biotech Bulletin. 1993. Survey shows wisconsin dairy farmers resistant to bgh. October 27.

Biotech Reporter. 1993. Agristar/Ambico develop edible vaccines. September, 1.

Birkenhead, K., S. S. Manian, and F. O'Gara. 1988. Dicarboxylic acid transport in *Bradyrhizobium japonicum:* Use of *Rhizobium meliloti dct* gene(s) to enhance nitrogen fixation. *Journal of Bacteriology, 170,* 184–89.

Bol, J. F., H. J. M. Linthorst, and B. J. Cornelissen. 1990. Plant pathogenesis-related proteins induced by virus infection. *Annual Review of Phytopathology, 28,* 113–38.

Bonning, B. C., A. T. Merryweather, and R. D. Possee. 1991. Genetically engineered baculovirus insecticides. *AgBiotech News and Information, 3,* 21–29.

Boulter, D., A. M. R. Gatehouse, and V. Hilder. 1990. Engineering enhanced natural resistance to insect pests—A case study. In *Plant gene transfer,* 267–73. New York: Alan R. Liss Inc.

Brattsten, L. B. 1979. Biochemical defense mechanisms in herbivores against plant allelochemicals. In *Herbivores: Their interactions with secondary metabolites,* ed. G. A. Rosenthal and D. H. Janzen, 199–270. New York: Academic Press.

Braun, C. J., and C. L. Hemenway. 1992. Expression of amino-terminal portions or full length viral replicase genes in transgenic plants confer resistance to potato virus X infection. *Plant Cell, 4,* 735–44.

Brenner, Carliene. 1991. *Biotechnology and developing country agriculture: The case of maize.* Paris: Organization for Economic Cooperation and Development (OECD).

Brill, Winston, J. 1981. Agricultural microbiology. *Scientific American, 245,* 198–215.

———. 1985. Safety concerns and genetic engineering in agriculture. *Science, 227,* 381–84.

———. 1991. The use of microorganisms for crop agriculture. In *Agricultural biotechnology at the crossroads,* ed. J. F. MacDonald, 91–96. Report 3. Ithaca: National Agricultural Biotechnology Council.

Browning, Graeme. 1992. Biotech rules ripen slowly. *National Journal, 13,* 47.

Broglie, K., I. Chet, M. Holliday, R. Cressman, P. Biddle, S. Knowlton, C. J. Mauvais, and R. Broglie. 1991. Transgenic plants with enhanced resistance to the fungal pathogen *Rhizoctonia solani. Science, 254,* 1194–97.

Bud, Robert. 1993. *The uses of life.* Cambridge: Cambridge University Press.

Buhler, T. A., et al. 1990. Rabbit b-cassein promoter directs secretion of human interleukin-2 into the milk of transgenic rabbits. *Bio/Technology, 8,* 140–43.

Burill, G. Steven, and Kenneth B. Lee, Jr. 1992. *Biotech 93: Accelerating commercialization.* San Francisco: Ernst & Young.

Burk, Dan L., Kenneth Barovsky, and Gladys H. Monroy. 1993. Biodiversity and biotechnology. *Science, 260,* 1900–1901.

Burns, Sara. 1989. *Pastoral inventions.* Philadelphia: Temple University Press.

Burris, R. H., and G. P. Roberts. 1993. Biological nitrogen fixation. *Annual Review of Nutrition, 13,* 317–35.

Busch, L., W. B. Lacy, J. Burkhardt, and L. R. Lacy. 1991. *Plants, power and profit.* Oxford: Basil Blackwell.

Busch, Lawrence, and William B. Lacy. 1983. *Science, agriculture and the politics of research.* Boulder: Westview Press.

Butler, L. J. 1991. Economic evaluation of bst for on farm use. In *Bovine somatotropin and emerging issues,* ed. M. C. Hallberg. Boulder: Westview Press.

Buttel, Frederick H. 1989. Modern biotechnology: Its prospective production and socioeconomic impacts. In *Innovation in resource management,* ed. L. Richard Meyers. Proceedings of the Ninth Agricultural Sector Symposium. Washington, D.C.: The World Bank.

———. 1990. Biotechnology, agriculture, and rural America: Socioeconomic and ethical issues. In *Agricultural bioethics,* ed. S. M. Gendel, A. D. Kline, D. M. Warren, and F. Yates. Ames: Iowa State University Press.

Buttel, Frederick H., and William L. Flinn. 1975. Sources and consequences of agrarian values in american society. *Rural Sociology, 40,* 134–51.

Byers, Floyd N., and Paul G. Thompson. 1991. Animal growth biotechnology in a quandary. In *Agricultural biotechnology at the crossroads,* ed. J. F. Macdonald, 264–98. Report 3. Ithaca: National Agricultural Biotechnology Council.

Byrnes, Kathleen. 1993. Synthesis: Choices/consequences. In *The dairy debate,* ed. William C. Liebhardt. Davis: University of California Sustainable Agriculture Research and Education Program.

Campbell, David. 1993. The economic and social viability of rural communities: BGH vs. rotational grazing. In *The dairy debate*, ed. William C. Liebhardt. Davis: University of California Sustainable Agriculture Research and Education Program.

Candelier-Harvey, P., and R. Hull. 1993. Cucumber mosaic virus genome is encapsidated in alfalfa mosaic virus coat protein expressed in transgenic tobacco plants. *Transgenic Research 2*, 277–85.

Cannon, F. C., J. Beynon, T. Hankinson, R. Kwiatkowski, R. P. Legocki, H. Ratcliffe, C. Ronson, W. Szeto, and M. Williams. 1988. Increasing biological nitrogen fixation by genetic manipulation. In *Nitrogen fixation: A hundred years after*, ed. H. Bothe, F. J. de Bruijn, and W. E. Newton, 735–40. Stuttgart: Gustav Fischer.

Cannon, Frank. 1990. Former Director of Research, Biotechnica. Interview, December 10.

Carlson, Peter. 1992. Chief Scientific Officer, Crop Genetic International. Interview, March 10.

Carlton, Bruce. 1992. Ecogen. Personal communication, January 6.

Carlton, Bruce C., C. Gawron-Burke, and T. B. Johnson. 1990. Exploiting the genetic diversity of *Bacillus thuringiensis* for creation of new bioinsecticides. *Fifth International Colloquium on Invertebrate Pathology and Microbial Control*, 18–22. Adelaide, Australia: Society for Invertebrate Pathology.

Carr, J. P., L. E. Marsh, G. P. Lomonossoff, M. E. Sekiya, and M. Zaitlin. 1992. Resistance to tobacco mosaic virus induced by the 54-kDa gene sequence requires expression of the 54-kDa protein. *Molecular Plant-Microbe Interactions, 5*, 397–404.

Carson, Rachel. 1962. *Silent spring.* New York, Fawcett Crest.

Carter, W. 1973. *Insects in relation to plant disease.* 2d ed. New York: John Wiley & Sons.

Caswell, M. F., K. O. Fuglie, and C. A. Klotz. 1994. *Agricultural biotechnology: An economic perspective.* Agricultural Economic Report 687. Washington, D.C.: Resources and Technology Division, Economic Resources Service, U.S. Department of Agriculture. May.

Chaleff, R. S. 1983. Isolation of agronomically useful mutants from plant cell cultures. *Science, 219*, 676–82.

Chaleff, R. S., and C. J. Mauvois. 1984. Acetolactate synthase is the site of action of two sulfonylurea herbicides. *Science, 223*, 1443–45.

Chaleff, R. S., and T. B. Ray. 1984. Herbicide-resistant mutants from tobacco cell cultures. *Science, 223*, 1148–51.

Chassan, Rebecca. 1993. Harvesting virus recombinants. *Plant Cell, 5*, 1489–91.

———. 1994. Disease resistance: Beyond the *R* genes. *Plant Cell, 6*, 461–63.

Chemical and Engineering News. 1991. Bovine growth hormone found safe for use. May 13, 7–8.

Chilton, Mary-Dell. 1991. Executive Director, Biotechnology Research, Ciba-Geigy Corporation. Interview, March 1.

Clark, A. J., H. Bessos, J. O. Bishop, P. Brown, S. Harris, R. Lathe, M. Mc-Clenaghan, C. Prowse, J. P. Simons, C. B. A. Whitelaw, and I. Wilmut. 1989. Expression of human anti-hemophilic factor ix in the milk of transgenic sheep. *Bio/Technology, 7,* 487–92.

Clark A. J., P. Simons, I. Wilmut, and R. Lathe. 1987. Pharmaceuticals from transgenic livestock. *Trends in Biotechnology, 5,* 20–25.

Clark, Ellie. 1994. U.S. Environmental Protection Agency, Biotechnology Program. Interview, March 15.

Coble, Harold. 1991. Professor, North Carolina State University. Interview, February 28.

Cochrane, Willard W. 1958. *Farm prices: Myth and reality.* Minneapolis: University of Minnesota Press.

———. 1993. *The development of American agriculture.* Minneapolis: University of Minnesota Press.

Colborn, T., F. S. vom Saal, and A. M. Soto. 1993. Developmental effects of endocrine disrupting chemicals in wildlife and humans. *Environmental Health Perspectives, 101,* 378–84.

Colwell, R. K. 1989. Nature and unnatural history: Biological diversity and genetic engineering. In *Scientists and their responsibilities,* ed. W. R. Shea and B. Sitter. Canton: Watson Publishing.

Comai, L., D. Faccoitti, W. R. Hiatt, G. Thompson, R. E. Rose, and D. M. Stalker. 1985. Expression in plants of a mutant aroA gene from *Salmonella typhimurium* confers tolerance to glyphosate. *Nature, 317,* 741–44.

Commission of the European Communities (CEC). 1992. *Second report from the commission to the council and to the parliament concerning bovine somatotropin (BST).* January 16. Brussels: CEC.

Comstock, Gary. 1992. What obligation have scientists to transgenic animals? *Ethics and patenting of transgenic organisms.* Ithaca: National Agricultural Biotechnology Council.

Corey, Beverly. 1990. Bovine growth hormone: Harmless for humans. *FDA Consumer,* April, 17–18.

Cramer, C., G. Bowman, M. Brusko, K. Cicero, B. Hofstetter, and C. Shirley, eds. 1991. Controlling weeds with fewer chemicals. *The new farm.* Emmaus: Rodale Institute.

Cramer, H. H. 1967. Plant protection and world crop production. *Pflanzenschutz Nachr. Bayer, 20,* 1.

Crapo, Eric. 1993. Genetically engineered fish: Moving toward the table. *Gene Exchange, 3,* 2.

Curwen, E. Cecil, and Gudmund Hatt. 1961. *Plough and pasture: The early history of farming.* New York: Collier Books.

Daughaday, William, and David M. Barbano. 1990. Bovine somatotropin supplementation of dairy cows. *Journal of the American Medical Association, 264,* 1003–5.

Davis, James H. 1994. Vice President, Research and Development, Crop Genetics International. Personal communication, June 22.

DeBlock, M., J. Botterman, M. Vandewiele, J. Docks, C. Thoen, V. Gossele,

N. Movva, C. Thompson, M. Van Montagu, and J. Leemans. 1987. Engineering herbicide resistance in plants by expression of a detoxifying enzyme. *EMBO Journal*, 6, 2513–18.

Decision Resources, Inc. (DRI). 1992. *Biotechnology in agriculture: The next decade*. February. Burlington, Mass.: Decision Resources.

Dekker, Jack. 1991. Professor, Iowa State University. Interview, February 20.

Department of Health and Human Services (DHHS). 1982. National Institutes of Health. Guidelines for research involving recombinant DNA molecules. *Federal Register*, 47, 17180–98.

de Wit, P. J. G. M. 1992. Molecular characterization of gene-for-gene systems in plant fungus interactions and the application of avirulence genes in control of plant pathogens. *Annual Review of Phytopathology*, 30, 391–418.

de Zoeten, G. A. 1991. Risk assessment: Do we let history repeat itself? *Phytopathology*, 81, 585–86.

Dillon, John. 1993. Farmers may earn more from BST-free milk. *Sunday Rutland Herald*. October 10.

Dixon, B. 1990. Researchers pursue *Nod* genes' trigger. *Bio/Technology*, 8, 897.

———. 1990. Biotech's effects on biodiversity debated. *Bio/Technology*, 8, 499.

———. 1994. Keeping an eye on *B. thuringiensis*. *Bio/Technology*, 12, 435.

Dixon, R. A., F. C. Cannon, and A. Kondorosi. 1976. Construction of a P-plasmid carrying nitrogen fixation genes from *Klebsiella*. *Nature*, 260, 268–71.

Donnelley, Strachan, Charles R. McCarthy, and Rivers Singleton, Jr. 1994. The brave new world of animal biotechnology. *Hastings Center Report*, 24 (Special Supplement 1).

Dosi, Giovanni, Christopher Freeman, Richard Nelson, Gerald Silverberg, and Luc Soete, eds. 1988. *Technical change and economic theory*. London: Pinter.

Douglas, Mary. 1966. *Purity and danger*. London: Ark Paperbacks.

Dowling, D. N., and W. J. Broughton. 1986. Competition for nodulation of legumes. *Annual Review of Microbiology*, 40, 131–57.

Doyle, Jack. 1985. *Altered harvest: Agriculture, genetics, and the future of the world's food supply*. New York: Viking.

Drobniewski, F. A. 1994. The safety of *Bacillus* species as insect vector control agents. *Journal of Applied Biotechnology*, 76, 101–9.

Dubois, N. R., R. C. Reardon, and K. Mierzejewski. 1993. Field efficacy and deposit analysis of *Bacillus thuringiensis*, Foray 48B, against gypsy moth (Lepidoptera: Lymantriidae). *Journal of Economic Entomology*, 86, 26–33.

Duffey, S. S. 1980. Sequestration of plant natural products by insects. *Annual Review of Entomology*, 25, 447–77.

Duke, Stephen, O. 1988. Glyphosate. In *Herbicides—chemistry, degrada-*

tion, and mode of action, ed. P. C. Kearney and D. D. Kaufman, 1–70. New York: Dekker.

Duke, Stephen O., A. Lawrence Christy, Dana F. Hess, and Jodie S. Holt. 1991. *Herbicide-resistant crops.* Ames: Council for Agricultural Science and Technology.

Ebert, Karl M., James P. Selgrath, Paul DiTullio, Julie Denman, Thomas E. Smith, Mushtaq A. Memon, Joanne E. Schindler, Glen M. Monastersky, James A. Vitale, and Katherine Gordon. 1991. Transgenic production of a variant of human tissue-type plasminogen activator in goat milk: Generation of transgenic goats and analysis of expression. *Bio/Technology,* 9, 835–38.

The Economist. 1988. The genetic alternative: A survey of biotechnology. *307*(7548), 1–18 [special supplement after 52].

———. 1990. Beef growth hormone: Bad moos. *316*(7667), 66, 70.

———. 1991. Promises, promises, promises. *320*(7727), 69–70.

Edwards, Clive A. 1993. The impact of pesticides on the environment. In *The pesticide question,* ed. D. Pimental and H. Lehman, 13–46. New York: Chapman & Hall.

Eliade, M. 1963. *Myth and reality.* Translated by W. R. Trask. New York: Harper.

Elkington, J. 1985. *The gene factory: Inside the biotechnology business.* London: Carroll & Graf.

Environmental Protection Agency. 1989. EPA imposes risk reduction measures of bromoxynil pesticide. *Environmental News,* May 9.

———. 1993. *Modification of consent order for P-92–403.* Unpublished contract. EPA Chemical Control Division, Office of Prevention, Pesticides and Toxic Substances, Washington, D.C.

Epstein, Samuel S. 1990. Potential public health hazards of biosynthetic milk hormones. *International Journal of Health Services, 20,* 73–84.

Evans, H. M., and J. A. Lang. 1921. Characteristic effects upon growth, oestrus and ovulation induced by the intraperitoneal administration of fresh anterior hypophyseal substance. *Proceedings of the National Academy of Sciences of the United States of America, 8,* 38–39.

Executive Branch of the Federal Government. 1994. *Use of bovine somatotropin (BST) in the United States: Its potential effects.* January. Washington, D.C.: Government Printing Office.

Falk, B. W., and G. Bruening. 1994. Will transgenic crops generate new viruses and new diseases? *Science, 263,* 1395–96.

Fallert, Richard, Tom McGuckin, Carolyn Betts, and Gary Bruner. 1987. *BST and the dairy industry: A national regional and farm-level analysis.* Agriculture Economic Report 579. Washington, D.C.: Resources and Technology Division, Economic Resources Service, U.S. Department of Agriculture. Washington, D.C.: Government Printing Office.

Farinelli, L., P. Malnoe, and G. F. Collet. 1992. Heterologous encapsidation of potato virus strain O (PVY) with the transgenic coat protein of PVY strain N (PVYN) in *Solanum tuberosum* cv. Bintje. *Bio/Technology, 10,* 1020–25.

Feder, B. J. 1991. Du Pont joins in a venture on pesticides. *New York Times* December 28.

Federal Insecticide, Fungicide, and Rodenticide Act Amendments of 1988. 1988. Public Law 100–532. 102 STAT. 2654–88, October 25.

Feenstra, Gail. 1993. Is BGH sustainable? The consumer perspective. In *The dairy debate,* ed. William C. Liebhardt. Davis: University of California Sustainable Agriculture Research and Education Program.

Feitelson, J. S., J. Payne, and L. Kim. 1992. *Bacillus thuringiensis:* Insects and beyond. *Bio/Technology, 10,* 271–75.

Fellman, Bruce. 1992. Splice genes? Nature did it long before geneticists. *Boston Globe,* April 6, 45.

Ferré, J., M. D. Real, J. Van Rie, S. Jansens, and M. Peferoen 1991. Resistance to the *Bacillus thuringiensis* bioinsecticide in a field population of *Plutella xylostella* is due to a change in a midgut membrane receptor. *Proceedings of the National Academy of Sciences of the United States, 88,* 5119–23.

Fincham, J. R. S., and J. R. Ravetz. 1991. *Genetically engineered organisms: Benefits and risks.* Toronto: University of Toronto Press.

Fischer, R., and L. Rosner. 1959. Toxicology of the microbial insecticide, thuricide. *Agricultural Food Safety, 10,* 686–88.

Fischhoff, David A. 1991. Research Group Leader, Insect Control Projects, Monsanto Agricultural Company. Interview, January 16.

Fischhoff, David A., K. S. Bowdish, F. J. Perlak, P. G. Marrone, S. M. Mc-Cormick, J. G. Niedermeyer, D. A. Dean, K. Kusano-Kretzmer, E. J. Mayer, D. E. Rochester, S. G. Rogers, and R. T. Fraley. 1987. Insect tolerant transgenic tomato plants. *Bio/Technology, 5,* 807–13.

Fitchen, J. H., and R. N. Beachy. 1993. Genetically engineered protection against viruses in transgenic plants. *Annual Review of Microbiology, 47,* 739–63.

Flavell, R. B., E. Dart, R. L. Fuchs, and R. Fraley. 1992. Selectable marker genes: Safe for plants? *Bio/Technology, 10,* 141.

Fliegel, Frederick C., and J. C. van Es. 1983. The diffusion-adoption process in agriculture: Changes in technology and changing paradigms. In *Technology and social change in rural areas,* ed. Gene F. Summers. Boulder: Westview Press.

Food and Drug Administration. 1992. Department of Health and Human Services. Statement of policy: Foods derived from new plant varieties. *Federal Register, 57,* 22984–23005.

Food and Chemical News. 1993a. Monsanto accused of using coelho to influence bst policy. *35*(32), 35–36.

———. 1993b. Scientist: Environmental benefits could result from BST. *35*(33), 21–22.

Fowler, Cary, Eva Lachkovics, Pat Mooney, and Hope Shand. 1988. *The laws of life: Development dialogue.* Volumes 1 and 2. Uppsala, Sweden: Dag Hammerskjold Foundation.

Fox, J. L. 1991. Bt resistance prompts early planning. *Bio/Technology, 9,* 1319.

Fox, Michael W. 1992. *Superpigs and wondercorn.* New York: Lyons & Burford.

Fuchs, Roy L. 1993. Risk assessment: A technical perspective. In *Agricultural biotechnology: A public conversation about risk,* ed. J. F. Macdonald, 55–64. Report 5. Ithaca: National Agricultural Biotechnology Council.

Fuchs, Roy, L., J. E. Ream, B. G. Hammond, M. W. Naylor, R. M. Leimgruber, and S. A. Berberich. 1993. Safety assessment of the neomycin phosphotransferase II (NPTII) protein. *Bio/Technology, 11,* 1543–46.

Fujimoto, H., K. Itoh, M. Yamamoto, J. Kyozuka, and K. Shimamoto. 1993. Insect resistant rice generated by introduction of a modified *d*-endotoxin gene of *Bacillus thuringiensis. Bio/Technology, 11,* 1151–55.

Fulton, R. W. 1986. Practices and precautions in the use of cross protection for plant virus disease control. *Annual Review of Phytopathology, 24,* 67–81.

Gaffney, T., L. Friedrich, B. Vernooij, D. Negrotto, G. Nye, S. Uknes, E. Ward, H. Kessman, and J. Ryals. 1993. Requirement of salicylic acid for the induction of systemic acquired resistance. *Science, 261,* 754–56.

Gal, S., B. Pisan, T. Hohn, N. Grimsley, and B. Hohn. 1992. Agroinfection of transgenic plants leads to viable cauliflower mosaic virus by intermolecular recombination. *Virology, 187,* 525–33.

Gallagher, Barney. 1992. Director, Biologicals Research and Development, Sandoz Agro. Interview, March 3.

Garraway, James L. 1991. Pesticides: Biological and chemical agents as insecticides, fungicides and herbicides. In *Biotechnology: The science and the business,* ed. V. Moses and R. E. Cape. London: Harwood Academic Publishers.

Gasser, Charles S., and Robert T. Fraley. 1989. Genetically engineering plants for crop improvement. *Science, 244,* 1293–99.

———. 1992. Transgenic crops. *Scientific American, 266,* 62–69.

Gelernter, Wendy, D. 1990. Targeting insecticide-resistant markets. In *Managing resistance to agrochemicals,* ed. M. B. Green, H. M. LeBaron, and W. K. Moberg, 105–17. ACS Symposium Series 421. Washington, D.C.: American Chemical Society.

———. 1992. Director of Product Development, Mycogen. Interview, March 4.

Gene Exchange. 1994a. Public interest groups oppose approval of transgenic herbicide-tolerant cotton. *4*(3–4), 1, 10.

———. 1994b. Herbicide-tolerant crops. *5*(1), 6–9.

———. 1995. EPA okays Bt spud. *5*(3).

Gene Report. 1993. Bovine growth hormone banned. No. 3. Fitzroy: Australian Gen-Ethics Network.

Georghiou, George P. 1988 Implications of Potential Resistance to Biopesticides. In *Biotechnology, biological pesticides and novel plant-pest resistance for insect pest management,* ed. D. W. Roberts and R. R. Granados, 137–45. Ithaca: Boyce Thompson Institute for Plant Research, Cornell University.

Georghiou, G. P., and A. Lagunes-Tejeda. 1991. *The occurrence of resistance to pesticides in arthropods.* Rome: Food and Agriculture Organization of the United Nations.

Giaquinta, Robert T. 1990. Manager, Biotechnology, Agricultural Products Department, E. I. Du Pont de Nemours & Co. Interview, December 17.

Gibbons, Ann. 1990. FDA publishes bovine growth hormone data. *Science, 249,* 852–53.

Gibbs, M. 1994. Risks of using transgenic plants? *Science, 264,* 1650–51.

Gill, S. S., E. A. Cowles, and P. V. Pietrantonio. 1992. The mode of action of *Bacillus thuringiensis* endotoxins. *Annual Review of Entomology, 37,* 615–36.

Gluckstein, Fritz P., Martha H. Glock, and James G. Hill. 1990. *Current bibliographies in medicine: Bovine somatotropin.* Washington, D.C.: National Library of Medicine No. 90–13.

Goldburg, Rebecca. 1991. Chair, Biotechnology Program, Environmental Defense Fund. Interview, February 7.

———. 1992. Environmental concerns with the development of herbicide-tolerant plants. *Weed Technology, 6,* 647–52.

Goldburg, Rebecca, and D. Douglas Hopkins. 1992. Environmental Defense Fund. Letter to David Kessler, Commissioner, FDA, October 15.

———. 1993. Letter to Chief, Regulatory Analysis and Development, USDA/APHIS. Environmental Defense Fund. November 9.

Goldburg, Rebecca, Jane Rissler, Hope Shand, and Chuck Hassebrook. 1990. *Biotechnology's bitter harvest.* A Report of the Biotechnology Working Group.

Goldburg, R. J., and G. Tjaden. 1990. Are *B.t.k.* plants really safe to eat? *Bio/Technology, 8,* 1011–15.

Gonsalves, D., P. Chee, R. Provvidenti, R. Seem, and J. L. Slightom. 1992. Comparison of coat protein mediated and genetically-derived resistance in cucumbers to infection by cucumber mosaic virus under field conditions with natural challenge inoculations by vectors. *Bio/Technology, 10,* 1562–70.

Goodman, David, Bernardo Sorj, and John Wilkinson. 1987. *From farming to biotechnology.* Oxford: Basil Blackwell.

Goodman, Robert. 1990. Former Director of Research, Calgene. Interview, December 23.

Goolsby, D. A., R. C. Coupe, and D. J. Markovchick. 1991. Distribution of selected herbicides and nitrate in the Mississippi River and its major tributaries, April through June 1991. *U.S. Geological Survey, water-resources investigations report 91–4163.* Denver: USGS Water Resources Division.

Gordon, Katherine, Eric Lee, James A. Vitale, Alan E. Smith, Heiner Westphal, and Lothar Hennighausen. 1987. Production of human tissue plasminogen activator in transgenic mouse milk. *Bio/Technology, 5,* 1183–187.

Gordon-Kamm, W. J., T. M. Spencer, M. L. Mangano, T. R. Adams, R. J.

Daines, W. G. Start, J. V. O'Brien, S. A. Chambers, W. R. Adams Jr., N. G. Willetts, T. B. Rice, C. J. Mackey, R. W. Krueger, A. P. Kausch, and P. G. Lemaux. 1990. Transformation of maize cells and regeneration of fertile transgenic plants. *Plant Cell, 2,* 603–18.

Goss, J. R., and B. J. Mazur. 1989. A kaleidoscopic view of crop herbicide resistance. *Proceedings of the Western Society of Weed Science, 42,* 17–28.

Gotesky, Rubin. 1952. The nature of myth and society. *American Anthropologist, 54,* 523–31.

Gottesman, Susan. 1995. Review of nitrogen fixing *Rhizobium meliloti.* Biotechnology Science Advisory Committee, EPA. Letter to Elizabeth Milewski, Office of Prevention, Pesticides and Toxic Substances, EPA. March 6.

Gould, Fred. 1988a. Evolutionary biology and genetically engineered crops. *BioScience, 38,* 26–33.

———. 1988b. Ecological-genetic approaches for the design of genetically-engineered crops. In *Biotechnology, biological pesticides and novel plant-pest resistance for insect pest management,* ed. D. W. Roberts and R. R. Granadow, 146–51. Ithaca: Boyce Thompson Institute for Plant Research, Cornell University.

———. 1989. Integrating biotechnology into agricultural systems: The need for more experimental agriculture at the farm level. In U.S. Congress, Senate, Committee on Agriculture, Nutrition, and Forestry, *Reform and innovation of science and education: Planning for the 1990 Farm Bill.* 101th Cong., 101–61, December. 117–24. Washington, D.C.: Government Printing Office.

———. 1991. Professor, North Carolina State University. Interview, March 21.

Gould, Fred, A. Martinez-Ramirez, A. Anderson, J. Ferré, F. J. Silva, and W. J. Moar. 1992. Broad-spectrum resistance to *Bacillus thuringiensis* toxins in *Heliothis virescens. Proceedings of the National Academy of Sciences in the United States, 89,* 7986–90.

Greaser, George L. 1992. BST impacts on resource needs and on beef and veal output. In *Bovine somatotropin and emerging issues,* ed. M. C. Hallberg, 196. Boulder: Westview Press.

Green, Margaret, M. Heumann, R. Sokolow, L. R. Foster, R. Bryant, and M. Skeels. 1990. Public health implications of the microbial pesticide *Bacillus thuringiensis:* An epidemiological study, Oregon 1985–86. *American Journal of Public Health, 80,* 848–52.

Greene, A. E., and R. F. Allison. 1994. Recombination between viral RNA and transgenic plant transcripts. *Science, 263,* 1423–25.

Gressel, Jonathan. 1988. Multiple resistances to wheat selective herbicides: New challenges to molecular biology. *Oxford Surveys of Plant Molecular and Cell Biology, 5,* 195–203.

———. 1992. Addressing real weed science needs with innovations. *Weed Technology, 6,* 509–25.

———. 1993. Advances in achieving the needs of biotechnologically-derived herbicide resistant crops. *Plant Breeding Reviews, 11,* 155–98.

———. 1995. Department of Plant Genetics, Weizmann Institute of Science, Rehevot, Israel. Personal communication, August.

Grigg, D. B. 1974. *The agricultural systems of the world.* Cambridge: Cambridge University Press.

Grobstein, C. 1979. *A double image of the double helix.* San Francisco: W. H. Freeman.

Guest, Gerald B. 1991. Director, Center for Veterinary Medicine, FDA. Letter to David Kowalczyk, Regulatory Affairs Manager, Monsanto Agricultural Company, January 9.

———. 1993. Testimony before the Joint Center for Food Safety and Applied Nutrition/Center for Veterinary Medicine Advisory Committee, May 6.

Hacking, Andrew J. 1986. *Economic aspects of biotechnology.* Cambridge Studies in Biotechnology 3. Cambridge: Cambridge University Press.

Hadley, W. M., S. W. Burchiel, T. D. McDowell, J. P. Thilsted, C. M. Hibbs, J. A. Whorton, P. W. Day, M. B. Friedman, and R. E. Stoll. 1987. Five-month oral (diet) toxicity/infectivity study of *Bacillus thuringiensis* insecticides in sheep. *Fundamentals of Applied Toxicology, 8,* 136–242

Hairston, N. G., F. E. Smith, and L. B. Slobodkin. 1960. Community structure, population control, and competition. *American Naturalist, 94,* 421–25.

Hallberg, Milton C., ed. 1992. *Bovine somatotropin and emerging issues.* Boulder: Westview Press.

Hamilton, W. F., J. Vila, and M. D. Dibner. 1990. Patterns of strategic choice in emerging firms: Positioning for innovation in biotechnology. *California Management Review, 32,* 73–86.

Hamilton, F. 1990. The dynamics of technology and strategy. *European Journal of Operational Research, 47,* 141–52.

Hammock, B. D., B. C. Bonning, R. D. Possee, T. N. Hanzlik, and S. Maeda. 1990. Expression and effects of the juvenile hormone esterase in a baculovirus vector. *Nature, 344,* 458–60.

Hankinson, Thomas. 1992. Senior scientist, EcoScience. Interview, January 20.

Hannay, C. L., and P. C. Fitz-James. 1955. The protein crystals of *Bacillus thuringiensis* Berliner. *Canadian Journal of Microbiology, 1,* 694.

Hansen, Michael K., Consumer Policy Institute, Consumer Union. Testimony, Joint Meeting, Food Advisory Committee and the Veterinary Medicine Advisory Committee, May 6, 1993.

Haq, T. A., H. S. Mason, J. D. Clements, and C. J. Arntzen. 1995. Oral immunization with a recombinant bacterial antigen in transgenic plants. *Science, 268,* 714–16.

Harbison, Earle H. Jr. 1990. Biotechnology commercialization: An economic engine for future agricultural and industrial growth. Speech given to the World Economic Forum, Davos Switzerland, February 5.

Harlander, Susan. 1989. Food biotechnology: Yesterday, today, and tomorrow. *Food Technology, 43,* 194–206.

———. 1991a. Social, moral and ethical issues in food biotechnology. *Food Technology*, 45, 152–56.

———. 1991b. Biotechnology: A means for improving our food supply. *Food Technology*, 45, 84–95.

Harris, Marvin K. 1991. *Bacillus thuringiensis* and pest control. Letters. *Science*, 253, 1075.

Harsanyi, Zsolt, and Nelson Schneider. 1984. *Investment strategies in biotechnology: The race to commercialization.* New York: EIC/Intelligence.

Haselkorn, R. 1986. Organization of the genes for nitrogen fixation in photosynthetic bacteria and cyanobacteria. *Annual Review of Microbiology*, 40, 525–47.

Hayenga, M., L. C. Thompson, C. Chase, and S. Kaaria. 1992. Economic and environmental implications of herbicide-tolerant corn and processing tomatoes. *Journal of Soil and Water Conservation*, 47, 411–17.

Hebblethwaite, J. 1991. Director of Technology Management and Acquisitions, Monsanto Agricultural Company. Interview, January 16.

Hecht, Donald W. 1991. Bovine somatotropin safety and effectiveness: An industry perspective. *Food Technology*, 45, 118–19, 124–25.

Helz, G. E., I. L. Baldwin, and E. B. Fred. 1927. Strain variation and host-specificity of root-nodule bacteria of the pea group. *Journal of Agricultural Research*, 35, 1039–55.

Hess, Dana F. 1992a. Director of Biological and Biochemical Research, Sandoz Agro Inc. Interview, March 3.

———. 1992b. Director of Biological and Biochemical Research, Sandoz Agro Inc. Personal communication, November 14.

HHS News. 1994. FDA news release. May 18.

Hicks J. R. 1932. *The theory of wages.* London: Macmillan.

Hilder, V. A., A. M. R. Gatehouse, S. E. Sheerman, R. F. Barker, and D. Boulter. 1987. A novel mechanism of insect resistance engineered into tobacco. *Nature*, 330, 160–63.

Hileman, Bette. 1993. Bovine growth hormone found safe for use. *Chemical and Engineering News* 7–8 (May 13).

Hilts, Philip. 1990. U.S. calls milk free of antibiotics. *New York Times*, February 6.

Hirano, Susan S., and Christen D. Upper. 1985. Ecology and physiology of *Pseudomonas syringae*. *Biotechnology*, 3, 1073–78.

Hirsh, A. M., K. J. Wilson, J. D. G. Jones, M. Bang, V. V. Walker, and F. M. Ausubel. 1984. *Rhizobium meliloti* nodulation genes allow *Agrobacterium tumefaciens* and *Escherichia coli* to form pseudonodules on alfalfa. *Journal of Bacteriology*, 158, 1133–43.

Hoban, Thomas J., and Patricia Kendall. 1992. *Consumer attitudes about the use of biotechnology in agriculture and food production.* Raleigh: North Carolina State University.

Hobbelink, Henk. 1987. Plant patents: Who benefits? *Gene Watch*, 4, 6–7.

———. 1991. *Biotechnology and the future of world agriculture.* London: Zed Books.

Hodgson, John. 1992. Whole animals for wholesale protein production. *Bio/Technology, 10,* 863–66.

Hodgson, John, and Kirsty Barlow. 1993. Does biotechnology measure up? Facts and feats of a biotechnological nature. *Bio/Technology, 11,* 1003–6.

Höfte, Herman, and H. R. Whiteley. 1989. Insecticidal crystal proteins of *Bacillus thuringiensis. Microbiological Reviews, 53,* 242–55.

Holt, Jodie S., and Homer M. LeBaron. 1990. Significance and distribution of herbicide resistance. *Weed Technology, 4,* 141–49.

Holt, J. S., S. B. Powles, and J. A. M. Holtum. 1993. Mechanisms and agronomic aspects of herbicide resistance. *Annual Review of Plant Physiology and Plant Molecular Biology, 44,* 203–9.

Honée, G., and B. Visser. 1993. The mode of action of *Bacillus thuringiensis* crystal proteins. *Entomologia Experimentalis et Applicata, 69,* 145–55.

Hopkins, D. Douglas, Rebecca Goldburg, and Steven A. Hirsch. 1991. *A mutable feast: Assuring food safety in the era of genetic engineering.* New York: Environmental Defense Fund.

Hoyle, Russ. 1992. Small step for biopesticides. *Bio/Technology, 10,* 123.

Hubbard, Ruth, and Elijah Wald. 1993. *Exploding the gene myth.* Boston: Beacon Press.

Hull, R. 1994. Risks in using transgenic plants? *Science, 264,* 1649–50.

Hutton, J. B. 1957. The effect of growth hormone on the yield and composition of milk. *Journal of Endocrinology, 15,* 115–25.

Ibrahim, M. A., G. G. Bond, T. A. Burke, P. Cole, F. N. Dost, P. E. Enterline, M. Gough, R. S. Greenberg, W. E. Halperin, E. McConnell, J. A. Munro, S. H. Swenberg, S. H. Zahm, and J. D. Graham. 1991. Weight of the evidence on the human carcinogenicity of 2,4–D. *Environmental Health Perspectives, 96,* 213–22.

Iowa State University, Office of Biotechnology. 1991. A benefit/risk assessment for the introduction of herbicide tolerant crops in Iowa. *Biotechnology Update, 5,* 1–14.

————. 1992. Practical farmers of Iowa reduce weed pressure in ridge-till. *Sustainable Agriculture.* Iowa State University Extension Service, Ames. July.

James, W. C., P. S. Teng, and F. W. Nutter. 1991. Estimated losses of crops from plant pathogens. In *CRC handbook of pest management,* ed. D. Pimentel and A. A. Hansen. 1:15–50. Boca Raton: CRC Press.

Jeffcoat, Roger. 1991. The impact of biotechnology on the food industry. In *Biotechnology: The science and the business,* ed. V. Moses and R. E. Cape, 463–80. London: Harwood Academic Publishers.

Jepson, P. C., B. C. Croft, and G. E. Pratt. 1994. Test systems to determine the ecological risks posed by toxin release from *Bacillus thuringiensis* genes in crop plants. *Molecular Ecology, 3,* 81–89.

Joel, D. M., Y. Kleifeld, D. Loshner-Goshen, G. Herzlinger, and J. Gressel. 1995. Transgenic crops against parasites. *Nature 374,* 220–21.

Johnson, Donald E., Gerald M. Ward, and Joan Torrent. 1992. The environmental impact of bovine somatotropin use in dairy cattle. *Journal of Environmental Quality, 2*, 157–62.

Journal of Commerce. 1992. Herman, the biotech bull, may sire new drug era. December 29.

Juskevich, J. C., and C. G. Guyer. 1990. Bovine growth hormone: Human food safety evaluation. *Science, 264*, 875–84.

Kaiser, Harry M., Clifford W. Scherer, and David M. Barbano. 1992. Consumer perceptions and attitudes towards bovine somatotropin. *Northeastern Journal of Agricultural and Resource Economics, 21*, 10–20.

Kalter, R. J., R. Milligan, W. Lesser, W. Magrath, L. Tauer, and D. Bauman. 1985. *Biotechnology and the dairy industry: Production costs, commercial potential, and the economic impact of the bovine growth hormone.* A.E. Research 85–20. Ithaca: Department of Agricultural Economics, Cornell University.

Kamien, Morton I., and Nancy L. Schwartz. 1982. *Market structure and innovation.* London: Cambridge University Press.

Kaniewski, W., C. Lawson, B. Sammons, L. Haley, J. Hart, X. Delannay, and N. E. Tumer. 1990. Field resistance to transgenic Russet Burbank potato effects of infection by potato virus x and potato virus Y. *Bio/Technology, 8*, 750–54.

Kapuscinski, A. R., and E. M. Hallerman. 1990. Transgenic fishes. *Fisheries, 15*, 2–5.

Kareiva, Peter, and John Stark. 1994. Environmental risk in agricultural biotechnology. *Industry and Chemistry*, 17 January, 52–55.

Kennedy, G. G., and M. E. Whalon. 1995. Managing pest resistance to *Bacillus thuringiensis* endotoxins: Constraints and incentives to implementation. *Journal of Economic Entomology, 88*, 454–60.

Kenney, Martin. 1986. *Biotechnology: The university industrial complex.* New Haven: Yale University Press.

Kessler, David A., Michael R. Taylor, James H. Maryanski, Eric L. Flamm, and Linda S. Kahl. 1992. The safety of foods developed by biotechnology. *Science, 256*, 1747–49, 1832.

Kidd, G. 1994. The dramatic fall and rise of Agracetus. *Bio/Technology, 12*, 122.

Kim, Leo. 1992. Vice President, Mycogen. Interview, March 4.

Kinnucan, Henry, Joseph J. Molnar, and Upton Hatch. 1989. Theories of technical change in agriculture with implications for biotechnologies. In *Biotechnology and the new agricultural revolution*, ed. J. J. Molnar and H. Kinnucan. Boulder: Westview Press.

Klee, Harry J., Maria B. Hayford, Keith A. Kretzmer, Gerard F. Barry, and Ganesh M. Kishore. 1991. Control of ethylene synthesis by expression of a bacterial enzyme in transgenic tomato plants. *Plant Cell, 3*, 1187–93.

Klein, T. M., M. Fromm, A. Weissinger, D. Tomes, S. Schaaf, M. Sletten, and J. C. Sanford. 1988. Transfer of foreign genes into intact maize cells with high-velocity microprojectiles. *Proceedings of the National Academy of Sciences in the United States, 85,* 4305–9.

Kondo, A., and S. Maeda. 1991. Host range expansion by recombination of the baculovirus *Bombyx mori* nuclear polyhedrosis virus and *Autographa californica* nuclear polyhedrosis virus. *Journal of Virology, 65,* 3625–32.

Kong, D. 1992. Slow times in the organic market. *Boston Globe,* June 17, 37, 40.

Koziel, M. G., G. L. Beland, C. Bowman, N. B. Carozzi, R. Crenshaw, L. Crossland, J. Dawson, N. Desai, M. Hill, S. Kadwell, K. Launis, K. Lewis, D. Maddox, K. McPherson, M. R. Meghji, E. Merlin, R. Rhodes, G. W. Warren, M. Wright, and S. V. Evola. 1993. Field performance of elite transgenic maize plants expressing an insecticidal protein derived from *Bacillus thuringiensis. Bio/Technology, 11,* 194–200.

Kramer, Matthew, Rick Sanders, Hassan Bolkan, Curtis Waters, Raymond E. Sheehy, and William R. Hiatt. 1992. Postharvest evaluation of transgenic tomatoes with reduced levels of polygalacturonase: Processing, firmness, and disease resistance. *Postharvest Biology and Technology, 1,* 241–55.

Krimpenfort, Paul, Adriana Rademakers, Will Eyestone, Adriaan van der Schans, Sandra van der Broek, Patricia Kooiman, Erika Kootwijk, Gerard Platenburg, Frank Pieper, Rein Strijker, and Herman de Boer. 1991. Generation of transgenic dairy cattle using 'in vitro' embryo production. *Bio/Technology, 9,* 844–47.

Krimsky, Sheldon. 1982. *Genetic alchemy: The social history of the recombinant DNA controversy.* Cambridge: MIT Press.

———. 1991. *Biotechnics and society: The rise of industrial genetics.* New York: Praeger Publishers.

Krimsky, Sheldon, and Alonzo Plough. 1988. *Environmental hazards: Communicating risks as a social process.* Dover: Auburn House.

Kroger, Manfred. 1992. Food safety and product quality. In *Bovine somatotropin and emerging issues,* ed. M. C. Hallberg. Boulder: Westview Press.

Kronfeld, David S. 1993. Recombinant bovine growth hormone: Cow responses delay drug approval and impact public health. In *The dairy debate,* ed. William C. Liebhardt. Davis: University of California Sustainable Agriculture Research and Education Program.

Kuc, J. 1982. Induced immunity to plant disease. *BioScience, 32,* 854–60.

Kuhn, Thomas. 1962. *The structure of scientific revolutions.* Chicago: University of Chicago Press.

Kunik, T., R. Salomon, D. Zamir, N. Navot, M. Zeiden, I. Michelson, Y. Gafni, and H. Czosnek. 1994. Transgenic tomato plants expressing the tomato yellow leaf curl virus capsid protein are resistant to the virus. *Bio/Technology, 12,* 500–504.

Lakatos, Imre, and Alan Musgrave, eds. 1970. *Criticism and the growth of knowledge.* Cambridge: Cambridge University Press.

Lambert, B., and M. Peferoen. 1992. Insecticidal promise of *Bacillus thuringiensis. BioScience, 42,* 112–22.

LeBaron, Homer, M. 1989. Herbicide resistance in plants. In *Biotechnology and sustainable agriculture: Policy alternatives*, ed. J. F. MacDonald, 92–102. NABC report 1. Ithaca: National Agricultural Biotechnology Council.

———. 1991. Senior Scientist, New Technology and Basic Research, Ciba-Geigy Corporation. Interview, March 5.

LeBaron, H. M., and J. E. McFarland. 1990. Resistance to herbicides. *Chemtech, 20*, 508–11.

Lecoq, H., M. Ravelonandro, C. Wipf-Schneibel, M. Monsion, B. Raccah, and J. Dunez. 1993. Aphid transmission of an aphid nontransmissible strain of zucchini yellow mosaic potyvirus from transgenic plants expressing capsid protein of plum pox virus. *Molecular Plant-Microbe Interactions, 6*, 403–6.

Lee, M. O., and N. K. Schaffer. 1933. Anterior pituitary growth hormone and the composition of growth. *Journal of Nutrition, 7*, 337–63.

Lee, Thomas F. 1993. *Gene future: The promise and perils of the new biology*. New York: Plenum Press.

Leemans, Jan. 1993. Ti to tomato, tomato to market. *Biotechnology, 11*, S22–S26.

Leonard, L. T. 1930. A failure of Australian winter peas apparently due to nodule bacteria. *Journal of the American Society of Agronony, 22*, 277–80.

Levidow, Les. In press. Codes, commodities, and combat: Agricultural biotechnology as clean surgical strike. In *Perspectives on the environment II*, ed. S. Elworthy et al. Aldershot, U.S.: Avebury Press.

Levy, Stuart. 1992. *The antibiotic paradox*. New York: Plenum Press.

Liebhardt, William C., ed. 1993. *The dairy debate*. Davis: University of California Sustainable Agriculture Research and Education Program.

Liebman, Matthew, and Rhonda R. Janke. 1990. Sustainable weed management practices. In *Sustainable agriculture in temperate zones*, ed. C. A. Francis, C. B. Flora, and L. D. King, 111–43. New York: John Wiley.

Lin, W., C. S. Anuratha, K. Datta, I. Potrykus, S. Muthukrishnan, and S. K. Datta. 1995. Genetic engineering of rice for resistance to sheath blight. *Bio/Technology, 13*, 686–91.

Lindemann, Julianne, Gareth J. Warren, and Trevor V. Suslow. 1986. Letter: Ice-nucleating bacteria. *Science, 231*, 536.

Lindow, S. E. 1982. Population dynamics of epiphytic ice nucleation active bacteria on frost sensitive plants and frost control by means of antagonistic bacteria. In *Plant cold hardness and freezing stress*, ed. A. Sakai and P. H. Li, 395–416. New York: Academic Press.

———. 1983. Methods of preventing frost injury caused by epiphytic ice-nucleation-active bacteria. *Plant Disease, 67*, 327–33.

———. 1985. Ecology of *Pseudomonas syringae* relevant to the field use of ice minus deletion mutants constructed in vitro for plant frost control. In *Engineered organisms in the environment: Scientific issues*, ed. H. O. Halvorson, D. Pramer, and M. Rogul, 23–25. Washington, D.C.: American Society for Microbiology.

Ling, K., S. Namba, C. Gonsalves, J. L. Slightom, and D. Gonsalves. 1991. Protection against detrimental effects of potyvirus infection in transgenic tobacco plants expressing the papaya ringspot virus coat protein gene. *Bio/Technology, 9,* 752–58.

Locke, Michelle. 1991. Battle over cow growth hormone. *Los Angeles Times* Dec. 8.

Loew, Franklin M. 1993. Turning ploughshares into Volvos: Changing american attitudes toward livestock. *Journal of Agricultural and Environmental Ethics, 6* (Special Supplement 1), 105–9.

Love, John M., and William Lesser. 1989. The potential impact of ice-minus bacteria as a frost protectant in New York fruit production. *Northeastern Journal of Agricultural and Resource Economics, 18,* 26–34.

Lovins, Amory. 1977. *Soft energy paths.* Cambridge: Ballinger.

Lyon, B. R., D. J. Llewellyn, J. L. Huppatz, E. S. Dennis, and W. J. Peacock. 1989. Expression of a bacterial gene in transgenic tobacco plants confers resistance to the herbicide 2,4–dichlorophenoxyacetic acid. *Plant Molecular Biology, 13,* 533–40.

Macer, Darryl R. J. 1990. *Shaping genes.* Christchurch, New Zealand: Eubios Ethics Institute.

MacFarlane, S. A., and J. W. Davies. 1992. Plants transformed with a region of the 201–kilodalton replicase gene from pea early browning virus RNA1 are resistant to virus infection. *Proceedings of the National Academy of Sciences, USA, 89,* 5829–33.

Macfarlane, N. A. A., ed. 1992. *Biotechnological innovations in animal productivity.* Oxford: Butterworth-Heinemann.

MacIntosh, Susan C., T. B. Stone, S. R. Sims, P. L. Hunst, J. T. Greenplate, P. G. Marrone, F. J. Perlak, D. A. Fischhoff, and R. L. Fuchs. 1990. Specificity and efficacy of purified *Bacillus thuringiensis* proteins against agronomically important insects. *Journal of Invertebrate Pathology, 56,* 258–66.

Maeda, S. 1989. Expression of foreign genes in insects using baculovirus vectors. *Annual Review of Entomology, 34,* 351–72.

Maki, Leroy R., Elizabeth L. Galyan, Mei-mon Chang-Chien, and Daniel R. Caldwell. 1974. Ice nucleation induced by *Pseudomonas syringae. Applied Microbiology, 28,* 456–59.

Malinowski, Bronislaw. 1926. *Myth in primitive psychology.* New York: W. W. Norton.

Mallet, J. 1989. The evolution of insecticide resistance: Have the insects won? *Trends in Ecology and Evolution, 4,* 336–40.

Mallet, James, and Patrick Porter. 1992. Preventing insect adaptation to insect-resistant crops: Are seed mixtures of refugia the best strategy? *Proceedings of the Royal Society of London, B, 250,* 165–69.

Marrone, Pamela. 1992. President, Novo Nordisk Entotech, Inc. Interview, March 2.

———. 1995. Former CEO Novo Nordisk Entotech. Personal communication, January 16.

Marrone, Pamela G., and Ruedi Sandmeier. 1991. Biological control: Making it work. In *Biotechnology and sustainable agriculture: Policy alternatives*, ed. J. F. MacDonald. NABC report 3. Ithaca: National Agricultural Biotechnology Council.

Martin, Sam, and Joyce Tait. 1992. *Release of genetically modified organisms: Public attitudes and understanding*. Milton Keynes, U.K.: The Open University,

Marx, Jean. 1990. Animal carcinogen testing challenged. *Science, 250*, 743–45.

Mauch, F., B. Mauch-Mani, and T. Boller. 1988. Antifungal hydrolases in pea tissue II. Inhibition of fungal growth by combinations of chitinases and B-1,3–glucanase. *Plant Physiology, 88*, 936–42.

McBride, B. W., J. L. Burton, and J. H. Burton. 1988. The influence of bovine growth hormone (somatotropin) on animals and their products. *Research and Development in Agriculture, 5*, 1–21.

McCutchen, B. F., P. V. Choudary, R. Crenshaw, D. Maddox, S. G. Kamita, N. Palekar, S. Volrath, E. Fowler, B. D. Hammock, and S. Maeda. 1991. Development of a recombinant baculovirus expressing an insect-selective neurotoxin: Potential for pest control. *Bio/Technology, 9*, 848–52.

McGaughey, W. H. 1985. Insect resistance to the biological insecticide *Bacillus thuringiensis*. *Science, 229*, 193–95.

McGaughey, W. H., and D. E. Johnson. 1992. Indianmeal moth (Lepidoptera: Pyralidae) resistance to different strains and mixtures of *Bacillus thuringiensis*. *Journal of Economic Entomology, 85*, 1594.

McGaughey, W. H., and M. E. Whalon. 1992. Managing insect resistance to *Bacillus thuringiensis* toxins. *Science, 258*, 1451–55.

McHughen, A., and F. A. Holm. 1995. Transgenic flax with environmentally and agronomically sustainable attributes. *Transgenic Research, 4*, 3–11.

McMurray, Scott. 1993. New calgene tomato might have tasted just as good without genetic alteration. *Wall Street Journal*, January 12, B1.

McPherson, Sylvia, A., F. J. Perlak, R. L. Fuchs, P. G. Marrone, P. B. Lavrik, and D. A. Fischhoff. 1988. Characteristics of a coleopteran-specific protein of *Bacillus thuringiensis* subsp. *tenebrionis*. *Bio/Technology, 6*, 61–66.

Meade, Harry, Liora Gates, Elizabeth Lacy, and Nils Lonberg. 1990. Bovine alpha-s1–casein gene sequences direct high level expression of active human urokinase in mouse milk. *Bio/Technology, 8*, 443–46.

Meadows, M. P. 1992. Environmental release of *Bacillus thuringiensis*. In *Release of genetically engineered and other micro-organisms*, ed. J. C. Fry and M. J. Day, 120–36. Cambridge: Cambridge University Press.

Mellon, M. 1995. Why UCS resists Bt crops. *Gene Exchange, 5*, 2, 15.

Mepham, T. B. 1991. Bovine somatotropin and public health. *British Medical Journal , 302*, 483.

Merryweather, A. T., U. Weyer, M. P. G. Harris, M. Hirst, T. Booth, and R. D. Possee. 1990. Construction of genetically engineered baculovirus insecticides containing the Bacillus thuringiensis subsp. kurstaki HD-73 delta endotoxin. *Journal of General Virology, 71*, 1535–44.

Métraux, J. P., P. Ahl-Goy, T. Staub, J. Speich, A. Steinemann, J. Ryals, and E. Ward. 1991. Induced systemic resistance in cucumber in response to 2,6-dichloro-isonicotinic acid and pathogens. In *Advances in molecular genetics of plant-microbe interactions*, ed. H. Hennecke and D. P. S. Verma. 1:432–39. Dordrecht, the Netherlands: Kluwer.

Metz, Sally. 1991. Technology Manager, Monsanto Agricultural Company. Interview, January 16.

Miller, Amy. 1993. City to distribute $5 million federal loan to biotech firms for needed lab space. *Cambridge Chronicle*, April 8, 5.

Miller, Dale A. 1990. Environmentalism and the new agriculture. Speech delivered at the Ag Bankers Association Annual Meeting, Denver, Colorado, November 12. *Vital Speeches of the Day, 57,* 221–24.

Miller, David. 1992. Vice President, Research and Development, Ecoscience. Interview, March 24.

Miller, Henry. 1993. Perceptions of biotechnology risks: The emotional debate. *Bio/Technology, 11,* 1075–76.

———. 1994. A need to reinvent biotechnology regulation at the EPA. *Science, 226,* 1815–18.

Miller, Henry I., Susanne L. Huttner, and Roger Beachy. 1993. Risk assessment experiments for "genetically modified" plants. *Bio/Technology, 11,* 1323–24.

Miller, Melanie. 1991. The promise of biotechnology. *Journal of Environmental Health, 54,* 13–14.

Moffat, A. S. 1990. Nitrogen-fixing bacteria finding new partners. *Science, 250,* 910–12.

———. 1992. Improving plant disease resistance. *Science, 257,* 482–83.

———. 1994. Mapping the sequence of disease resistance. *Science, 265,* 1804–5.

———. 1995. Exploring transgenic plants as a new vaccine source. *Science, 268,* 658–60.

Molnar, J. J., and H. Kinnucan. 1989. Conclusion: Biotechnology, farming, and agriculture into the 21st century. In *Biotechnology and the new agricultural revolution*, ed. J. J. Molnar and H. Kinucan. Boulder: Westview Press.

Molnar, Joseph J., Keith A. Cumming, and Peter F. Nowak. 1990. Bovine somatotropin: Biotechnology products and social issues in the United States dairy industry. *Journal of Dairy Science, 73,* 3084–93.

Moore, Dale A., and Lawrence J. Hutchinson. 1992. BST and animal health. In *Bovine somatotropin and emerging issues*, ed. M. C. Hallberg. Boulder: Westview Press.

Moses, V., and R. E. Cape. 1991. *Biotechnology the science and the business.* London: Harwood Academic Publishers.

Murry, L. E., L. G. Elliot, S. A. Capitant, J. A. West, K. K. Hanson, L. Scarafia, S. Johnston, C. DeLuca-Flaherty, S. Nichols, D. Cunanan, P. S. Dietrich, I. J. Mettler, S. Dewald, D. A. Warnick, C. Rhodes, R. M. Sinibaldi, and K. J. Brunke. 1993. Transgenic corn plants expressing MDMV

Strain B coat protein are resistant to mixed infections of Maize Dwarf Mosaic Virus and Maize Chlorotic Mottle Virus. *Bio/Technology, 11*, 1559–64.

National Academy of Sciences (NAS). 1987. Committee on the Introduction of Genetically-Engineered Organisms into the Environment. *Introduction of recombinant-DNA engineered organisms into the environment: Key issues.* Washington, D.C.: National Academy Press.

National Institutes of Health Technology Assessment Panel (NIH-TAP). 1991. Bovine somatotropin and the safety of cow's milk: National institutes of health technology assessment conference statement. *Nutrition Reviews, 49,* 227–32.

National Institutes of Health (NIH). 1991. NIH technology assessment conference statement on bovine somatotropin. *Journal of the American Medical Association, 265,* 1423–25.

National Research Council (NRC). 1989. *Alternative agriculture.* Washington, D.C.: National Academy Press.

Nawrath, C., Y. Poirier, and C. Somerville. 1994. Targeting of the polyhydroxybutyrate biosynthetic pathway to the plastids of *Arabidopsis thaliana* results in high levels of polymer accumulation. *Proceedings of the National Academy of Sciences in the United States, 91,* 12760–64.

Nejidat, A., and R. N. Beachy. 1990. Transgenic tobacco plants expressing a coat protein gene of tobacco mosaic virus are resistant to some other tobamoviruses. *Molecular Plant-Microbe Interactions, 3,* 247–51.

Nelson, R. S., S. M. McCormick, X. Delannay, P. Dubé, J. Layton, E. J. Anderson, M. Kaniewska, R. K. Proksch, R. B. Horsch, S. G. Rogers, R. T. Fraley, and R. N. Beachy. 1988. Virus tolerance, plant growth, and field performance of transgenic tomato plants expressing coat protein from tobacco mosaic virus. *Bio/Technology, 6,* 403–9.

Neuhaus Jean-Marc, P. Ahl-Goy, U. Hinz, S. Flores, and F. Meins Jr. 1991. High-level expression of tobacco chitinase gene in *Nicotiana sylvestris:* Susceptibility of transgenic plants to *Cercospora nicotianae* infection. *Plant Molecular Biology, 16,* 141–51.

Newhouse, K., B. Singh, D. Shaner, and M. Stidham. 1991. Mutations in corn (*Zea mays* L.) conferring resistance to imidazolinone herbicides. *Theoretical and Applied Genetics, 83,* 65–70.

Norris, Robert, F. 1992. Have ecological and biological studies improved weed control strategies? In *Proceedings of the first international weed control congress,* 7–33. Melbourne, Australia: Weed Science Society of Victoria.

Obukowicz, M. G., F. J. Perlak, K. Kusano-Kretzmer, E. J. Mayer, S. L. Bolten, and L. S. Watrud. 1986. Tn5–mediated integration of the delta-endotoxin gene from *Bacillus thuringiensis* into the chromosome of root-colonizing pseudomonads. *Journal of Bacteriology, 168,* 982–89.

Odum, Eugene P. 1985. Biotechnology and the biosphere. *Science, 229,* 1338.

Office of Science and Technology Policy (OSTP), Executive Office of the President. 1986. Proposal for a coordinated framework for regulation of biotechnology. *Federal Register, 51,* 23309–93.

———. 1992. Exercise of federal oversight within scope of statutory authority: Planned introductions of biotechnology products into the environment. *Federal Register, 57,* 753–6762.

Office of Technology Aassessment (OTA), U.S. Congress. 1981. *Impacts of applied genetics: Micro/organisms, plants, and animals.* OTA-HR-32. Washington, D.C.: Government Printing Office.

———. 1984. *Commercial biotechnology: An international analysis.* Washington, D.C.: Government Printing Office.

———. 1986. *Technology, public policy, and the changing structure of American agriculture.* OTA-F 285. Washington, D.C.: Government Printing Office.

———. 1988. *New developments in biotechnology: U.S. investment in biotechnology—special report.* OTA-BA-360. Washington, D.C.: Government Printing Office.

———. 1989. *New developments in biotechnology: Patenting life.* Special report 5, OTA-BA-370. Washington, D.C.: Government Printing Office.

———. 1991a. *Biotechnology in a global economy.* OTA-BA-494. Washington, D.C.: Government Printing Office.

———. 1991b. *U.S. dairy industry at a cross road: Biotechnology and policy choices.* Special report, OTA-F-470. Washington, D.C.: Government Printing Office.

Okie, Susan. 1987. NIH scientists introduce genetic code of AIDS virus into mice. *Washington Post,* December 6.

Olson, David. 1995. Director of Regulatory Affairs, Ecogen, Inc. Personal communication, August 28.

Olson, Steve. 1986. *Biotechnology: An industry comes of age.* Washington, D.C.: National Academy Press.

O'Reilly, D. R., and L. Miller. 1991. Improvement of a baculovirus pesticide by deletion of the egt gene. *Bio/Technology, 9,* 1086–89.

Orsenigo, Luigi. 1989. *The emergence of biotechnology: Institutions and markets in industrial innovation.* New York: St. Martin's Press.

Osborne, J. K., S. Sarkar, and T. M. A. Wilson. 1990. Complementation of coat protein-defective TMV mutants in transgenic plants expressing TMV coat protein. *Virology, 179,* 921–25.

Osteen, Craig. 1993. Pesticide use trends and issues in the United States. In *The pesticide question,* ed. D. Pimentel and H. Lehman, 309–36. New York: Chapman & Hall.

Ostrach, Michael. 1991. Financing biotechnology companies. In *Biotechnology: The science and the business,* ed. V. Moses and R. E. Cape. London: Harwood Academic Publishers.

Ott, Stephen, L. 1990. Supermarket shoppers' pesticide concerns and willingness to purchase certified pesticide residue-free fresh produce. *Agribusiness, 6,* 593–602.

Padgette, Stephen. 1991. Plant Molecular Biology Group, Monsanto Agricultural Company. Interview, January 16.

———. 1992. Plant Molecular Biology Group, Monsanto Agricultural Company. Personal communication, March 5.

Padgette, S. R., G. della-Cioppa, D. M. Shah, R. T. Fraley, and G. M. Kishore.

1989. Selective herbicide tolerance through protein engineering. In *Cell culture and somatic cell genetics of plants*. 6:441–76. New York: Academic Press.

Palmiter, R. D., R. L. Brinster, R. E. Hammer, M. E. Trumbauer, M. G. Rosenfeld, N. C. Brinberg, and R. M. Evans. 1982. Dramatic growth of mice that develop from eggs microinjected with metallothionein—growth hormone fusion genes. *Nature, 300,* 611–15.

Palukaitis, P. 1991. Virus-mediated genetic transfer in plants. In *Risk asessment in genetic engineering*, ed. M. Levin and H. Strauss, 140–62. New York: McGraw-Hill.

Panetta, Joseph. 1992. Director of Regulatory Affairs, Mycogen. Interview, March 4.

Patton, R. A., and C. W. Heald. 1992. Management of BST-supplemented cows. In *Bovine somatotropin and emerging issues*, ed. M. C. Hallberg. Boulder: Westview Press.

Perkins, John H. 1980. The quest for innovation in agricultural entomology, 1945–1978. In *Pest control: Cultural and environmental aspects*, ed. D. Pimentel and J. H. Perkins, 23–80. Boulder: Westview Press.

Perlak, Frederick, J., R. L. Fuchs, D. A. Dean, S. L. McPherson, and D. A. Fischhoff. 1991. Modification of the coding sequence enhances plant expression of insect control protein genes. *Proceedings of the National Academy of Sciences, USA, 88,* 3324–28.

Perlak, Frederick, J., R. W. Deaton, T. A. Armstrong, R. L. Fuchs, S. R. Sims, J. T. Greenplate, and D. A. Fischhoff. 1990. Insect resistant cotton plants. *Bio/Technology, 8,* 939–43.

Perlak, Frederick J., T. B. Stone, Y. M. Muskopf, L. J. Petersen, G. B. Parker, S. A. McPherson, J. Wymam, S. Love, D. Reed, D. Biever, and D. A. Fischhoff. 1993. Genetically improved potatoes: Protection from damage by Colorado potato beetles. *Plant Molecular Biology, 22,* 313–21.

Perseley, Gabrielle J. 1991. *Beyond Mendel's garden: Biotechnology in the service of world agriculture*. Wallingford, U.K.: C. A. B. International.

Peters, S., R. Janke, and M. Böhlke. 1992. *Rodale's farming systems trial, 1986–1990*. Kutztown: Rodale Institute Research Center.

Pimentel, D., E. C. Terhune, W. Dritschi, D. Gallahn, N. Kinner, D. Nafus, R. Peterson, N. Zareh, and J. Misiti. 1977. Pesticides, insects in foods, and cosmetic standards. *BioScience, 27,* 178–85.

Pimentel, David, et al. 1992. Environmental and economic cost of pesticide use. *BioScience, 42,* 750–60.

Pisano, Gary P. 1991. The governance of innovation: Vertical integration and collaborative arrangements in the biotechnology industry. *Research Policy, 20,* 237–49.

Poirier, Y., C. Nawrath, and C. Somerville. 1995. Production of polyhydroxy-alkanoates, a family of biodegradable plastics and elastomers, in bacteria and plants. *Bio/Technology, 13,* 142–50.

Powell-Abel, Patrica, R. S. Nelson, B. De, N. Hoffman, S. G. Rogers, R. T. Fraley, and R. N. Beachy. 1986. Delay of disease development in transgenic plants that express the tobacco virus coat protein gene. *Science,* 232, 738–43.

Quemada, Hector. 1994. Assistant Director of Vegetable Biotechnology, Asgrow Seed Company. Interview, June 2.

Regal, Philip J. 1994. Scientific principles for ecologically based risk assessment of transgenic organisms. *Molecular Ecology,* 3, 5–13.

Research Seeds. 1993. *Third biannual report 1992, 1993 field trials.* St. Joseph, Mo.: Research Seeds Inc., Urbana Laboratories.

Rhodes, C. A., D. A. Pierce, I. J. Mettler, D. Mascarenhas, and J. J. Detmer. 1988. Genetically transformed maize plants from protoplasts. *Science,* 240, 204–7.

Rissler, Jane. 1991. Staff Scientist, National Biotechnology Policy Center, National Wildlife Federation. Interview, February 6.

Rissler, Jane, and Margaret Mellon. 1993. *Perils amidst the promise: Ecological risks of transgenic plants in a global market.* Cambridge: Union of Concerned Scientists.

Roberts, Leslie. 1988. Genetic engineers build a better tomato. *Science,* 241, 1290.

Rochow, W. F. 1977. Dependent virus transmission from mixed infections. In *Aphids as virus vectors,* ed. K. F. Harris and K. Maramorosch, 253–77. New York: Academic Press.

Rogers, E. 1983. *Diffusion of innovations.* New York: Free Press.

Rogoff, Martin H., and Stephen L. Rawlins. 1987. Food security: A technological alternative. *BioScience,* 37, 800–807.

Rollin, B. E. 1986. The Frankenstein thing: The moral impact of genetic engineering of agricultural animals on society and future science. In *Genetic engineering of animals: An agricultural perspective,* ed. J. W. Evens and A. Hollander, 285–97. New York: Plenum Press.

Ronson, C. W., A. Bosworth, M. Genova, S. Gudbrandsen, T. Hankinson, R. Kwiatkowski, H. Ratcliffe, C. Robie, P. Sweeney, W. Szeto, M. Williams, and R. Zablotowicz. 1990. Field release of genetically-engineered *Rhizobium meliloti* and *Bradyrhizobium japonicum* strains. In *Nitrogen fixation: Achievements and objectives,* ed. P. M. Gresshoff, L. E. Roth, G. Stacey, and W. E. Newman, 397–403. New York: Chapman and Hall.

Ross, A. F. 1961. Systemic acquired resistance induced by localized virus infections in plants. *Virology,* 14, 340–58.

Roush, Richard. 1992. Letter to the editors. *Gene Exchange,* 3, 2.

Rowan, Andrew N. 1989. The development of the animal protection movement. *Journal of the National Institutes of Health Research,* 1, 97–100.

RTD Updates. 1993a. *Iowa/Illinois study links agricultural production and natural resource data.* Washington, D.C.: United States Department of Agriculture, Economic Research Services, Resources and Technology Division. November.

———. 1993b. *Upper Snake River Basin area study links agricultural production and natural resource data.* Washington, D.C.: United States Department of Agriculture, Economic Research Services, Resources and Technology Division. December.

Russell, Dick. 1993. Miracle or myth? *Amicus Journal, 15,* 20–24.

Russell, Katherine A. 1991. Managing a biotechnology business. In *Biotechnology: The science and the business,* ed. V. Moses and R. E. Cape. London: Harwood Academic Publishers.

Ryals, John. 1994. Agricultural Biotechnology Research Unit, Ciba-Geigy Corporation, Research Triangle Park, N.C. Personal Communication, May.

Ryals, J., E. Ward, and J. Métraux. 1992. Systemic acquired resistance: An inducible defense mechanism in plants. In *Inducible plant proteins: Their biochemistry and molecular biology,* ed. L. Wray, 205–55. Cambridge: Cambridge University Press.

Saari, L. L., J. C. Cotterman, and D. C. Thill. 1994. Resistance to acetolactate synthase-inhibitor herbicides. In *Herbicide resistance in plants: Biology and biochemistry,* ed. S. B. Powles and J. A. M. Holtum, 83–139. Chelsea, Mich.: Lewis Press.

Salameh, Roger. 1994. Market Analyst, Calgene. Interview, June 23.

Salquist, Roger. 1991. Chair and Chief Executive Officer, Calgene. Interview, January 6.

Samples, J. R., and H. Buettner. 1983. Corneal ulcer caused by a biological insecticide (*Bacillus thuringiensis*). *American Journal of Ophthalmology, 95,* 258–60.

Sandmeier, Ruedi. 1992. Vice President, Research, Sandoz Agro. Interview, March 3.

Sanford, J. C. 1988. The biolistic process. *Tibtech, 6,* 299–302.

Sanford, J. C., and S. A. Johnston. 1985. The concept of parasite-derived resistance-deriving resistance genes from the parasite's own genome. *Journal of Theoretical Biology, 113,* 395–405.

Schafer, Joseph. 1936. *The social history of American agriculture.* New York: Macmillan.

Schell, Jozef, Bruno Gronenborn, and Robert T. Fraley. 1989. Improving crop plants by the introduction of isolated genes. In *A revolution in biotechnology,* ed. J. L. Marx. Cambridge: Cambridge University Press.

Schlumbaum, A., F. Mauch, U. Vogeli, and T. Boller. 1986. Plant chitinases are potent inhibitors of fungal growth. *Nature, 324,* 365–67.

Schmickle, Sharon. 1993. Germany's shunning of gene altered food frustrates scientists. *Minneapolis Star Tribune,* March 16.

Schneider, Keith. 1990. A drug for cows churns up opposition. *New York Times,* May 20.

———. 1991. Deadly pesticide may face U.S. ban. *New York Times,* March 26, A20.

———. 1992. Court expands pesticide ban to cover many used in food. *New York Times,* July 9, A1, A16.

———. 1993. U.S. approves use of drug to raise milk production. *New York Times,* November 6, 1, 8.

———. 1994a. Study finds risk of making plants viral resistant. *New York Times,* March 11.

———. 1994b. FDA warns the dairy industry not to label milk hormone-free. *New York Times*, February 8, A1.

Schneider, William. 1992. EPA, Office of Pesticide Programs. Personal communication, August.

Schneiderman, H. A., and W. D. Carpenter. 1990. *Planetary patriotism: Sustainable agriculture for the future.* St. Louis: Monsanto Agricultural Company.

Schoelz, J. E., and W. M. Wintermantel. 1993. Expansion of viral host range through complementation and recombination in transgenic plants. *Plant Cell, 5,* 16669–79.

Scholthof, Karen-Beth G., H. B. Scholthof, and A. O. Jackson. 1993. Control of plant virus diseases by pathogen-derived resistance in transgenic plants. *Plant Physiology, 102,* 7–12.

Schroth, M. N., and A. H. McCain. 1991. The nature, mode of action, and toxicity of bactericides. In *CRC handbook of pest management*, ed. D. Pimentel and A. A. Hensen. 2:497–505. Boca Raton: CRC Press.

Schumpeter, J. 1934. *The theory of economic development.* Cambridge: Harvard University Press.

Seabrook, Jeremy. 1991. Biotech bondage. *New Statesman and Society, 4,* 17, 19.

Seabrook, John. 1993. Tremors in the hothouse. *The New Yorker,* July 19, 32–41.

Sedivy, John M., and Alexandra L. Joyner. 1992. *Gene targeting.* New York: W. H. Freeman.

Senker, Jacqueline, and Wendy Faulkner. 1992. Industrial use of public sector research in advanced technologies: A comparison of biotechnology and ceramics, *R&D Management, 22,* 157–75.

Shade, R. E., H. E. Schroeder, J. J. Pueyo, L. M. Tabe, L. L. Murdock, T. J. V. Higgins, and M. J. Chrispeels. 1994. Transgenic pea seeds expressing the α-amylase inhibitor of the common bean are resistant to bruchid beetles. *Bio/Technology, 12,* 793–96

Shand, H. J. 1994. Agricultural biotechnology and the public good. In *Agricultural biotechnology and the public good*, ed. J. F. MacDonald, 73–86. NABC report 6. Ithaca: National Agricultural Biotechnology Council.

Sheehy, Raymond E., Matthew Kramer, and William R. Hiatt. 1988. Reduction of polygalacturonase activity in tomato fruit by antisense RNA. *Proceedings of the National Academy of Sciences of the United States, 85,* 8805–9.

Shiva, Vandana. 1990. Biodiversity, biotechnology and profit: The need for a people's plan to protect biological diversity. *The Ecologist, 20,* 44–47.

———. 1993. *Monocultures of the mind: Biodiversity, biotechnology and scientific agriculture.* London: Zed Books.

Show, James R., Edward C. Mather, and Mary M. Noel. 1992. Comparative study of the knowledge, attitudes, and behaviors of large animal veterinarians, dairy farmers,, and dairy processors in Michigan on bovine somatotropin. *Journal of the American Veterinary Association, 201,* 548–52.

Sibbison, J. B. 1990. USA: Concerns about BST. *Lancet, 336,* 1498–99.

Smith, S. R. L. 1980. Single cell protein. Royal Society of London, *Philosophical Transactions, B, 290,* 341–54.

Spalding, B. J. 1992. Transgenic pharming advances. *Bio/Technology, 10,* 498–99.

———. 1993. Ag biotech firms increase R&D spending 39.6 percent. *Bio/Technology, 11,* 875.

Speth, Gus. 1989. A Luddite recants. *The Amicus Journal,* March.

Spoor, C. 1990. Hormone helps African cows give more milk longer. *African Farmer,* November, 36.

Stalker, D. M., K. E. McBride, and L. D. Malyj. 1988. Herbicide resistance in transgenic plants expressing a bacterial detoxification gene. *Science, 242,* 419–22.

Staskawicz, B. J., F. M. Ausubel, B. J. Baker, J. G. Ellis, and J. D. G. Jones. 1995. Molecular genetics of plant disease resistance. *Science, 268,* 661–66.

Steinrucken, H. C., and N. Amrhein. 1980. The herbicide glyphosate is a potent inhibitor of 5–enolpyruvyl-shikmatic acid-3–phosphate synthase. *Biochemical and Biophysical Research Communications, 94,* 1207–12.

Stevens, W. K. 1992. Power of natural pest-killer wanes from overuse. *New York Times,* December 29, C1, C6.

———. 1993. Are gene-altered plants an ecological threat? Test is devised. *New York Times,* June 22, C4.

Stewart, L. D., M. Hirst, M. L. Ferber, A. T. Merryweather, P. J. Cayley, and R. D. Possee. 1991. Construction of an improved baculovirus insecticide containing an insect-specific toxin. *Nature, 352,* 85–88.

Stewart, Richard B. 1991. Regulatory law. In *The genetic revolution,* ed. B. D. Davis, 212–38. Baltimore: Johns Hopkins University Press.

Stonard, Richard. 1992. Research Manager, Monsanto. Personal communication, February 18.

Stone, Christopher D. 1987. *Earth and other ethics.* New York: Harper and Row.

Stone, R., ed. 1994. Reaping human vaccines from plants. *Science, 263,* 1211.

Stricker, P., and F. Grueter. 1928. Action du lobe antérier de l'hypophyse sur la montée laiteuse. *Compte Rendus, 99,* 1978–80.

Sugarman, Carole. 1989. Chains refuse engineered milk products. *Washington Post,* August 24, A6.

Summers, Gene F. 1993. *Technology and social change.* Boulder: Westview Press.

Swanson, M. E., et al. 1992. Production of functional human hemoglobin in transgenic swine. *Bio/Technology, 10,* 557–59.

Tabashnik, B. E. 1994. Evolution of resistance to *Bacillus thuringiensis. Annual Review of Entomology, 39,* 47–79.

Tabashnik, B. E., N. L. Cushing, N. Finson, and M. W. Johnson. 1990. Field development of resistance to *Bacillus thuringiensis* in diamondback moth (Lepidoptera: Plutellidae). *Journal of Economic Entomology, 83,* 1671–76.

Tabashnik, B. E., N. Finson, and M. W. Johnson. 1991. Managing resistance to *Bacillus thuringiensis:* Lessons from the diamondback moth (Lepidoptera: Plutellidae). *Journal of Economic Entomology, 84,* 49–55.

Taylor, Paul W. 1986. *Respect for nature.* Princeton: Princeton University Press.

Taylor, Steven. 1993. Allergic reactions to bioengineered foods: Do we know enough? *AAAS93 Program/Abstracts.* Annual Meeting of the American Association for the Advancement of Science, February 11–16, Boston.

Tepfer, M. 1993. Viral genes and transgenic plants: What are the potential environmental risks. *Bio/Technology, 11,* 1125–32.

Teubal, Morris, Tamar Yinnon, and Ehud Zuscovitch. 1991. Networks and market creation, *Research Policy, 20,* 381–92.

Thill, D. C., J. M. Lish, R. H. Callihan, and E. J. Bechinski. 1991. Integrated weed management a component of pest management. *Weed Technology, 5,* 648–56.

Tiedje, James M. 1992. Director, Center for Microbial Ecology, Michigan State University. Interview, April 22.

Tokar, Brian. 1992. The false promise of biotechnology. *Z Magazine,* February.

Tolin, S. A. 1991. Persistence, establishment, and mitigation of phytopathogenic viruses. In *Risk assessment in genetic engineering,* ed. M. Levin and H. Strauss, 114–39. New York: McGraw-Hill.

Tomalski, M. D., and L. K. Miller. 1991. Insect paralysis by baculovirus mediated expression of a mite neurotoxin. *Nature, 352,* 82–85.

Triplett, E. W. 1990. Construction of a symbiotically effective strain of *Rhizobium leguminosarum* bv. *trifolii* with increased nodulation competitiveness. *Applied Environmental Microbiology, 56,* 98–103.

Triplett, E. W., and M. J. Sadowsky. 1992. Genetics of competition for nodulation of legumes. *Annual Review of Microbiolology, 46,* 399–428.

Truve, E., A. Aaspôllu, J. Honkanen, R. Puska, M. Mehto, Anja Hassi, T. H. Teeri, M. Kelve, P. Seppänen, and M. Saarma. 1993. Transgenic potato plants expressing mammalian 2'-5' Oligoadenylate synthetase are protected from potato virus X infection under field conditions. *Bio/Technology, 11,* 1048–51.

Uknes, S. J., B. Mauch-Mani, M. Moyer, S. Potter, S. Williams, S. Dincher, D. Chandler, A. Slusarenko, E. R. Ward, and J. Ryals. 1992. Acquired resistance to Arabidopsis. *Plant Cell, 4,* 645–56.

United States Food and Drug Administration (USFDA). 1993. Food labeling: Foods derived from new plant varieties. *Federal Register, 58,* April 28, 25837–41.

United States General Accounting Office (USGAO). 1992. *Food safety and quality: FDA strategy needed to address animal drug residues in milk.* Washington, D.C.: U.S. General Accounting Office.

United States Department of Agriculture (USDA). 1976. *Agricultural Statistics 1976.* Washington, D.C.: Government Printing Office.

———. 1986. *Agricultural Statistics 1986.* Washington, D.C.: Government Printing Office.

———. 1987. *The magnitude and costs of groundwater contamination from agricultural chemicals: A national perspective.* Staff Report AGES870318. Washington, D.C.: U.S. Department of Agriculture, Economic Research Service.

———. 1993a. *Agricultural chemical usage: 1992 field crops summary.* Ag Ch 1 (93). Washington, D.C.: National Agricultural Statistics Service.

———. 1993b. *Environmental release permit: Issued permits.* Animal and Plant Health Inspection Service, Biotechnology, Biologics, and Environmental Protection.

———. 1993c. *Agricultural statistics 1993.* Washington, D.C.: Government Printing Office.

University of California. 1986. Biological frost control experiment fact sheet.

Vaeck, M., A. Reynaerts, H. Höfte, S. Jansens, M. De Beuckleer, C. Dean, M. Zabeau, M. Van Montagu, and J. Leemans. 1987. Transgenic plants protected from insect attack. *Nature, 328,* 33–37.

Van Loon L. C., and J. F. Antoniw. 1982. Comparison of the effects of salicylic acid and ethephon with virus-induced hypersensitivity and acquired resistance in tobacco. *Netherlands Journal of Plant Pathology, 88,* 237–56.

Van Rie, J., W. H. McGaughey, D. E. Johnson, B. D. Barnett, and H. Van Mellaert. 1990. Mechanism of insect resistance to the microbial insecticide *Bacillus thuringiensis. Science, 247,* 72–74.

Voelker, T. A., A. C. Worrell, L. Anderson, J. Bleibaum, C. Fan, D. J. Hawkins, S. E. Radke, and H. M. Davies. 1992. Fatty acid biosynthesis redirected to medium chains in transgenic oilseed plants. *Science, 257,* 72–74.

Wacek, Thomas. 1993. Research Microbiologist, Research Seeds. Interview, December 29.

Walgate, R. 1990. *Miracle or menace? Biotechnology in the third world.* London: Panos Institute.

Walton, J. D., and D. C. Panaccione. 1993. Host-selective toxins and disease specificity: Perspectives and progress. *Annual Review of Phytopathology, 31,* 275–303.

Ward, E. R., S. J. Uknes, S. C. Williams, S. S. Dincher, and D. L. Wiederhold. 1991. Coordinate gene activity in response to agents that induce systemic acquired resistance. *Plant Cell, 3,* 1085–94.

Watts, Susan. 1990. Drug safety body refuses to keep quiet on BST. *New Scientist,* September 22, 25.

Weintraub, Pamela. 1992. The coming of the high-tech harvest. *Audubon,* July–August, 94, 96–100, 103.

Whalon, M. E., D. L. Miller, R. M. Hollingworth, E. J. Graflus, and J. R. Miller. 1993. Selection of a Colorado potato beetle (Coleoptera: Chrysomelidae) strain resistant to *Bacillus thuringiensis. Journal of Economic Entomology, 86,* 226–33.

Whiteley, H. R., and H. E. Schnepf. 1986. The molecular biology of parasporal crystal body formation in *Bacillus thuringiensis. Annual Review of Microbiology, 40,* 549–76.

Wilkinson, C. F. 1990. Introduction and overview. In *The effects of pesti-*

cides on human health, proceedings of a workshop May 9–11, 1988, Keystone, Colorado, ed. S. R. Baker and C. F. Wilkinson, 5–33. Princeton: Princeton Scientific Publishing.

Williams, S., L. Friedrich, S. Dincher, N. Carozzi, H. Kessman, E. Ward, and J. Ryals. 1992. Chemical regulation of *Bacillus thuringiensis* δ-endotoxin expression in transgenic plants. *Bio/Technology, 10,* 540–43.

Wilms, Heinz. 1994. Dietary IGF-1 and rBST. Talk Paper T94–17, March 16.

Wilson, M., and S. E. Lindow. 1993. Release of recombinant microorganisms. *Annual Review of Microbiololgy, 47,* 913–44.

Wilson, P. W. 1940. *The biochemistry of symbiotic nitrogen fixation.* Madison: University of Wisconsin Press.

Wilson, T. M. A. 1993. Strategies to protect crop plants against viruses: Pathogen-derived resistance blossoms. *Proceedings of the National Academy of Sciences of the United States of America, 90,* 3134–41.

Woloshuk, C. P., J. S. Meulenhoff, M. Sela-Buurlage, P. J. M. van den Elzen, and B. J. C. Cornelissen. 1991. Pathogen-induced proteins with inhibitory activity toward *Phytophthora infestans. Plant Cell, 3,* 619–28.

Wood, Alan. 1993. Virologist, Boyce Thompson Institute for Plant Sciences. Interview, June 17.

Wrage, Karol. 1993a. Molecular farming: A new American agriculture roles out. *Biotech Reporter,* November, 1, 3.

———. 1993b. Agracetus developing plant bioreactors. *Biotech Reporter,* November, 4.

———. 1994. Calgene to determine BXN cotton pricing. *Biotech Reporter,* January, 2–3.

———. 1995. Plastic producing plants. *Biotech Reporter, 12,* 1, 4.

Wrubel, Roger. 1993. Ice-minus revisted. *Gene Watch, 8,* 4.

Wrubel, Roger P., and Jonathan Gressel. 1994. Are herbicide mixtures useful for delaying the rapid evolution of resistance? A case study. *Weed Technology, 8,* 635–48.

Wrubel, R. P., S. Krimsky, and M. D. Anderson. 1995. Has regulatory oversight inhibited innovation of genetically engineered microorganisms? [In preparation.]

Wrubel, R. P., S. Krimsky, and R. E. Wetzler. 1992. Field testing transgenic plants. *BioScience, 42,* 280–89.

Wyke, Alexandra. 1988. The genetic alternative: A survey of biotechnology. *The Economist, 307*(7548), 1–18 [special supplement after 52].

Yonkers, Robert D. 1992. Potential adoption and diffusion of BST among dairy farmers. In *Bovine somatotropin and emerging issues,* ed. M. C. Hallberg, 100. Boulder: Westview Press.

Yu, S. H., et al. 1989. Functional human CD4 protein produced in milk of transgenic mice. *Molecular Biology and Medicine, 6,* 255–61.

Zessman, H., T. Staub, C. Hofmann, T. Maetzke, J. Herzog, E. Ward, S. Uknes, and J. Ryals. 1994. Induction of systemic acquired resistance in plants by chemicals. *Annual Review of Phytopathology, 32,* 439–59.

Zimmerman, Burke K. 1984. *Biofuture.* New York: Plenum Press.

Index

SHELDON KRIMSKY is professor in the Department of Urban and Environmental Policy at Tufts University. He received B.S. and M.S. degrees in physics from Brooklyn College and Purdue University, respectively, and M.A. and Ph.D. degrees in philosophy from Boston University. He has published numerous essays and reviews on the social and regulatory aspects of science appearing in such journals as *The American Journal of Public Health, Nature, The Bulletin of the Atomic Scientists, The American Scientist, BioScience,* and *Science, Technology and Human Values.* He is the author of *Genetic Alchemy: The Social History of the Recombinant DNA Controversy, Environmental Hazards: Communicating Risk as a Social Process* (with Alonzo Plough), *Biotechnics and Society: The Rise of Industrial Genetics,* and *Social Theories of Risk* (a volume edited with Dominic Golding).

ROGER WRUBEL is assistant professor of urban and environmental policy at Tufts University. He received a B.A. degree in political science from Hunter College, an M.S. in environmental science from the University of Virginia, and a Ph.D. in entomology from the University of California, Berkeley. He has published articles on agriculture and biotechnology in *BioScience, Weed Technology,* and *Technology Review.*